CAMBRIDGE CLASSICAL STUDIES

General Editors
M.F.BURNYEAT, M.K.HOPKINS, M.D.REEVE, A.M.SNODGRASS

THE METAMORPHOSIS OF PERSEPHONE

THE METAMORPHOSIS OF PERSEPHONE
Ovid and the self-conscious Muse

STEPHEN HINDS

Assistant Professor of Greek and Latin, University of Michigan
Formerly Fellow of Girton College, Cambridge

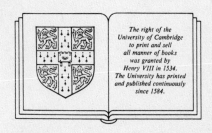

The right of the
University of Cambridge
to print and sell
all manner of books
was granted by
Henry VIII in 1534.
The University has printed
and published continuously
since 1584.

CAMBRIDGE UNIVERSITY PRESS

CAMBRIDGE

NEW YORK   NEW ROCHELLE   MELBOURNE   SYDNEY

Published by the Press Syndicate of the University of Cambridge
The Pitt Building, Trumpington Street, Cambridge CB2 1RP
32 East 57th Street, New York, NY 10022, USA
10 Stamford Road, Oakleigh, Melbourne 3166, Australia

First published 1987

Printed in Great Britain by the University Press, Cambridge

British Library cataloguing in publication data
Hinds, Stephen
The metamorphosis of Persephone:
Ovid and the self-conscious Muse.
– (Cambridge classical studies)
1. Ovid. Metamorphosis
I. Title
871'.01   PA6519.M9

Library of Congress cataloguing in publication data
Hinds, Stephen.
The metamorphosis of Persephone.
(Cambridge classical studies)
Bibliography.
Includes indexes.
1. Ovid, 43 B.C. – 17 or 18 A.D. Metamorphoses.
2. Persephone (Greek deity) in literature.
3. Metamorphosis in literature.
I. Title.   II. Series.
PA6519.M9H5 1987   873'.01   86-26923

ISBN 0 521 33506 X

TO ALFRED AND MURIEL HINDS

CONTENTS

ACKNOWLEDGEMENTS

My greatest debt is to Ted Kenney, my former research super-
visor, who in conversation and in published work has more
than anyone else shaped my appreciation of things Ovidian.
His encouragement and moral support made my task a much
lighter one than it would otherwise have been. Nor could this
book have been written without the stimulus provided by the
weekly (or sometimes fortnightly) research seminar at Cambridge devoted to Latin (or sometimes Greek) poetry. To all of
its members in recent years, but especially to John Henderson,
an inspiring critic, my thanks are due.

I would like to acknowledge the help too of Anna Wilson
(formerly Crabbe), Ian Du Quesnay, Denis Feeney and Alfred
Hinds, all of whom read, and by their comments helped me to
reread, the penultimate version of the book; as also the various
contributions of Neil Hopkinson, Duncan Kennedy, Guy Lee,
Dorothy Thompson, Robert Wardy, Donald Wormell and
Maria Wyke. Towards the end, I had many important discussions with Barbara Goff, who, as well as encouraging me in the
completion of the present work, did much to show me the way
ahead to future critical inquiry.

Conceived in Trinity College, Dublin, this study was begun
on paper in St John's College, Cambridge, and finished on
screen in Girton College, Cambridge. I am indebted to the
Master and Fellows of the one Cambridge college, for their
award in 1979 of a Research Studentship; and to the Mistress
and Fellows of the other, for their award in 1983 of a Research
Fellowship.

For their professional help, and for their kind interest in my
work, I am grateful to June Ethridge of the Classics Faculty
Library, and to Pauline Hire and Susan Moore of Cambridge
University Press. Some of the final preparation of the book for
publication was undertaken in the course of a visit to Geneva

made possible by the generosity of the Fondation Hardt and of the British Academy.

These acknowledgements give me an opportunity to bid farewell to the Cambridge Classics Faculty and to Girton College, two communities in which I have thoroughly enjoyed life as an Ovidian, *felix pariter studioque locoque*. I end by expressing my heartfelt thanks to my parents, dedicatees of this volume, and to all the friends in Cambridge, Dublin and elsewhere who have helped to see me through the years of research here represented.

S.E.H.

Ann Arbor, Michigan
1987

PREFACE

A new *aetas Ovidiana* in the criticism of Latin literature has
dawned: so modern studies of the poet from Sulmona are wont
to introduce themselves. Their general expressions of goodwill,
however, are not always backed up by re-examination in detail:
the new Ovid, one might almost say, is a poet more honoured
than read. Critics still tend to hang back from the close, word-
by-word and line-by-line engagement which any Ovidian text
deserves; and nowhere are they more guilty of underreading
than in the *Metamorphoses*—whether because the easy fluency
and geniality of its narrative makes a more painstaking approach seem ungracious, or because the poem's great length
seems to render such an approach impracticable. In either case,
they do their poet a disservice; for Ovid's mastery is above all
a mastery of words. When I began work on the *Metamorphoses*
some years ago, it was the complexity of Ovid's language, its
activity and wealth of nuance, which surprised and delighted
me most; and my surprise and delight have continued to grow
ever since.

Hence, partly, this book: not a general reassessment of the
Metamorphoses, but a reading, designedly specific, of one episode from the *Metamorphoses*: the account in Book 5 of the
rape of Persephone. In the first part of my study I give detailed
consideration to two short passages which serve in different
ways to set the scene for the rape. My reading of these can be
regarded as generating the discussion in Part II, which ranges
much more widely without, I hope, sacrificing the closeness of
focus achieved in the early chapters.

My choice of episode is by no means a random one. Ovid
treats the rape of Persephone not once in his writings but twice;
and my discussion, as it progresses, becomes increasingly interested in the parallel version which we find in the fourth book
of the *Fasti*, and in how this relates to the version in *Metamor-*

phoses 5. The twin Persephone episodes constitute a remarkable exercise in extended cross-reference, offering food for thought not just to the critic of Latin poetry but, perhaps, to any student of narrative: my investigation, the most extensive yet undertaken of the Persephone myth in Ovid, can lay some claim here to a broader relevance.

My third and fourth chapters present a literary historical context in which to read the two episodes. The *Homeric Hymn to Demeter*, all but ignored in earlier *Quellenforschung*, is discovered to be central to the inspiration of both; so that what ensues is an exploration not just of allusion, but of allusion in parallel to a literary predecessor.

A concern with poetic self-reference informs my study throughout, and nowhere more so than in the final two chapters. In these, I address the questions raised by Richard Heinze's famous attempt to distinguish between an epic narrative manner in the *Metamorphoses* version of the rape and an elegiac narrative manner in the *Fasti* version. That attempt, to which Ovid's two Persephones owe such celebrity as they possess in the present century, has come to be regarded by most critics as, at best, a noble failure. However, my reading of the twin accounts, a reading newly alive to the undercurrents there of Ovidian self-commentary, will suggest that Heinze did indeed ask the right questions, even if he came up with some of the wrong answers. I shall offer a radical redefinition of the terms of the long-standing controversy, a redefinition which will seek first and foremost to shed new light on *Metamorphoses* 5 and *Fasti* 4 themselves, but which may also be seen as contributing to a wider debate on Augustan literary polemic and practice.

But I end my preface by emphasising once more my belief in the importance of close and energetic engagement with the texts under consideration, in all their detail. I hope that my readers will respond to my pleasure in teasing out the implications of Ovid's words; and that this book will be felt to proceed with due care and literary tact in the quest, which it does not presume to complete, for the Ovidian Persephone.

vos mihi sacrarum penetralia pandite rerum
et vestri secreta poli: qua lampade Ditem
flexit Amor; quo ducta ferox Proserpina raptu
possedit dotale Chaos quantasque per oras
sollicito genetrix erraverit anxia cursu

Claudian, De Raptu Proserpinae 1.25–9

... Ah, the master's touch
So suave, mere word-play, that can do so much!

Donald Davie, 'The Fountain of Cyanë' I

PART I

TWO SETTINGS FOR A RAPE

CHAPTER 1

METAMORPHOSES 5.256–64:
THE HELICONIAN FOUNT

Two hundred and fifty lines into Book 5, the goddess Pallas brings Ovid's *Metamorphoses* to the home of the Muses:

> hactenus aurigenae comitem Tritonia fratri
> se dedit: inde cava circumdata nube Seriphon
> deserit, a dextra Cythno Gyaroque relictis,
> quaque super pontum via visa brevissima, Thebas
> virgineumque Helicona petit; quo monte potita
> constitit et doctas sic est adfata sorores[1]
>
> (*Met.* 5.250–5)

Ever since Hesiod's famous encounter at the beginning of the *Theogony* (most famously remembered by Callimachus in fragment 2 of the *Aetia*), the introduction into any poem of the Heliconian Muses,[2] patron goddesses of literature itself, has always been a moment for the poet to turn in on himself (or rather, perhaps, to stand outside himself) so as to contemplate more obtrusively than elsewhere the nature of his own craft. The narrative of the *Metamorphoses* embraces the whole world of Graeco-Roman myth from the Creation down to the Augustan present; but we may still reasonably expect Mount Helicon here in Book 5 to be more than just another setting, and its inhabitants more than just another group of mythological characters.

A cursory glance ahead at once suggests that Ovid is not unaware of his responsibilities to the tradition. We do indeed seem set to find out something about the pursuit of literature in this Heliconian section of the *Metamorphoses*: the main piece of action recounted here turns out to be nothing less than a contest for supremacy in poetic recitation, involving the Muses and a rival band of artists, the daughters of Pieros.

The Muses' entry in this contest, sung by Calliope and reproduced verbatim at *Met.* 5.341–661, is an account of the rape of the maiden goddess Persephone by Dis, king of the

Underworld, and of the quest for Persephone by her mother Ceres, goddess of agriculture. This will be the concern of chapters 2–6. However, in the present chapter I want to dwell a little on the setting which will see the tale of Persephone told; and to consider in its own right, as a sort of *hors d'œuvre* to my main study, that other myth which has brought about Pallas' visit to Mount Helicon in the first place: viz., the tale of the origin of the Hippocrene.

> 'fama novi fontis nostras pervenit ad aures,
> dura Medusaei quem praepetis ungula rupit.
> is mihi causa viae: volui mirabile factum
> cernere; vidi ipsum materno sanguine nasci.'
> excipit Uranie: 'quaecumque est causa videndi
> has tibi, diva, domos, animo gratissima nostro es.
> vera tamen fama est: est Pegasus huius origo
> fontis', et ad latices deduxit Pallada sacros.
> quae mirata diu factas pedis ictibus undas
>
> (*Met.* 5.256–64)

Apparent here, I think, as later in Book 5, is an awareness of what it is to bring the Muses into a literary work: the subject of this brief exchange between Pallas and Uranie, of more than passing interest to any *doctus poeta* or *doctus lector*, is a hoof-blow which marks the birth of poetry and of poetic inspiration as later ages know them.

ii

> 'vera tamen fama est: est Pegasus huius origo
> fontis' ...
>
> (*Met.* 5.262–3)

Uranie, weighing her words carefully, as a good Muse should, provides us immediately with a modest illustration of how active Ovidian language can be, even in the most straightforward of sentences.

'Pegasus is the originator of this spring.' Riley's translation[3] is unexceptionable, as far as it goes; but it gives little idea of the suggestiveness here of Ovid's *origo*. In the first place, the word serves to advertise the fact that this story of an 'originator'

4

comes into a literary category especially beloved of poets in the Alexandrian tradition: as for instance in the case of the poetry enjoined on Gallus by Linus in Virgil's sixth *Eclogue*

> his [sc. calamis] tibi Grynei nemoris dicatur origo
> (Virgil, *Ecl.* 6.72)

origo functions as a quasi-technical term to suggest the Greek αἴτιον, and identifies the myth as an exercise in aetiology.[4]

Another, equally learned *origo* may come to mind too. Notably absent in this discussion of the *novi fontis* is the actual name of the spring, which it traditionally owes, of course, to this very myth of the ἴχνιον ὀξέος ἵππου (Callimachus, *Aet.* fr. 2.1): Ἵππου κρήνη, *Hippocrene*.[5] However, can one perhaps discern in Ovid's *est Pegasus huius origo | fontis* a pointer towards this missing element? *origo* is amongst other things the standard term in Latin for the etymological derivation of a word:[6] so that inherent in the statement here of Pegasus' responsibility for the new spring is, arguably, a hint at his further responsibility for its name.

This nuance is the more readily perceived because of a second verbal derivation implied in the sentence. Etymological word-play is a favourite mannerism of the learned poet;[7] and Uranie, no disgrace to her *doctas ... sorores* (*Met.* 5.255), is, I think, doubly allusive here. Pegasus, a horse, gives a name to *Hippo-crene*; but also his *own* name, *Pegasus*, makes him a peculiarly apposite figure to create any flow of water. *Pegasus* is derived in antiquity from πηγή, an etymology especially likely to command attention in that it occurs in Hesiod:[8]

> τῷ μὲν [sc. Πηγάσῳ] ἐπώνυμον ἦν, ὅτ' ἄρ' Ὠκεανοῦ παρὰ πηγὰς
> γένθ' ...
> (Hesiod, *Theog.* 282-3)

πηγή translates into Latin as *fons*; and a *fons* is precisely what Πήγ-*asus* originates in Uranie's etymologically charged sentence.[9]

Finally, note how close comes this *origo*, for all its mythological reference, to the language of normal geographical description. The *origo* of this *fons* is Pegasus; but other *origines*

fontium are more simply aquatic, as in Horace, *Carm.* 4.14.45–6
fontium qui celat origines | Nilus ... and, later, in Seneca's and
Pliny's natural histories.[10]

Well, then, may Uranie preface her confirmation of the
origin of the spring with the assertion *vera tamen fama est*.
What Pallas has heard as a mere report (*Met.* 5.256 *fama ...
nostras pervenit ad aures*) is indeed true: aetiologically, etymologically and geographically true.[11]

It may be worth pressing the word *fons* a little further in
the light of all these *origines*. The cliché *fons et origo* is not
yet current in Ovid's time;[12] but the former noun does have
various figurative senses which render it almost synonymous
with the latter. *fons* is even used by Varro in his treatise on the
Latin language to refer to verbal derivation, as it is by Horace,
with full consciousness of the metaphor, at *A.P.* 52–3 *et nova
fictaque nuper habebunt verba fidem, si | Graeco fonte cadent
parce detorta*.[13] What is the effect on Uranie's sentence of this
near-equivalence? Does it encourage one to see the *fons* of the
Hippocrene as itself a kind of symbol for all its own *origines*?[14]

iii

Be that last speculation as it may, there is one further kind of
'well-spring' which is of some importance in these verses. One's
reading of any piece of Latin poetry is enriched by consideration of its literary sources. The Ovidian Persephone is to bear
strong witness to this later in my discussion; and here in the
opening chapter *Met.* 5.256–64 will prove no less amenable to
analysis along these lines. However, *Quellenforschung* always
finds itself hampered to a greater or lesser degree by *lacunae* in
the ancient evidence; and in the present instance, the manner in
which a literary historical picture takes shape will be such as to
draw our attention to its incompleteness, as it has come down
to us.

The first step is, strangely enough, forward in time:

> '... est Pegasus huius origo
> fontis', et ad latices deduxit Pallada sacros.
> quae mirata diu factas pedis ictibus undas
>   (*Met.* 5.262–4)

Bömer's commentary, that mine of information for the Ovidian critic, gives the information ad loc. that line 264 offers the first attested instance in Latin of the *iunctura pedis ictus*. The second instance, we are told, is at Germanicus, *Arat*. 220; and an examination of the relevant part of the astronomical work in question reveals the parallel to be rather more interesting than Bömer seems to have allowed:

> Gorgonis hic proles; in Pierio Helicone,
> vertice cum summo nondum decurreret unda,
> Musaeos fontis dextri pedis ictibus hausit.
> inde liquor genitus nomen tenet: Hippocrenen
> fontes nomen habent; sed Pegasus aethere summo
> velocis agitat pennas et sidere gaudet
> (Germanicus, *Arat*. 218–23)

Not only is the *iunctura* in the same case and in the same metrical *sedes* as in *Met*. 5.264, which could be mere coincidence; but the *pes* here belongs to exactly the same mythological character as it does in the *Metamorphoses* passage and, moreover, to exactly the same moment in that character's mythological career. A firm literary historical link between the two instances of the *iunctura* can surely be considered established.[15]

But, before the obvious conclusion is drawn, viz. that the Germanican passage alludes directly to *Metamorphoses* 5, there is something else to be taken into account. Germanicus' poem is, remember, a translation, albeit a free one, of a celebrated Hellenistic astronomical work, the *Phaenomena* of Aratus; and a look at the Aratean lines rendered by Germanicus in the passage quoted above rather complicates matters:

> κεῖνον δὴ καί φασι καθ' ὑψηλοῦ Ἑλικῶνος
> καλὸν ὕδωρ ἀγαγεῖν εὐαλδέος Ἱππουκρήνης.
> οὐ γάρ πω Ἑλικὼν ἄκρος κατελείβετο πηγαῖς,
> ἀλλ' Ἵππος μιν ἔτυψε· τὸ δ' ἀθρόον αὐτόθεν ὕδωρ
> ἐξέχυτο πληγῇ προτέρου ποδός· οἱ δὲ νομῆες
> πρῶτοι κεῖνο ποτὸν διεφήμισαν Ἱππουκρήνην.
> ἀλλὰ τὸ μὲν πέτρης ἀπολείβεται, οὐδέ ποτ' αὐτὸ
> Θεσπιέων ἀνδρῶν ἑκὰς ὄψεαι· αὐτὰρ ὁ Ἵππος
> ἐν Διὸς εἰλεῖται καί τοι πάρα θηήσασθαι
> (Aratus, *Phaen*. 216–24)

Germanicus varies, condenses and expands Aratus in many details; but one detail in which he does remain essentially faithful to his Greek 'original' is that very *iunctura* which we have been discussing in connexion with Ovid. Germanicus' *dextri pedis ictibus* is virtually a straight translation of Aratus' πληγῇ προτέρου ποδός, but for the greater specificity (assuming that *dextri* stands for *dextri e prioribus*) of the Latin epithet.

So how do we now plot the position of the Ovidian passage? If there is circumstantial identity between *Met.* 5.264 and the later Germanicus 220, as pointed out above, there is also circumstantial identity between *Met.* 5.264 and the earlier Aratus 219–20, the avowed model of the Germanican line. Germanicus' *pedis ictibus* demonstrably derives from Aratus' πληγῇ ... ποδός: is it not natural to trace Ovid's *pedis ictibus* too to the same source? Aratus 216–23 is, for all its brevity, the principal pre-Ovidian account of the origin of the Hippocrene to survive antiquity;[16] and, given the extraordinary esteem in which Aratus' *Phaenomena* was held by the *literati* of Rome, inspiring as it repeatedly did comment, allusion and wholesale translation, the importance of his version can safely be assumed.[17]

Thus, when Ovid's Pallas wonders at the *factas pedis ictibus undas*, it is more than a little tempting to see specific allusion to the ἀθρόον ... ὕδωρ which pours out πληγῇ προτέρου ποδός at the identical moment in Aratus 219–20. Note that Ovid's *pedis* occurs in the same metrical *sedes* as its etymological cognate ποδός, and that, despite syntactical differences, *undas* finds itself in the same *sedes* as its cognate ὕδωρ.[18] Ovid, unlike Germanicus, offers no equivalent for προτέρου: but, as I shall argue later, this is interpretable as a highly pointed omission.

Moreover, if the Aratean provenance of *Met.* 5.264 seems plausible, there is another detail in Ovid's version of events which one may refer to the same source. Aratus introduces the Hippocrene myth as something spread by report at 216 κεῖνον δὴ καί φασι ... ; and, following up this common poetic mannerism[19] in an unusually precise way, he goes on to specify just who is responsible for having begun this process of dissemination: 220–1 οἱ δὲ νομῆες | πρῶτοι κεῖνο ποτὸν διεφήμισαν

Ἱπποκρήνην.[20] Ovid too uses the idea of report in his treatment of the myth; and, by a process not dissimilar to that which operates in the case of Aratus' φασι and διεφήμισαν, his etymologically cognate[21] *fama* (*Met.* 5.256) is followed up in such a way (*Met.* 5.262 *vera tamen fama est*) as to deepen our interest in the workings of the report concerned: see my discussion above. Thus the Ovidian detail may well owe something to the Aratean one. Is it going too far, indeed, to see here an allusive conceit whereby the *fama novi fontis* which has reached Pallas' ears in *Met.* 5.256 can actually be envisaged as filtering through from none other than those Aratean herdsmen who πρῶτοι κεῖνο ποτὸν διεφήμισαν in Aratus 221? Or, still more archly, can the source of Pallas' information be envisaged as being Aratus' poetry itself?

We must evidently consider anew where the Ovidian and the Germanican passages stand *vis-à-vis* each other. It is unlikely that each would have hit on precisely the same phrase independently in rendering Aratus 219–20. Ovid is on oath to no-one; and even for a closer translator than we know Germanicus habitually to have been, the resources of the Latin language open up many paths to Aratus 219–20 other than that of *pedis ictus* (to say nothing of the various combinations of number, case and line-position in which this previously unattested *iunctura* might itself occur).[22] One only has to consider the quite different verbal detail of Avienius' later version:

> ... cornuque excita repente
> lympha Camenalem fudit procul Hippocrenen
> (Avienius, *Arat.* 495–6)

No; more likely is that Germanicus, in rendering Aratus 219–20, deliberately built into his version a verbal acknowledgement of the earlier echo by Ovid of the same Aratean verses. The technique of alluding to a model both directly and through an intermediary is a well-established one in Roman poetry (see chapter 3, n.16 below).

This is a tidy enough reconstruction. However, beside the link between Germanicus and Ovid, as strong verbally as it is circumstantially, the suggested allusion in Ovid to Aratus himself may seem, although interestingly subtle, a little lacking in self-assertiveness. How much longer would Ovid's debt here to the Aratean tradition have remained buried, one is tempted to ask, without that post-Ovidian prompt from the adoptive son of Tiberius? Another venture into literary detective work will, I think, uncover more information about this tradition in which *Met.* 5.256–64 participates; and will put us in a position, if not to elucidate it, at least to account better for some of its obscurities. Again, the approach to be taken is a somewhat oblique one.

Ovid's exile in A.D. 8 found him with not one, but two major poems in his study awaiting publication. When the blow fell, both the hexameter *Metamorphoses* and the elegiac *Fasti* were, he says, in an unfinished state:

> carmina mutatas hominum dicentia formas,
>   infelix domini quod fuga rupit opus
>   (*Trist.* 1.7.13–14)

> sex ego Fastorum scripsi totidemque libellos,
>   cumque suo finem mense volumen habet,
> idque tuo nuper scriptum sub nomine, Caesar,
>   et tibi sacratum sors mea rupit opus
> . . . .
> dictaque sunt nobis, quamvis manus ultima coeptis
>   defuit, in facies corpora versa novas
>   (*Trist.* 2.549–52, 555–6)

... *rupit opus*: the verbal echo of *Trist.* 1.7.14, where the *opus* is the *Metamorphoses*, in *Trist.* 2.552, where it is the *Fasti*, further underlines the parallelism in circumstances. One suspects, of course, that the *Metamorphoses* was rather more, and the *Fasti* rather less, finished than Ovid seems to claim.[23] However, the fact that he can make such statements at all forbids one to believe that either work was disseminated in a completed state before A.D. 8. Whether Ovid switched between the two poems every minute, every day, every month or every year; whether, as some hold, he wrote most of the *Metamorphoses* before starting the *Fasti*;[24] or whether, as a few others argue, he wrote most of the *Fasti* before starting the *Metamorphoses*;[25] it should in any of these cases be evident that he was in a position to revise both poems freely up to the time of his exile. They

10

are in some sense what most Ovidian scholars have held them to be, simultaneous compositions.[26] Nor are there internal grounds for disputing this conclusion: even where the subject-matter of the *Metamorphoses* and the *Fasti* coincides, no consistent pattern of priority can be found to emerge.[27]

I mention this literary historical circumstance partly to prepare the way for my discussion of the Persephone myth in chapters 2–6. Its pertinence to the present context, however, arises from the existence in *Fast*. 3.455–6 of a second Ovidian version of the very moment under consideration here, viz. the moment of the mythological origin of the Hippocrene.

> iamque ubi caeruleum variabunt sidera caelum,
>   suspice: Gorgonei colla videbis equi.
> creditur hic caesae gravida cervice Medusae
>   sanguine respersis prosiluisse iubis.
> huic supra nubes et subter sidera lapso
>   caelum pro terra, pro pede pinna fuit;
> iamque indignanti nova frena receperat ore
>   cum levis Aonias ungula fodit aquas.
> nunc fruitur caelo, quod pinnis ante petebat,
>   et nitidus stellis quinque decemque micat
>   (*Fast*. 3.449–58)

We have here a nice piece of circumstantial evidence supporting our findings about the literary origins of the *Metamorphoses* version. There were no stars in *Met*. 5.256–64; but the passage seemed nevertheless to be rooted in a piece of astronomical poetry by Aratus. Now in this other Ovidian version of the myth, belonging to the same phase in the poet's career, there *are* stars; and there is good reason to think, moreover, that they are Aratean stars. The fact is that, just as on its aetiological side,

> tempora cum causis Latium digesta per annum
>   (*Fast*. 1.1)

the *Fasti* looks back to Callimachus, so the main inspiration for the poem's astronomy,

> lapsaque sub terras ortaque signa canam
>   (*Fast*. 1.2)

famously derives from none other than Aratus.[28]

11

Here in the third book of the *Fasti*, just as in Aratus, the origin of the Hippocrene is mentioned in the course of a discussion of the constellation of the Horse. Note especially how Ovid ends his discussion at *Fast.* 3.457–8 by moving straight from the Hippocrene to a concluding remark about the Horse's place in the sky, just as Aratus does at lines 223–4 of the *Phaenomena*. Perhaps, moreover, the exhortation to look for the constellation with which the Ovidian discussion begins (*Fast.* 3.450 *suspice ... videbis*) may be seen as influenced by the remark, also explicitly addressed to the star-gazing reader, with which the Aratean one ends (Aratus 224 καί τοι πάρα θηήσασθαι).

Nor is this the end of the parallelism between the literary connexions of Ovid's two references to the Hippocrene myth. Not only do they both seem to recall Aratus, but the *Fasti* passage, as well as the *Metamorphoses* one, looks as if it may well have served as an intermediary between Aratus and his later translator Germanicus. Compare the three versions of that concluding remark about the Horse's place in the sky:

... αὐτὰρ ὁ ῞Ιππος
ἐν Διὸς εἰλεῖται καί τοι πάρα θηήσασθαι
(Aratus 223–4)

nunc fruitur caelo, quod pinnis ante petebat,
et nitidus stellis quinque decemque micat
(*Fast.* 3.457–8)

... sed Pegasus aethere summo
velocis agitat pennas et sidere gaudet
(Germanicus 222–3)

Quite apart from those wings, Germanicus does not get the touch of 'inner life' in *sidere gaudet* from Aratus' ἐν Διὸς εἰλεῖται, and it is more than a little tempting to trace it to Ovid's *fruitur caelo. fruitur* can imply, though it need not (thus *frui* 'to have as one's lot'[29]), an imputation of emotion to the Horse; but *gaudet* enforces the implication and intensifies the emotion. Thus a line of descent can plausibly be traced from Aratus' emotionally neutral version through Ovid's *fruitur* to Germanicus' *gaudet*.

A further detail in the *Fasti* passage begs comparison with Germanicus' version of the Horse constellation:

> iamque indignanti nova frena receperat ore
> (*Fast.* 3.455)

> spumanti mandit sed qua ferus ore lupata
> (Germanicus 212)

In Aratus, where the Horse of heaven and Hippocrene is not named as Pegasus, a bridle, like wings, is altogether absent.[30] Ovid adds it; and Germanicus' line may betray specific indebtedness to Ovid's in its reproduction of the configuration *-anti . . . ore*.

Further than this it is not safe to venture. However, these new data do encourage speculation. Germanicus now seems to have gone to remarkable lengths, even for a *doctus poeta*, to enrich his Greek original's account of the Horse constellation. To have located and used as an intermediary one Aratean allusion from an independent poem (i.e. not a translation of Aratus) would be commendable enough; to locate and conflate *two* such allusions, and from different Ovidian poems, suggests a truly labyrinthine approach to the translation of the Aratean episode. Perhaps that was indeed Germanicus' approach. However, a more economical explanation of the patterns of allusion discovered does suggest itself – an explanation which, let it be emphasised, is and must remain entirely conjectural.

The fact is that at some point in his career Ovid himself, like Germanicus after him, produced a version (an abbreviated one, it seems) of Aratus' *Phaenomena*.[31] It is natural to assume that it was an early work: the translation of the well-known Hellenistic poem is surely the sort of exercise that Ovid would have set himself while first trying out his powers, rather than in his maturity, when daring innovation in subject-matter was his rule.[32]

Thus, could it be that Ovid, a poet given more than any other to self-echo,[33] drew for his allusions to Aratus in *Met.* 5.256–64 and *Fast.* 3.449–58 on the language of his own earlier translation of the relevant part of the *Phaenomena*; so that when Germanicus seems to us, with our limited access to

13

Augustan writings, to be elaborately pulling together recondite allusions in the *Metamorphoses* and *Fasti* for his version of Aratus' Horse constellation, his eye is not in fact on those two passages at all, but on their immediate common source: what Germanicus is echoing is, more obscurely for us but much more naturally for him, the translation of the Horse episode in Ovid's *Phaenomena*, his direct and possibly his most important precursor in the Latin Aratean tradition?

A corollary is worth stating. If things were as I propose, then Ovid's allusion to Aratus in *Met.* 5.256–64 and *Fast.* 3.449–58 will originally have stood out as such more clearly than it does now, by virtue of the additional signalling given in each passage by verbal echoes of Ovid's own earlier *Phaenomena*.[34]

But enough of guesswork: the picture resists final completion. However, what has emerged is not inconsiderable. In the past, investigators have always traced the inspiration of the Hippocrene passage in *Met.* 5.256–64 to Nicander's lost *Heteroioumena*, thus bringing the modern reader up against something of an impasse.[35] It is indeed the case that a brief prose epitome at Antoninus Liberalis 9 allows us with some certainty to trace the basic idea for the Heliconian song contest just below in Ovid's narrative (*Met.* 5.300ff.) to the fourth book of the *Heteroioumena*: the correspondence is amongst those most frequently cited in discussions of the influence of Nicander's poem on the *Metamorphoses*.[36] And it is also the case that the Nicandrian version of the contest appears to have included in its action, just before the transformation of the losers into birds, a blow from the hoof of Pegasus:

ὅτε μὲν οὖν αἱ θυγατέρες ᾄδοιεν τοῦ Πιέρου, ἐπήχλυεν πάντα καὶ οὐδὲν ὑπήκουεν πρὸς τὴν χορείαν, ὑπὸ δὲ Μουσῶν ἵστατο μὲν οὐρανὸς καὶ ἄστρα καὶ θάλασσα καὶ ποταμοί, ὁ δ' Ἑλικὼν ηὔξετο κηλούμενος ὑφ' ἡδονῆς εἰς τὸν οὐρανόν, ἄχρις αὐτὸν βουλῇ Ποσειδῶνος ἔπαυσεν ὁ Πήγασος τῇ ὁπλῇ τὴν κορυφὴν πατάξας

(Antoninus Liberalis 9.2)

Rival Pierid singers metamorphosed by the Muses (the name is elsewhere in the mythological tradition applied to the Muses themselves) are unique to Antoninus' report of Nicander and to *Met.* 5.300ff.;[37] so that, even before one takes into account the inherent appropriateness of any allusion in the *Metamorphoses* to that previous poem on tranformations, Ovid's use of the Nicandrian song contest for his song contest in the latter part of *Metamorphoses* 5 looks overwhelmingly likely.

Given that likelihood, it also seems reasonable to infer that this same Nicandrian passage did something to prompt Ovid's account, adjacent to his song contest, of the momentous hoof-blow of Pegasus. However, it should already have been clear before the present study that the *detail* of *Met.* 5.256–64 was unlikely to be Nicandrian. Whereas Pegasus' act constitutes an essential part of the song contest in the *Heteroioumena*, the two events are associated in *Metamorphoses* 5 only by conversational juxtaposition in the ears of Pallas; and, whereas Ovid's concern is first and last with the flow of the Hippocrene, the Nicandrian account seems to focus on a bizarre swelling of the mountain itself,[38] to the complete exclusion (in Antoninus' epitome at least) of any mention of the spring.

Working from a wholly different starting-point, we have traced Ovid's version of the Hippocrene myth to a second, distinct literary tradition, that of Aratus.[39] For us this tradition is surely the more interesting one. Whereas any peculiarly Nicandrian touches in *Met.* 5.256–64 are effectively veiled from our sight by the blandness of Antoninus' synopsis, the debt to Aratus, as my discussion here perhaps shows, is sufficiently recoverable to allow a real attempt at literary critical appreciation.

Maybe this was the side of the passage's literary history which Ovid regarded as most important too. At any rate, one element in his presentation of the myth, which has not so far been considered, is interpretable as a sly programmatic[40] hint pointing to its Aratean inspiration. Out of the nine Muses, the one who speaks up in *Met.* 5.260ff. to confirm the *fama* about the origin of the Hippocrene, and who actually leads Pallas to the sacred spring in *Met.* 5.263, is Uranie. Rigid differentiation of the Muses' literary functions is post-Augustan: but is it not rather appropriate that the self-appointed guide to this particular Hippocrene should be that Muse whose very name (Uranie, Greek Οὐρανίη) already marks her as an expert in

15

the field on which Ovid draws for details of his treatment here, viz. astronomical poetry?[41]

And a final underlining of the Aratean allusion may be discerned in the *positioning* of *Met.* 5.256–64 within the structure of Ovid's narrative.[42] The visit to the Hippocrene is immediately preceded in the *Metamorphoses* by the rescue of Andromeda, chained to a rock through the folly of her mother Cassiope, and the resultant battle in the royal hall of her father Cepheus (*Met.* 4.663–5.241). An apt conjunction; for in the structure of Aratus' *Phaenomena*, the description of the Horse who is the origin of the Hippocrene (*Phaen.* 205–24) is immediately preceded by a family of three constellations (*Phaen.* 179–81): none other than Cepheus (*Phaen.* 182–7), Cassiope (*Phaen.* 188–96) and Andromeda (*Phaen.* 197–204).

iv

One detail which may be especially sharpened by recognition of its Aratean origins comes in the line which has been the main focus of attention in these recent pages. Where Aratus writes that the Hippocrene first flowed πληγῇ προτέρου ποδός (220), and Germanicus later translates *dextri pedis ictibus* (220), in the *Metamorphoses* the spring shown by Uranie to Pallas is created, more simply, *pedis ictibus* (5.264). Ovid's omission of an adjective corresponding to Aratus' προτέρου or to Germanicus' *dextri* leaves *pedis* unqualified: but this, I would suggest, far from impoverishing his version of the phrase, actually opens up in it a new stratum of meaning.

Remember that we are on Mount Helicon, a place uniquely devoted to the making of poetry, and that what is under discussion here is the fount of poetic inspiration itself. In this environment, do not the blows of Pegasus' hoof exploit an ambiguity available in the phrase *pedis ictus* to take on a distinctly prosodic aspect? Few word-plays are more familiar in Latin poetry than the one between the bodily and metrical senses of the word *pes*.[43] Sometimes the pun is quite plainly spelled out, as at Catullus 14.21–3 *vos hinc interea valete abite | illuc, unde malum pedem attulistis, | saecli incommoda, pessimi poetae*, or, even more, Horace, *A.P.* 80 (where the foot to be 'shod' is an iambus) *hunc socci cepere pedem grandesque cothurni*, Ovid, *Am.* 3.1.8 (of the personified Elegy) *et, puto, pes illi longior alter erat*, and *Trist.* 1.1.15–16 *vade, liber, verbisque meis loca grata saluta:* | *contingam certe quo licet illa pede*; more often it is obliquely evoked. And what of *ictus*? This word for the 'blows' administered by Pegasus' hoof is also, as it happens, the technical term in Latin for the 'beat' of a metrical *pes*: see e.g. Horace, *A.P.* 251–3 *syllaba longa brevi subiecta vocatur iambus,* | *pes citus; unde etiam trimetris accrescere iussit* | *nomen iambeis, cum senos redderet ictus*, and *Carm.* 4.6.35–6 *Lesbium servate pedem meique pollicis ictum.*[44] Is not Ovid, then, foreshadowing the *result* of the flow of the Hippocrene through a covert pun in his description of its *cause*? The blows of a horse's hoof are ultimately responsible for the creation of rhythmical verse: *pedis ictus* of one kind will lead to *pedis ictus* of another.[45]

Without labouring the point, one may perhaps suggest a corresponding ambiguity in the grammatical case of *ictibus*: the *factas pedis ictibus undas*, the 'waters made *by* the blows of the hoof', are, fleetingly, 'waters made *for* rhythmical verse'.[46]

There exist two instances of the *iunctura pedis ictus* from later in the first century A.D. which lie rather interestingly in between the two poles of meaning under review: Pliny, *Nat.* 2.209 *sunt et in Nymphaeo parvae [insulae], Saliares dictae, quoniam in symphoniae cantu ad ictus modulantium pedum moventur*; Quintilian, *Inst.* 9.4.51 *tempora ... metiuntur et pedum et digitorum ictu*. In each case the *pedes* are unambiguously of the bodily kind; but in each case the *ictus* which these *pedes* stamp out are distinctly prosodic: no random impacts, they are the beats of a regular rhythm. The fact is that there is no complete separation in Latin usage between *ictus* as a term of prosody and *ictus* denoting an actual bodily blow: some oscillation in thought between metre in the abstract and the visible movements which accompany it is inherent in any ancient discussion of prosody.[47]

This circumstance makes the word-play in *Met.* 5.264 all the more natural; and it may even encourage a secondary suggestion, whereby the *ictus* of Pegasus' bodily *pes* are fantastically envisaged as moving in time to the *ictus* of the metrical *pes* which will be the consequence of his action.

V

> ... et ad latices deduxit Pallada sacros.
> quae mirata diu factas pedis ictibus undas
> (*Met.* 5.263–4)

In view of this latest manifestation in *Met.* 5.264 of the power of poetry on Mount Helicon, can the verb in the preceding line, I wonder, remain entirely innocent? Uranie 'led down', *deduxit*, Pallas to the sacred waters of the Hippocrene. The walk to the spring arises naturally out of the immediately preceding conversation; but the choice of verb seems to be such as to add a further nuance to Uranie's playing of the Muse's part.

The fact is that *deducere*, although a commonplace word, carries for a writer like Ovid some very powerful programmatic associations. With a noun like *carmen* as object, *deducere* functions as a key term of Augustan poetics, descriptive of the kind of composition which adheres to the Μοῦσαν ... λεπταλέην enjoined at Callimachus, *Aet.* fr. 1.23–4:

> ... 'pastorem, Tityre, pinguis
> pascere oportet ovis, deductum dicere carmen'[48]
> (Virgil, *Ecl.* 6.4–5)

> at tibi saepe novo deduxi carmina versu
> (Propertius 1.16.41)

The origins of the usage are not entirely clear; but it comes to be regarded as a metaphor from *deducere* 'to draw out a thread in spinning, spin'.[49] Just as the spinner spins a thin thread from the wool on the distaff, so the Callimachean poet forms something thin and fine from a mass of formless material:

> cum lamentamur non apparere labores
> nostros et tenui deducta poemata filo
> (Horace, *Ep.* 2.1.224–5)

deducere is a word, therefore, which crops up again and again in discussions of poetic composition;[50] and it seems to me a piquant touch here in *Met.* 5.263 that Uranie, even whilst doing something as simple as walking about, should not be able altogether to shake off the language of her job: in the very detail of her deportment, she reminds us of her status as Muse.

If such a reference to programmatic *deducere* appears implausibly oblique, it may be helpful to consider some other instances in Ovid of what seems to be equally allusive evocation of the term.

But first let us take the opportunity to look at the proem of the *Metamorphoses* itself, where *deducere* is used programmatically in a way which, while more straightforward, is by no means entirely so. In the poet's opening request to the gods

> ... primaque ab origine mundi
> ad mea perpetuum deducite tempora carmen
> (*Met.* 1.3–4)

perpetuum ... carmen has long been seen to imply an alignment of the *Metamorphoses* with the ἓν ἄεισμα διηνεκές abhorred at Callimachus, *Aet.* fr. 1.3;[51] but it is only recently that a second, opposing implication in the sentence has also been recovered.[52] With reference to the chronology of the *carmen*, the imperative *deducite* means simply 'bring down' or 'carry through'. However, a further, specifically poetic suggestion in the word strongly asserts itself too. For, if the gods do what Ovid asks them to do here, viz. *deducite ... carmen*, then what will be the literal result of their action but, precisely, a *deductum carmen*? In the very act of repudiating Callimachean principles, Ovid seems to let them in again by the back door. More of this paradox later: for now, simply let the slightly allusive nature of the employment here of *deducere* be noted.

The obliquity of reference envisaged in *Met.* 5.263 is clearly of a greater order of magnitude than this; but consider the following instances, in which, as in the present passage, *deducere* takes as object something quite other than a *carmen*:[53]

> risit Amor pallamque meam pictosque cothurnos
> sceptraque privata tam cito sumpta manu;

> hinc quoque me dominae numen deduxit iniquae,
> deque cothurnato vate triumphat Amor
>> (*Am.* 2.18.15–18)

The poet's mistress 'drew him away from' tragedy and back to love elegy; and *deduxit* also suggests, by a fleeting reference to the programmatic sense, that this marked a return to Callimachean values.[54]

> ipsum nos carmen deduxit Pacis ad aram:
> haec erit a mensis fine secunda dies
>> (*Fast.* 1.709–10)

'The song itself has brought me to the altar of Peace'; but, in isolation, the wording of the first four spondees prompts the momentary thought that an expected statement involving programmatic *deducere*, viz. *nos carmen deduximus*, has been stood on its head, with the *carmen* absurdly 'composing' the poet rather than *vice versa*. *ipsum* facilitates the ambiguity by seeming to express surprise at the position of *carmen* as subject of *deduxit*.[55]

> 'tu quoque' dic 'studiis communibus ecquid inhaeres,
>   doctaque non patrio carmina more canis?
> nam tibi cum fatis mores natura pudicos
>   et raras dotes ingeniumque dedit.
> hoc ego Pegasidas deduxi primus ad undas,
>   ne male fecundae vena periret aquae'
>> (*Trist.* 3.7.11–16)

As Luck's commentary ad loc. suggests, *hoc* sc. *ingenium* in 15 functions as an equivalent for *puellam ingeniosam*, so that once more *deducere* is being used of 'leading' a person; also, in anticipation of the metaphor in the following line, the sense 'to draw or lead water off, divert'[56] is present; but finally, since it is the nurturing of Perilla's poetic talent by Ovid that is under discussion, there is surely a reference to the programmatic connotations of the verb.

This final instance is perhaps more than merely illustrative: for does not *Trist.* 3.7.15 actually allude to *Met.* 5.263 and its context? Where previously Uranie led Pallas to the Hippocrene, now it is Ovid himself who, metaphorically, leads Perilla to the same spring. *deduxi* echoes *deduxit* in *Met.* 5.263 (same *sedes*); *ad undas* conflates *ad latices . . . sacros* in *Met.* 5.263 and *undas* in *Met.* 5.264; and the epithet *Pegasidas* has an eye to *Met.* 5.262–3 *est Pegasus huius origo | fontis.* As often in his exile poetry, Ovid redeploys one of his own earlier fictions in an autobiographical context.[57] The hint of programmatic *deducere* in *Trist.* 3.7.15 is, of course, no guarantee of the presence of a like ambiguity in *Met.* 5.263: but it is at least tempting to read the later reference as a commentary on the earlier, slightly more elusive one.

vi

Lastly in this chapter, let a small point be considered which arises out of the comparison between *Met.* 5.256ff. and the other Ovidian version of Pegasus' hoof-blow at *Fast.* 3.455–6. The duplication of the Hippocrene myth in the *Metamorphoses* and in the *Fasti* was seen earlier to raise a number of interesting questions: perhaps we may add a final, somewhat tentative one here.

Compare *Met.* 5.257 *dura Medusaei quem praepetis ungula rupit* with *Fast.* 3.456 *cum levis Aonias ungula fodit aquas.* Why is it that the hoof which taps the Hippocrene (*ungula rupit, ungula fodit*) is in the *Metamorphoses* version *dura*, but in the *Fasti* version *levis*? 'Variation des Ausdrucks', says Bömer's commentary on the *Metamorphoses* line; but I think that something more substantial may lie behind it. In our newly won Heliconian perspective, a contrast between these two adjectives, familiar 'opposites' in the imagery of Augustan literary debate, is distinctly susceptible to interpretation along programmatic lines. Could the hoof which creates the fount of poetry be *dura* in the *Metamorphoses* in keeping with the 'weighty', epic impulse behind Ovid's venture into hexameters; whereas the same hoof is *levis* in the *Fasti* in keeping with that poem's 'slighter', elegiac inspiration? For the common association of *durus* as a term of poetics with grand genres like epic, see e.g. Propertius 2.1.41–2 *nec mea conveniunt duro praecordia versu | Caesaris in Phrygios condere nomen avos*; for the associa-

21

tion of *levis* with humbler genres like elegy, see e.g. Ovid, *Am.*
2.1.21 *blanditias elegosque levis, mea tela, resumpsi;*[58] and,
for an earlier Ovidian play between the two terms (also, interestingly, involving the blow of a foot), see the words of the
personified Elegy to a grand rival, not Epic but Tragedy, in
Am. 3.1:[59]

> sum levis, et mecum levis est, mea cura, Cupido:
> non sum materia fortior ipsa mea
>
> . . . .
>
> quam tu non poteris duro reserare cothurno,
> haec est blanditiis ianua laxa meis
>
> > (*Am.* 3.1.41–2, 45–6)

Arguably, then, *Met.* 5.257 and *Fast.* 3.456 show two contrasted Hippocrenes which quite literally bear the stamp of
their respective generic contexts.[60] The idea is one which may
aptly be offered to the *Manes* of Richard Heinze, whose famous 1919 monograph *Ovids elegische Erzählung* sought to
establish a clear distinction between an epic narrative manner
in the *Metamorphoses* and an elegiac manner in the *Fasti*. The
generic classification of the *Metamorphoses* implied by the
suggested hoof image, as by Heinze's monograph itself, is not
unproblematic: issues are raised here which will have to be
faced squarely later in the present study (chapters 5 and 6).
However, even if Ovid's large-scale hexameter work has in it
more of the *carmen deductum* than Heinze recognised, it should
still be evident that its initial profession of alignment with the
carmen perpetuum of grand epic in *Met.* 1.4 conveys at least a
half-truth about weightiness in its inspiration.

And there is another circumstance which disposes one to
give credence to the studiedly casual cross-reference here envisaged. Ovid mentions Pegasus' *ungula* in just one other place in
his writings; and it is tempting to read the couplet in question,
which occurs in the exile poetry, as a rather wry postscript
to the game played in the earlier two passages. Ovid makes
reference to his Muse,

> quae quoniam nec nos unda summovit ab illa,
> ungula Gorgonei quam cava fecit equi
>
> > (*Pont.* 4.8.79–80)

The *ungula* which was *dura* or *levis* has now in *Pont*. 4.8 become *cava*. Once more, this is a reasonable 'Variation des Ausdrucks': one thinks, perhaps, of Ennius' description of hoofbeats:

> it eques et plausu cava concutit ungula terram
> (Ennius, *Ann.* 431 Sk.)

But once more, the variation looks as if it may carry a programmatic point.

In the *Tristia* and *Epistulae ex Ponto*, the alleged weakening of Ovid's literary powers in exile is a central preoccupation: so, earlier in *Pont*. 4.8, lines 65–6 *siquid adhuc igitur vivi, Germanice, nostro|restat in ingenio* ... Analogies are constantly accumulated to describe this decline; and prominent among these are images of decay. See, for example, the comparison of the poet's weakened powers to an idle ship,

> adde quod ingenium longa rubigine laesum
> torpet et est multo, quam fuit ante, minus
> . . . .
> vertitur in teneram cariem rimisque dehiscit,
> siqua diu solitis cumba vacavit aquis
> (*Trist.* 5.12.21–2, 27–8)

to an unfit body,

> cernis ut ignavum corrumpant otia corpus
> . . . .
> et mihi siquis erat ducendi carminis usus,
> deficit estque minor factus inerte situ
> (*Pont.* 1.5.5, 7–8)

and to a choked spring

> scilicet ut limus venas excaecat in undis,
> laesaque suppresso fonte resistit aqua,
> pectora sic mea sunt limo vitiata malorum,
> et carmen vena pauperiore fluit
> (*Pont.* 4.2.17–20)

In this context, a *cava ungula* is perhaps apt to take on the unhealthy connotations of, say, a *cavus dens*: the adjective *cavus* and its associated verb *cavare* are readily descriptive in

Latin of the kind of hollowness that results from decay[61]—or from erosion. This allied implication, indeed, may be still more relevant here. *cavus* occurs in the *Epistulae ex Ponto* only in the passage under discussion; but *cavare* occurs three times, each time expressing the erosion of rock by the constant impact of water, each time as an image descriptive of the general decline of Ovid. The first occurrence is in the very opening poem of Book 1,

> aequorei scopulos ut cavat unda salis
> . . . .
> sic mea perpetuos curarum pectora morsus,
> fine quibus nullo conficiantur, habent
> *(Pont.* 1.1.70, 73–4)

the second is in Book 2; and the third, which offers a somewhat defiant overturning of the image, comes two poems after the *cava ungula* in Book 4:

> iam dolor in morem venit meus, utque caducis
> percussu crebro saxa cavantur aquis,
> sic ego continuo Fortunae vulneror ictu,
> vixque habet in nobis iam nova plaga locum
> *(Pont.* 2.7.39–42)

> ecquos tu silices, ecquod, carissime, ferrum
> duritiae confers, Albinovane, meae?
> gutta cavat lapidem, consumitur anulus usu,
> atteritur pressa vomer aduncus humo.
> tempus edax igitur praeter nos omnia perdit:
> cessat duritia mors quoque victa mea
> *(Pont.* 4.10.3–8)

ungula Gorgonei quam cava fecit equi. The epic *Metamorphoses* had a Hippocrene created by a *dura ungula*; the elegiac *Fasti* had one created by a *levis ungula*: does not this Hippocrene too bear the mark of its literary surroundings? Sadly, Ovid intimates, the symbol used by him in his greatest years to characterise his poetic output has caved in under the pressures of life in exile: a Hippocrene remains, but it is the Hippocrene of a *cava ungula*, fit inspiration for the poetry of an 'eroded' talent.[62]

CHAPTER 2

METAMORPHOSES 5.385–91:
THE LANDSCAPE OF ENNA

Let us now move from the Heliconian setting into the poetry sung there. The account of the Pierid challenge given by one of the Muses to Pallas at *Met.* 5.300ff. is dominated by the full quotation in *Met.* 5.341–661 of Calliope's entry in the resultant poetic contest. Beginning with a hymnic preface devoted to Ceres (341–5), Calliope moves towards the main theme of her narrative, the rape of Persephone, via an account of the punishment of Typhoeus, whose attack on the gods was the Pierid singer's subject. Imprisoned beneath Mount Etna (346ff.), Typhoeus struggles so much that the god Dis, worried that the roof of his underworld realm may suffer structural damage, emerges and carries out a tour of inspection around Sicily. He is espied there by Venus, in residence in her Sicilian haunt of Mount Eryx. Bent on mischief, the goddess instructs Cupid (365–79) to shoot Dis with his arrows and, by coupling him with the divine maiden Persephone, to bring about a twofold triumph for the empire of love. Her son duly fits his choicest arrow to his bow-string and scores a direct hit on the underworld king (379–84).

This rapid sequence of cause and effect leaves the narrative poised for the moment of Persephone's abduction. That moment, when it comes, will again produce some fast-moving action. Persephone, whilst playing and gathering flowers with her companions (391–4), will almost at once be seen, loved and swept off by Dis, her cries for help uttered in vain as she is borne in his chariot across the changing terrain of Sicily (395ff.).

But, before this violence, there is a brief respite. The setting for the abduction is to be the landscape of Enna: and, after the bow-shot in line 384, the narrative hangs in suspension for a few verses as we are treated to a leisurely description, standing free of the action, of the tree-girt lake near the city walls whose calm is to be so rudely shattered.

25

ii

> haud procul Hennaeis lacus est a moenibus altae,
> nomine Pergus, aquae; non illo plura Caystros
> carmina cycnorum labentibus edit in undis.
> silva coronat aquas cingens latus omne suisque
> frondibus ut velo Phoebeos submovet ictus.
> frigora dant rami, Tyrios humus umida flores:
> perpetuum ver est. quo dum Proserpina luco
> ludit et aut violas aut candida lilia carpit
>
> (*Met.* 5.385–92)

This is a very attractive description. However, in order to give it due appreciation, we must first realise what it is not, viz. an exactly observed portrayal of a fully individualised natural scene. That is not to say that a lake, trees, flowers and cool shade offer an implausible version of nature, nor even necessarily to claim that they are false to anything in the real Enna, once visited by Ovid with his friend Macer (see *Pont.* 2.10.25).[1] But the concentration on these elements immediately suggests that the writer is working very much in a literary tradition of stereotyped beautiful landscapes, which is detectable in Greek literature from earliest times, and is first felt strongly in the pastoral poetry of Theocritus. The *locus amoenus*, as this pattern of landscape comes to be known when it is codified in later antiquity, is characterised in E.R. Curtius' classic discussion as

a beautiful, shaded natural site. Its minimum ingredients comprise a tree (or several trees), a meadow, and a spring or brook. Birdsong and flowers may be added. The most elaborate examples also add a breeze.[2]

Ovid's *Metamorphoses* constitutes an important stage, in fact, in the establishment of this stereotype: the present landscape is one of many in the poem, especially in Books 3, 4 and 5, which are constructed along lines essentially similar to each other, and to the pastoral landscapes of Theocritus and Virgil that precede them.[3]

Swans are no more than occasional visitors to such settings, and an extra touch of grace is added here by the singing of those birds on the waters of lake Pergus. But note the obliquity of their presentation, which is perhaps as responsible for the impression of grace as is any visual or audial reference in the sentence. The *labentibus ... undis*, with the *carmina cycnorum* therein, belong not to lake Pergus but to the river Cayster: in the language of *Met.* 5.386–7, the swans of Pergus are depicted wholly in terms of the Caystrian swans to which they are compared; or, more precisely, wholly in terms of the songs of those swans. The effect of the mention of the Cayster is to lend associations to the landscape which are literary as much as geographical, since that region in Asia Minor is established as the great haunt of swans in poetry from Homer on:

> ... ὥς τ' ὀρνίθων πετεηνῶν ἔθνεα πολλά,
> χηνῶν ἢ γεράνων ἢ κύκνων δουλιχοδείρων,
> Ἀσίῳ ἐν λειμῶνι, Καϋστρίου ἀμφὶ ῥέεθρα,
> ἔνθα καὶ ἔνθα ποτῶνται ἀγαλλόμενα πτερύγεσσι,
> κλαγγηδὸν προκαθιζόντων, σμαραγεῖ δέ τε λειμών⁴

(Homer, Il. 2.459–63)

And the concentration on the *songs* of the swans constitutes an affirmation of the familiar landscape pattern, since birdsong, if not generally the song of this particular water-dwelling species, is, as we saw, a recurrent feature of the *locus amoenus*.

Another element with a certain inherent distinctiveness is added to the scene in *Met.* 5.391 *perpetuum ver est*. This, coming after *Tyrios humus umida* [sc. *dat*] *flores* in the line above, alludes to the ever-blooming flowers which seem to have been an observable feature of the real Enna, and are prominent in earlier literary descriptions of the place at Cicero, *Verr.* 2.4.107 (a passage to which we shall have cause to return later) and Diodorus 5.3.2–3. However, the nature of the reference here is not really such as to bring us closer to 'experiencing' the landscape of Enna: contrast, perhaps, Diodorus' version, where a vivid anecdote almost fills our nostrils with the scent of the floral meadows:

διὰ δὲ τὴν ἀπὸ τῶν φυομένων ἀνθῶν εὐωδίαν λέγεται τοὺς κυνηγεῖν εἰωθότας κύνας μὴ δύνασθαι στιβεύειν, ἐμποδιζομένους τὴν φυσικὴν αἴσθησιν

(Diodorus Siculus 5.3.2)

The distinctiveness of the Ovidian detail lies rather in the evocation through *perpetuum ver* of a literary-mythological tradition of perennially beautiful landscapes situated in wonderful times (like the Golden Age: *Met.* 1.107 *ver erat aeternum*) and wonderful places (like Virgil's idealised Italy: *Geo.* 2.149 *hic ver assiduum*).[5] A 'supernatural charge' is thus given to the milieu, helping to set the mood for the momentous rape of goddess by god about to be enacted in it. As in the case of the swans, there is no radical departure here from the familiar landscape pattern: the pastoral *locus amoenus* is closely related in its conception to this idea of the place of supreme bliss.[6]

iii

The above remarks on the combination of distinctiveness and conventionality in certain aspects of the setting begin, I think, to suggest some answers to the question implied in my initial negative definition of the landscape: namely, if these lines do not offer an exactly observed portrayal of a fully individualised natural scene, what do they offer?

It may be instructive to return to first principles, and to note how the formal architecture of the verse helps to keep it instinct with life. This is simply to give a particular demonstration of the flexibility and expressiveness of Ovid's hexameter style which, happily, thanks to E.J. Kenney's 1973 study, it is no longer necessary to defend in general terms against any charge of monotony.

Consider the management of tempo. Following on, and in contrast to, a connected sequence of action expressed in a single, unbroken verse-period of over five lines,

> ... ille pharetram
> solvit et arbitrio matris de mille sagittis
> unam seposuit, sed qua nec acutior ulla
> nec minus incerta est nec qua magis audiat arcum,
> oppositoque genu curvavit flexile cornum
> inque cor hamata percussit harundine Ditem
>
> (*Met.* 5.379–84)

the piece-by-piece description of the landscape in *Met.* 5.385–91 is expressed in a number of short periods in which architecture of the line is nicely set off against architecture of

28

the sentence by the mixture of end-pause, mid-pause and en-jambment in almost equal proportions. The contrast between the two passages emphasises the rightness of the marriage of form and meaning in each.

The same felicity is apparent on the small scale within *Met.* 5.385–91. Note the sound-responsion of initial 'h' in 385 (*haud ... Hennaeis*), picking up the 'h's of 384 (*hamata ... harundine*), and giving an unobtrusive element of continuity over the 'para-graph' break; the 'c's of *Caystros* | *carmina cycnorum*, re-inforced by the distinctive Greek 'y's,[7] welding together the core of the line-straddling sentence in 386–7; the further cluster of [k] sounds in 388 allowing *cingens*, 'surrounding', to look away from its own participial phrase towards *coronat* and *aquas*, the main 'surrounding' and 'surrounded' words in the sentence; the interplay of 'o' and 'e' across the main caesura of 389 (*velo Phoebeos*),[8] giving a strong central articulation to both line and clause; the initial 'f' words beginning 389 and 390 and enclosing 390, reinforcing the rhythmical near-identity of the first halves of the two lines and the rhetorical antithesis between the two halves of the second, and helping thus to effect a sort of climax before the addition of the final, supernatural touch to the landscape in 391; and, at the end, the insertion of Persephone into the middle of the grove through 'pictorial' word order (*quo ... Proserpina luco*),[9] which, together with the pick-up of the final syllable of *perpetuum* in *dum* (both syllables with the verse-ictus) and likewise of the first syllable of *luco* in *ludit*, contributes to the ease of the transition back from static description to dynamic narrative.

A footnote is worth adding to one of the details of this analysis:

> frigora dant rami, Tyrios humus umida flores
> (*Met.* 5.390)

The line is loosely chiastic in arrangement, with the two al-literative scenic elements *frigora* and *flores* produced respec-tively, and in different ways, by the *rami* and the *humus umida*.[10] Although the first half is a sort of variation on the preceding *suisque* | *frondibus ... Phoebeos submovet ictus*, and

29

the second half is closely linked with the succeeding *perpetuum ver est*, the antithesis in line 390 stands free with its stylistic blend of the formal and the casual, a blend peculiarly appropriate to what is being said. On the one hand, the use of antithesis gives an air of organisation appropriate to the assembly of a set-piece description. On the other, there is understatement in the use of such a colourless verb as *dant* to carry out the assembly, understatement in the way that it economically performs two diverse duties by means of what can only be termed (with, I fear, less than commensurate understatement) an 'expanded' syllepsis,[11] and a general absence of rigidity in the antithetical arrangement. Ovid is not making something big here out of the *frigora* and the *flores*. Knowing, as we know, that the presence of these stock elements is no surprise, he directs them to their proper places with the easy familiarity due to a couple of regulars.

iv

silva coronat aquas cingens latus omne suisque
frondibus ut velo Phoebeos submovet ictus
(*Met.* 5.388–9)

C.P. Segal takes an interesting approach to the question of how landscape relates to action in the *Metamorphoses* (something touched on a little earlier with reference to the *perpetuum ver* of *Met.* 5.391). He sees settings like the present one as symbolically ambiguous, as at once contrasting with and foreshadowing the violence that subsequently takes place in them.[12] Thus in *Met.* 5.389 the shade is protective; but, says Segal, 'the particular phrasing ... (*Phoebeos ... ictus*) intimates the violence to follow'.[13] That is my reading of *Met.* 5.389 too; but, as it happens, I arrive at it rather differently from Segal.

What he sees in the phrase as intimating violence, specifically sexual violence, is an image in the word *ictus* of male ejaculation. The use of *ictus* in this sense is not widespread in Latin: it is found twice with a characteristically scientific nuance in Lucretius (4.1245, 1273), perhaps once in Juvenal (6.126: the authenticity of the line is in doubt), and at *Anth. Lat.* 712.19.[14]

Nonetheless, Segal is probably right to see an innuendo along these lines in the word when it occurs in a well-known simile in *Metamorphoses* 4, in a context which he shows to be otherwise rich in sexual symbolism:[15]

> ... cruor emicat alte
> non aliter, quam cum vitiato fistula plumbo
> scinditur et tenui stridente foramine longas
> eiaculatur aquas atque ictibus aera rumpit
> (*Met.* 4.121–4)

Not only are many details of the overtly envisaged *ictus* of water and blood here readily applicable also to sexual *ictus*; but also, supporting an evocation of this sense, there is much in the lines reminiscent of Lucretius, specifically of that very Lucretian passage in which the word *ictus* is openly used of male ejaculation, viz. the account of sexual attraction at the end of his fourth book.[16]

However, even granted the presence of innuendo in *Met.* 4.124, should one also read it into the *Phoebeos ... ictus* of *Met.* 5.389? Perhaps one should: the *Metamorphoses* 4 passage would afford a precedent; and, a little below line 389, when Persephone is engaged in the symbolically charged activity of plucking flowers,[17] it would take a cloistered mind not to see a hint of sexual *double entendre* prefiguring the physical outrage soon to be inflicted on her in the words *sinum ... | implet* (393–4).[18] However, for all that, *Met.* 5.389 cannot be said to offer the circumstantial detail and literary historical associations which encourage the ejaculatory ambiguity at *Met.* 4.124; and, to my mind at least, any such innuendo in these *Phoebeos ... ictus* yields the foreground to another more obvious and more contextually secure suggestion in the phrase.

The fact is that the primary reference in *Phoebeos ... ictus*, namely to the rays of the sun, is itself loaded with implication for the unwary Persephone: the image, envisaging the sun's rays as substantial things which strike what they encounter, is one which merits close consideration. An historical approach will be useful.

The 'striking' image is already found in the *Odyssey* where, as here, it is foliage that keeps the rays off:[19]

τοὺς [sc. δοιοὺς θάμνους] μὲν ἄρ' οὔτ' ἀνέμων διάη μένος ὑγρὸν ἀέντων,
οὔτε ποτ' ἠέλιος φαέθων ἀκτῖσιν ἔβαλλεν,
οὔτ' ὄμβρος περάασκε διαμπερές· ὣς ἄρα πυκνοὶ
ἀλλήλοισιν ἔφυν ἐπαμοιβαδίς ...

(Homer, Od. 5.478–81)

The rays of the sun are frequently described in Greek poetry of all periods as 'striking' things, especially by the words βάλλω and βολή. Sometimes there seems to be no more to the idea than this. However, it develops into an image of the rays as arrows: this is overt at Euripides, *H.F.* 1090 τόξα θ' ἡλίου and *tr. fr. adesp.* 546.7–8 θερμά θ' ἡλίου τοξεύματα; and such a development, if it does not reflect a long-existing interpretation of βάλλω etc. used of the sun's rays, cannot but colour subsequent readings of the usage.[20] Likewise the sun itself, when mentioned in connection with the 'striking' image, need not be personified as an archer, but is increasingly apt to be. Such a personification is probably bound up with identification of the sun with Apollo, something attested in Greece only from the fifth century B.C. on.[21]

So too in Latin the *icio* and *ictus* whereby the sun's rays strike things, like their Greek equivalents βάλλω and βολή,[22] need not always,[23] but readily will suggest the impact of arrows. And nowhere will this suggestion be more insistent than when either word is associated with the name of Phoebus: for under that name in Augustan writing the sun becomes identified, more than it ever was in classical Greece, with the god Apollo, traditional wielder of the bow.[24] Thus, here in *Met.* 5.389 the phrase *Phoebeos ... ictus* surely represents the fullest mythological form of the 'striking' image, with the sun's rays envisaged as the arrows of Phoebus, sun-god and archer.

The reason for spelling this out can now emerge. The 'particular phrasing' in *Met.* 5.389 does indeed intimate the violence to follow; but it does so with rather more precision and relevance to the context than Segal's symbolic interpretation allows. It will be remembered that just before the suspension of the narrative at 385 Cupid, acting on Venus' orders, had flexed his bow and shot Dis with one of *his* arrows. The appearance of the *Phoebeos ... ictus* five lines later cannot but invite comparison; and the point of the comparison soon becomes all too clear. This *locus amoenus* may be able to keep away (*submovet*) the arrows of Phoebus; but it is about to prove defenceless against the effects of that other arrow just loosed by Cupid. In 395–6 the love-struck Dis will invade the sheltered landscape and secure his prey; and the ineffectual shafts of Phoebus in 389 ironically presage this invasion through their evocation of the recent activity of the deadlier archer.

v

A different set of associations is generated by the words which immediately precede *Phoebeos ... ictus*: *Met*. 5.388–9 ... *suisque | frondibus ut velo* .... The simile, drawn from contemporary urban life, is as suggestive as it is economical. Bömer has a long note ad loc. on the origins and uses of *vela*, the 'awnings' whose most notable function was to keep off the sun in theatres and amphitheatres: 'Das *velum*, "Sonnensegel", mit dem man die Cavea des Theaters oder auch, kaum bekannt, das Atrium eines Hauses (*Met*. 10.595–6) überspannte, um die Menschen vor den Strahlen der Sonne zu schützen ...', he begins.[25] But, before we get caught up with 'kaum bekannt' uses of the *velum*, it will be worth our while to attend more closely to the circumstances attendant on this particular specimen:

> silva coronat aquas cingens latus omne suisque
> frondibus ut velo Phoebeos submovet ictus
> (*Met*. 5.388–9)

Enclosure of various kinds is common in the *loca amoena* of the *Metamorphoses*;[26] but the simile here lends to the pattern a peculiar significance. If the foliage of the trees constitutes a *velum*, the formation of those trees into a circular shape (*silva coronat aquas cingens latus omne*) surely has the effect of specifying one kind of *velum*, one kind of enclosure: the foliage, Ovid's sentence suggests, serves as awning to a natural amphitheatre;[27] and perhaps one may even supply supporting masts for an amphitheatrical *velum* from the trunks of the trees thus arranged.[28]

The effect is quite in the spirit of the ancient view of land-scape. Trees, water and shade have been formed into a distinctive and visually attractive configuration; but it is one in which, in accordance with the principle of Diana's cave in *Metamorphoses* 3, nature has imitated the work of man:

> ... in extremo est antrum nemorale recessu
> arte laboratum nulla: simulaverat artem
> ingenio natura suo; nam pumice vivo
> et levibus tofis nativum duxerat arcum[29].
>
> (*Met.* 3.157–60)

It is interesting to compare with the present passage the one previous reference in Ovid to *vela* as 'awnings'. At the beginning of a discussion of the rape of the Sabine women, the subject of theatre building in early Rome comes up:

> tunc neque marmoreo pendebant vela theatro,
> nec fuerant liquido pulpita rubra croco;
> illic quas tulerant nemorosa Palatia frondes
> simpliciter positae scena sine arte fuit;
> in gradibus sedit populus de caespite factis,
> qualibet hirsutas fronde tegente comas[30]
>
> (*A.A.* 1.103–8)

In the theatre of *Ars Amatoria* 1, foliage is quite literally pressed into service as a *velum*; here in the 'amphitheatrical' grove of *Metamorphoses* 5, again in the context of a rape, foliage serves as *velum* once more – but this time only in the world of metaphor.

The specifically amphitheatrical, rather than generally theatrical suggestion in the *velum* image at *Met.* 5.388–9 is worth emphasising. Once more, as earlier (section iv above), the description of the landscape of Enna is enriched by a vivid detail; but once more that detail seems to carry a warning of trouble ahead. Amphitheatres at Rome were violent places: here, not for the last time in the *Metamorphoses*, Ovid shows himself sensitive to their peculiarly grim associations. Compare the beginning of Book 11, where, all of Creation having been held in a peaceful trance by the singing of Orpheus (*Met.* 10.148–739), his 'theatre audience' (*Met.* 11.22 *Orphei ... theatri*)[31] is suddenly broken up by the incursion of a group of maenads. The audience dispersed, the frenzied women turn on the bard himself; and when in a simile at 25–7 the imagery of performance recurs, it has been contaminated by the violence: the theatre has become an amphitheatre (*Met*. 11.25 *structoque utrimque theatro*, with a strong pick-up at the line-end of *theatri* at the end of 22) and Orpheus, again on stage, is not now a singer, but a doomed stag about to be torn apart by dogs.

The above incident may be relevant to the present discussion in another way too. The milieu in which Orpheus has been singing is a *locus amoenus* (see *Met*. 10.86ff., 143–7), and that is why the imagery just analysed arises so naturally at *Met*. 11.22ff.; for not just there, but throughout Theocritean and Virgilian pastoral, its chief pre-Ovidian home, the *locus amoenus* is above all else a place of performance, a 'stage' on which herdsmen are wont to sing their songs.[32] Perhaps, then, the amphitheatrical suggestion in *Met*. 5.385ff. can likewise be regarded as an organic development from in-built associations of the *locus amoenus* with performance. As in *Met*. 11.25–7, if more obliquely, the topic has been grimly perverted: the familiar 'stage' of pastoral is here an amphitheatrical arena; and the performance scheduled for the spot is no bucolic song recital, but a cruel spectacle of which the maiden Persephone is destined to be the unwilling star.

> ... quo dum Proserpina luco
> ludit ...
> (*Met*. 5.391–2)

The very verb which introduces Persephone into the landscape may hint at what the imagery bodes for her. She 'sports'[33] in her Sicilian grove; but she has also been placed in a metaphorical arena in which she will be forced to 'play' out 'the spectacle'[34] of her own violent abduction.[35]

vi

Now if the landscape here can indeed be envisaged as an 'arena' which awaits the arrival of performers and spectacle, this is in no small measure due to the rhetorically free-standing character of *Met.* 5.385–91, mentioned at the beginning of the chapter, to the way in which narrative action hangs in suspension for these six-and-a-half lines while the description of the setting unfolds itself. Here, once more, are the two points of transition:

> ... curvavit flexile cornum
> inque cor hamata percussit harundine Ditem.
> haud procul Hennaeis lacus est a moenibus ...
>
> perpetuum ver est. quo dum Proserpina luco
> ludit et aut violas aut candida lilia carpit
>   (*Met.* 5.383–5, 391–2)

For my next approach to the landscape of Enna, I want to take a closer look at this common mannerism whereby the set-piece, 'ecphrastic' description of a place[36] marks itself off from preceding and succeeding narrative, through the use of standard phrases of introduction and conclusion.

In his note on Virgil, *Aen.* 4.480ff., R.G. Austin remarks thus on the characteristic Latin opening formula: 'Dido begins with an ecphrasis, in a traditional manner ...: *locus est*, or more commonly *est locus* is a conventional opening of such a passage.'[37] Some examples may be offered:[38]

> est locus Hesperiam quam mortales perhibebant
>   (Ennius, *Ann.* 20 Sk.)
>
> ultimus Aethiopum locus est, ubi maximus Atlas
> axem umero torquet stellis ardentibus aptum
>   (Virgil, *Aen.* 4.481–2)
>
> est locus extremis Scythiae glacialis in oris,
> triste solum, sterilis, sine fruge, sine arbore tellus
>   (*Met.* 8.788–9)

'... Elsewhere it is varied by the naming of the place or object described.' Thus, instead of *est locus* or *locus est*, one will find e.g. Virgil, *Geo.* 4.418 *est specus*, *Met.* 1.168 *est via*, *Met.* 8.624 *stagnum est* – or, here at *Met.* 5.385, *lacus est.*[39]

But this last variation stands out from the others in an interesting way. In *lacus est*, the specific 'place or object' used to vary the formula actually evokes by its sound and shape the standard *locus est* that, as it were, lies behind it. The two words are naturally susceptible to word-play of various kinds in Latin; and the pun may even be felt to have an etymological tinge. Amongst ancient derivations of the word *lacus* is this (false) one in Isidorus:

fontes labuntur in fluviis; flumina in freta discurrunt; lacus stat in loco nec profluit. Et dictus lacus quasi aquae locus

(Isidorus, *Orig*. 13.19.2)

Lucretius, that most committed of poetic etymologists, may already be familiar with the derivation, to judge from an interesting juxtaposition of line-ends in his second book:[40]

et variae volucres, laetantia quae loca aquarum
concelebrant circum ripas fontisque lacusque
(Lucretius 2.344–5)

Here in *Met*. 5.385, a punning allusion in *lacus est* to the *locus est* opening becomes all the more pointed if the pun involves the perception of a 'child–parent' etymological relationship between particular variation and standard formula.[41]

Consider now the typical close of these local descriptions set in narrative. Austin again: 'The descriptive opening is picked up by some word that marks the return to narrative proper.'[42] Generally what picks up the *locus*, or the 'place or object' varying it, is a simple demonstrative (sometimes a relative): thus e.g. Virgil, *Aen*. 1.530–4 *est locus – hic*; *Fast*. 4.337–9 *est locus – illic*; *Met*. 8.624–6 *stagnum est – huc*; *Met*. 11.592–616 *est ... spelunca – quo*. However, occasionally the close will occur in a fuller form, whereby the opening word is actually restated rather than, as above, merely pointed to: thus e.g. Sallust, *Cat*. 55.3 *est ... locus – in eum locum*; *Fast*. 5.707–8 *locus est – illo ... loco*.

Let us turn again to *Met*. 5.385ff. The description here, it has just been suggested, opens with a pun on the standard set-piece formula. Now an initial *locus est* would have created the expectation of a reference to (or perhaps, as just seen, a restatement of) the word *locus* at the moment of return to narrative. So what is it that returns our *actual* opening phrase in *Met*. 5.385, viz. *lacus est*, to narrative? The slightly unexpected answer is, in *Met.* 5.391, *quo ... luco*. Strictly speaking, *luco* picks up *silva* etc. in *Met.* 5.388ff., offering a not unparalleled exit via a more recent element in the description rather than via the initial one.[43] But, as in the case of the opening, the sound and shape of this closing word is such as to offer another, larger sense of what is going on. In the first place, *luco* is punningly suggestive of *lacus*, so that it almost seems to pick up the initial 'place or object' in the normal way: *lucus* and *lacus* are a common paronomasial pair in Latin.[44] But also, still more neatly, the standard *locus* is once again in view, with *quo ... luco* suggestive (in all but quantity) of *quo ... loco*, just as *lacus est* was of *locus est*: the association in word-play of *lucus* and *locus* is another well-established one.[45]

The word *locus*, then, is the unstated common factor as opening and close combine to make a composite pun, unmistakable in its double impact, on the standard formula for marking the boundaries of a set-piece description in narrative. The word-play is no idle one. It reveals Ovid in a typical attitude, not only painting a scene but also watching himself paint it. At *Met.* 8.624 he writes *haud procul hinc stagnum est ...*, and a pool appears. Here at *Met.* 5.385 he writes *haud procul Hennaeis lacus est ...*, and, while the pool appears just as clearly, there is also visible a poet writing about a pool, drawing attention by means of a nice pun to the fact that his description is constructed according to a well-established literary formula. There is no need for Bömer to comment ad loc. 'Die Darstellung beginnt mit einer Ekphrasis vom Typ "*est locus*"': Ovid has already made the point in his text.

A footnote, involving something of a digression, may be added to all this. Ovid's description setting the scene for the rape of Persephone in *Met.* 5.385–91 has a well-known literary predecessor. In E.J. Kenney's words, 'setting and subject would be apprehended in a moment by a public who needed to read no further than *haud procul Hennaeis ...* before recalling one of the most famous ecphrases in Roman literature, Cicero, *Verr.* 2.4.106–7'.[46] Ovid's awareness of this Ciceronian 'purple passage' finds expression, as I have already pointed out in print elsewhere,[47] in a rather striking verbal echo – not here in

Metamorphoses 5, however, but in that parallel poem which proved so pertinent to the consideration of the Hippocrene myth in chapter 1: the *Fasti*. Like the Hippocrene myth, but on a much more substantial scale, the story of the rape of Persephone is told twice by Ovid in the years before his exile; and the first couplet of the version in the *Fasti* distinctly calls to mind the climactic words of the *Verrine* ecphrasis:

Henna autem, ubi ea quae dico gesta esse memorantur, est loco perexcelso atque edito, quo in summo est aequata agri planities et aquae perennes, tota vero ab omni aditu circumcisa atque directa est; quam circa lacus lucique sunt plurimi atque laetissimi flores omni tempore anni, locus ut ipse raptum illum virginis, quem iam a pueris accepimus, declarare videatur

(Cicero, *Verr*. 2.4.107)

exigit ipse locus raptus ut virginis edam:
plura recognosces, pauca docendus eris
(*Fast*. 4.417–18)

Where Cicero has the verbal collocation *locus ut ipse raptum illum virginis*, Ovid has *ipse locus raptus ut virginis*. In the former passage the words form part of a single clause; in the latter they have been distributed between two clauses. *ipse locus*, which in Cicero refers to the geographical 'site' that is Enna, in Ovid means something quite different, the 'occasion' in the poem or calendar.

It is in this disjunction of meaning that the word-for-word correspondence acquires some piquancy. If the Ciceronian sense of *ipse locus* is mentally substituted in the Ovidian sentence, Ovid too can seem for a moment to be remarking on the way that the geographical site calls attention to the rape.[48] Of course, such a reading is strictly 'wrong' in the *Fasti* context: but note that what follows directly after the quoted couplet is a reference to Sicily, or Trinacris,

... a positu nomen adepta loci
(*Fasti*. 4.420)

which soon leads into a set-piece description of the very *locus* with which the Ciceronian sentence is concerned:

valle sub umbrosa locus est ...
(*Fast*. 4.427)

39

Thus Cicero's sense of *locus*, though suppressed by Ovid in the introductory *Fast.* 4.417, finds a kind of reinstatement in the subsequent movement of his account.[49]

plura recognosces in the pentameter of the couplet under discussion (*Fast.* 4.418) implies in the Alexandrian manner (cf. chapter 1, n. 19; chapter 3, p. 58 and n. 22) that the bulk of the ensuing narrative will consist of material attested elsewhere: in particular, as Merkel already saw, a programmatic cross-reference to our contemporaneous treatment in *Metamorphoses* 5 is surely intended.[50] However, in close-up, I think, the words *plura recognosces* also have a complex contribution to make to the Ciceronian allusion. First, coming as they do just after *Fast.* 4.417, they serve to administer a slightly mischievous nudge to the reader, alerting him to the presence in the immediate vicinity of a piece of near-verbatim allusion. Second, besides being in this way a comment on it 'from the outside', the words actually function as a *continuation* of the allusion, constituting (with the aid of the educational nuance lent by their antithesis in 418, *pauca docendus eris*) an oblique reference to Cicero's *quem iam a pueris accepimus*. On its own, a reference like this would not be felt; but, coming as it does in the wake of the close echo above, it is readily discernible.

To return to the matter in hand, this clear echo in *Fasti* 4 of the *Verrine* Enna tends to endorse the suggestion that Ciceronian associations will loom large for the reader of *Met.* 5.385ff. too. Indeed, the remarkable attentiveness to the detail of Cicero's set-piece evidenced in the *Fasti* allusion encourages a further piece of speculation. In my discussion of the opening and concluding phrases of the *Metamorphoses* 5 description of Enna, I supported the case for the various word-plays between *lacus*, *lucus* and an implied *locus* by pointing out the susceptibility of the three words to paronomasia elsewhere in Latin. The interesting fact now emerges that at every point I could have drawn my illustrations from the language of Cicero's Enna ecphrasis. The doublet *lacus lucique*,

quam circa lacus lucique sunt plurimi

(Cicero, *Verr.* 2.4.107)

40

is an especially distinctive element in that passage:[51] it is echoed by Cicero himself in a final prayer to Ceres and Persephone at the very end of the *Verrines*,

vos etiam atque etiam imploro atque appello, sanctissimae deae, quae illos Hennensis lacus lucosque incolitis

(Cicero, *Verr*. 2.5.188)

and it even finds its way thence into Pinarius' speech at Enna in Livy 24 before a massacre in the Second Punic War:[52]

vos, Ceres mater ac Proserpina, precor, ceteri superi infernique di, qui hanc urbem, hos sacratos lacus lucosque colitis

(Livy 24.38.8)

Back in *Verr*. 2.4.107, the verbal music of the *lacus lucique* doublet is picked up in the first word of Cicero's next, climactic clause, viz. *locus*,

quam circa lacus lucique sunt plurimi atque laetissimi flores omni tempore anni, locus ut ipse

(Cicero, *Verr*. 2.4.107)

and there is a reprise in the following sentence:

lacumque in eo loco repente exstitisse

(Cicero, *Verr*. 2.4.107)

May one not, then, see in *Met*. 5.385–91 a kind of redeployment in this parallel Ennaean context of those Ciceronian *lacus*, *luci* and *loci*? The allusion suggested is not so much to the actual words, as to the fact of a relationship between them: Ovid's creative appropriation of the Ciceronian model is effected by means of a redefinition of the Ciceronian verbal relationship into a new, and newly meaningful, word-play.

A final, and deliberately tendentious comment may be offered on this allusive piece of punning.

... quo dum Proserpina luco
ludit ...

(*Met*. 5.391–2)

After the word *luco* completes the play between ecphrastic opening and close, the next word, in prominent run-on position

41

and connected through strong assonance to *luco*, is *ludit*. Perhaps the verb has been pressed enough already (see the end of section v above). However, a reflexive twist in the language could encourage one to catch a brief glimpse of Persephone, not just playing *in* the *lucus*, but (as if the heroine were now her own 'author') playing *with the word lucus*,[53] in a fleeting, knowing reference to the pun which gives the landscape its rhetorical shape.

vii

Whatever the merits of this last suggestion, artistic self-definition does seem to have a considerable role to play in Ovid's description of Enna here in *Metamorphoses* 5. And reasons for this should be becoming apparent. In the first place, Cicero's depiction of Enna was, as noted above, one of the great set-piece descriptions of Roman literature, and Ovid could not but be aware of that as he inserted *his* Enna set-piece into his narrative. Thus it is entirely appropriate that he should see an occasion here to take a programmatic look at his own use of descriptive writing; and that the challenge of creating something worthy to stand beside Cicero's ecphrasis should produce seven such concentrated lines.

Another, even more special consideration also emerges from the discussion above. It has to do with the way in which this chapter, like the previous one, is finding the *Metamorphoses* correspondent in so much more than merely its date with the *Fasti*.

The invitation to compare and contrast the two poems goes right back to the beginning of each. The narrative of the *Metamorphoses* opens, in accordance with its professed intention (*Met.* 1.3–4), with an account of the origin of the universe, presented by Ovid as the transformation of Chaos:

> ante mare et terras et, quod tegit omnia, caelum
> unus erat toto naturae vultus in orbe,
> quem dixere Chaos ...

(Met. 1.5–7)

The *Fasti* opens, in accordance with *its* professed intention (*Fasti.* 1.1), with an account of the first day of the calendar year, the Kalends of January, in the form of a dialogue between Ovid and the god Janus. However, in the third line of Janus' first speech comes a small surprise, as we learn that he has an *alias*:

> 'disce metu posito, vates operose dierum,
>   quod petis, et voces percipe mente meas.
> me Chaos antiqui (nam sum res prisca) vocabant:
>   aspice quam longi temporis acta canam.
> lucidus hic aer et quae tria corpora restant,
>   ignis, aquae, tellus, unus acervus erat'
>   (*Fast.* 1.101–6)

– and so, here too, into a cosmogony. From that point on, one cannot but be alive to possibilities for cross-reference between the two poems; and the possibilities are not few. Particularly interesting are the handful of myths which are told at some length in both *Metamorphoses* and *Fasti*: Callisto (*Met.* 2.409–531, *Fast.* 2.153–92), Europa (*Met.* 2.836–3.2 and 6.103–7, *Fast.* 5.603–18), the apotheosis of Romulus (*Met.* 14.805–51, *Fast.* 2.475–512), Hippolytus/Virbius (*Met.* 15.495–546, *Fast.* 6.733–56) – and, several times longer than any of these, the rape of Persephone.

As far as correspondence with the *Fasti* is concerned, then, *Met.* 5.385–91 comes at the key point in the *Metamorphoses*: the ecphrastic description of Enna here inaugurates[54] a uniquely direct and extended confrontation between the parallel poems of Ovid's middle period.

A cross-reference to the *Metamorphoses* version of the rape of Persephone in the introductory couplet of the *Fasti* version has, as we saw, long been discerned: *Fast.* 4.418 *plura recognosces.* It can now further be suggested that both introductions mark this special moment with a particularly subtle demonstration of allusion in parallel to a literary predecessor. In each case a play on the word *locus* is central to the echo: in the *Metamorphoses*, the word is bound up with a *lacus* and a *lucus*; in the *Fasti* the pun involves two senses of *locus* itself.[55] This is not the first time in my study that treatments of the same subject in the *Metamorphoses* and *Fasti* have been traced to the same literary source; nor will it be the last.

Whereas the specific verbal echoes of the Ciceronian ecphrasis in the *Fasti* stand out quite clearly in their own right, it is arguable that the reader would never be able to notice Ciceronian affinities in the *lacus/lucus/locus* word-play in the *Metamorphoses* without having his mind first concentrated by the *Fasti* allusion. But, on the other hand, the programmatic cross-reference in *Fasti*. 4.418 *plura recognosces* suggests that the *Metamorphoses* version should be the one read first. No consistent pattern of priority between the two accounts emerges: here as elsewhere (cf. chapter 4, section ii) they seem to be mutually dependent.

viii

Why, finally, are the swan-songs of the lake adjoining Enna compared to the swan-songs of the river Cayster?

> haud procul Hennaeis lacus est a moenibus altae,
> nomine Pergus, aquae; non illo plura Caystros
> carmina cycnorum labentibus edit in undis
> (*Met.* 5.385-7)

One reason has already been offered: the Ἄσιος λειμών around the Cayster is the classic locale for swans in ancient poetry. However, a brief note by Haupt and Ehwald on *Met.* 5.385ff. suggests a further motive:

Der Ort der Entführung ward in den Sagen verschieden angegeben. In dem alten attischen Hymnus geschieht sie in dem nysischen Gefilde (17 Νύσιον ἂμ πεδίον: vielleicht hat Ovid in Erinnerung an diese Ortsangabe die caystrischen Schwäne erwähnt)

The rape of Persephone is a popular subject throughout antiquity, but the 'old Attic hymn', i.e. the *Homeric Hymn to Demeter*, is one of the earliest and most influential versions.[56] One probable instance of allusion to it in *Metamorphoses* 5 has already (n. 33) been noted in this chapter. Thus the idea adumbrated by Haupt and Ehwald is rather an attractive one. The comparison of the Sicilian rape site favoured by Ovid (as by most later Greek and Roman writers) with the Nysian site found in the *Homeric Hymn*[57] would draw attention to an important literary predecessor in a manner very appropriate to the obliquely programmatic mood of the passage; and such an unpredictable use of a predictable topic (the swans of the Cayster) would be most Ovidian.

But it may seem less than obvious that Caystrian swans should evoke the Νύσιον ... πεδίον of the *Homeric Hymn*, the λειμῶνα ... μαλακόν (*H.Dem.* 7) in which that earlier Persephone picked her flowers. A first move towards the association can be readily enough conceded. While there were many places called Nysa in the ancient world,[58] the only one with potential for geographical association with the Cayster, viz. Carian Nysa, was also the most important. Moreover, it is on record as having identified itself very strongly with the mythical rape: Strabo's description tells of a Plutonium with a temple of Pluto and Core in the Nysian κώμη of Acharaca (*Geog.* 14.1.44).[59] We learn, indeed, that the people of this Nysa were actually able to point to the supposed site of the rape nearby: thirty stadia from the town was a place identified as Persephone's λειμών.

It is worth quoting this portion of Strabo's account in full, as it contains a further piece of information vital to our argument:

ἀπὸ δὲ τριάκοντα σταδίων τῆς Νύσης ὑπερβᾶσι †[60] Τμῶλον τὸ ὄρος τὴν Μεσωγίδα ἐπὶ τὰ πρὸς τὸν νότον μέρη καλεῖται τόπος Λειμών, εἰς ὃν ἐξοδεύουσι πανηγυριοῦντες Νυσαεῖς τε καὶ οἱ κύκλῳ πάντες· οὗ πόρρω δὲ τούτου στόμιόν ἐστιν ἱερὸν τῶν αὐτῶν θεῶν [i.e. Πλούτωνός τε καὶ Κόρης], ὃ φασι καθήκειν μέχρι τῶν Ἀχαράκων. τοῦτον δὲ τὸν λειμῶνα ὀνομάζειν τὸν ποιητὴν φασιν, ὅταν φῇ,

Ἀσίῳ ἐν λειμῶνι,

δεικνύντες Καϋστρίου καὶ Ἀσίου τινος ἡρῷον καὶ τὸν Κάϋστρον πλησίον ἀπορρέοντα

(Strabo, *Geog.* 14.1.45)

In other words, the Nysians associated their meadow not only with the λειμών whence Persephone was abducted, but also, like Haupt and Ehwald, with the λειμών of Homer's Caystrian swans:

... ἢ κύκνων δουλιχοδείρων,
Ἀσίῳ ἐν λειμῶνι, Καϋστρίου ἀμφὶ ῥέεθρα
Homer, *Il.* 2.460–1

In terms of Strabo's account, then, the proposed interpretation of *Met.* 5.386–7 makes perfect sense.

Now one can readily countenance some general familiarity with the fact that Nysa in Caria was identified with the Nysian plain of Persephone's rape in the *Homeric Hymn to Demeter*: plotting well-known fictional places on the map has always been popular, as is testified by, for instance, Odyssean or Arthurian geography. However, to expect Ovid and his Roman readers to have known not only of the association of Carian Nysa with the rape, but also of its association with the celebrated swan-meadow of the Cayster, may seem a little over-optimistic.

Yet it can be argued that this was just the sort of knowledge expected of a man who claimed to be *doctus* in the Alexandrian fashion. Strabo will almost certainly not have been the first to write about the dual associations of this part of the Cayster: at an earlier point in his description of this area of Asia Minor, he himself speaks of his dependence on previous accounts of the region.[61] And such writing was far from being a literary backwater: river-lore, indeed, was a speciality of the Callimachean school, and Callimachus himself wrote a prose work Περὶ τῶν ἐν τῇ οἰκουμένῃ ποταμῶν (see Callimachus, fr. 457–9) – with which, incidentally, Strabo was familiar.[62]

Thus, there is nothing inherently implausible about the kind of geographical allusion being suggested here. However, given that Caystrian swans are something of a standard topic in ancient literature, it would be nice to have a little more encouragement in the Ovidian text for reading *Met.* 5.386–7 in this way. And such encouragement is, I think, forthcoming.

Met. 5.387 *carmina cycnorum labentibus edit in undis.* Swans' song tends to carry certain associations in Latin poetry: as Nisbet and Hubbard note, 'the story of the singing swan was encouraged by the bird's connection with Apollo ..., the Muses ..., and perhaps Orpheus ... Hence poets and other literary men are often compared or identified with swans.'[63] It is worth stressing the strength of this association. *TLL* and *OLD* between them offer eleven non-Ovidian examples of swans (*cycnus* or *olor*) envisaged specifically as singing birds from poetry up to the end of the Augustan period. In no fewer than nine of these, there are clear evocations of 'poets and other literary men'.[64] And a *full* survey of singing swans in Ovid (*Her.* 7.1–2; *Met.* 2.252–3, 5.386–7, 14.429–30; *Fast.* 2.108–10; *Trist.* 5.1.11–12) shows – leaving the present passage out of consideration – allusion to song of the literary kind in every case.[65]

Thus, independently of the programmatic suggestiveness of the Cayster, independently of all the other hints of artistic self-definition discerned in this landscape, there is already good reason to give the *carmina cycnorum* in *Met.* 5.387 a second look.[66]

> ... non illo plura Caystros
> carmina cycnorum labentibus edit in undis
> (*Met.* 5.386–7)

Ovid's lake near the walls of Enna is as rich in the singing of swans as is the proverbial Cayster; but is it not also the case that this Sicilian locale has an unusual wealth of the *literary* variety of swans' song? Not just here in the *Metamorphoses*, but also in the contemporary *Fasti*, the landscape of Enna finds itself involved in a major piece of narrative poetry; and it is perhaps possible to read the imagery as alluding to the fact.

Then, if the Cayster too exercises its programmatic weight, another claim, perhaps an even prouder one, can be elicited. The *carmina* of Ovid's Sicilian landscape are equal in wealth to any *carmina* which the Cayster, i.e. which the Carian setting of the *Homeric Hymn to Demeter*, can 'produce' (*Met.* 5.387 *edit*: note that *edere* also means in Latin 'to publish'[67]): the accounts of the rape of Persephone in *Metamorphoses* 5 and *Fasti* 4 are full worthy, the imagery seems to intimate, to stand beside their Greek literary predecessor.[68]

Once more, a footnote may be added. It was argued above that the openings of the two Ovidian accounts of the rape at *Met.* 5.385–91 and *Fast.* 4.417–18 make common allusion to

Cicero, in each case through a play on the word *locus*. Here, too, a subtle affinity between the two passages suggests itself. If the singing swans of the *Metamorphoses* serve programmatically to place the ensuing narrative in its literary historical context, so, more straightforwardly, does the initial appeal to memory in the *Fasti* (*Met.* 5.386–7 *non illo plura ...* | *carmina*; *Fast.* 4.418 *plura recognosces*). Also, in *Met.* 5.386–7 the site of the rape itself 'produces' (*edit*) ambiguously literary *carmina*; in *Fast.* 4.417 Ovid (in the first person) 'produces' (*edam*) his Persephone narrative; and he does so, moreover, at the behest of an *ipse locus* which is fleetingly felt to represent (see pp. 39–40 above) the site of the rape.

Whether or not such speculations seem attractive, it is clearly time to take a longer look at the question of the interaction of *Metamorphoses* 5 and *Fasti* 4; and, perhaps even more urgently, at the question of where both Ovidian narratives stand in relation to the *Homeric Hymn to Demeter*.

PART II

OVID'S TWO PERSEPHONES

CHAPTER 3

THE *HOMERIC HYMN TO DEMETER*: *FASTI* 4

The *Homeric Hymn to Demeter* is an archaic Greek poem in the Homeric and Hesiodic tradition composed at some time between 675 and 550 B.C. It may be useful to offer a rough summary of its contents. Stating its subject (1–3), the *Hymn* launches straight into its account of the rape of Persephone by Hades at the prompting of Zeus. Persephone is gathering flowers with her companions in the Nysian plain when the earth gapes open and the king of the underworld appears and carries her off, crying vainly for help, on his chariot (4–39). Her cries are finally heard by her mother who, stricken with grief, proceeds to search for her over the earth for nine days with burning torches in her hands, without eating, drinking or washing (39–51). After a meeting with Hecate, Demeter goes to see Helios, and finds out from him the circumstances of the rape. Unconsoled by his view that the match with Hades is no bad thing, Demeter leaves Olympus in her anger with Zeus and wanders on earth disguised as an old woman, ending up in Eleusis (52–97). As she sits sorrowfully by a well, she is met by the daughters of Celeus, ruler of Eleusis. Having told them a false story about her identity and circumstances, she offers herself as a servant, and is given a position as nurse to Celeus' baby son Demophoon (98–173). Received into the household by Celeus' wife Metaneira, she sits in silent grief until made to laugh by Iambe. She refuses to take wine, but gives instructions for the preparation of a barley and water mixture, which she then accepts (174–211). Demophoon flourishes under Demeter's supernatural care. At night she places him in the fire to make him immortal, but is detected and interrupted in this by a dismayed Metaneira (212–50). Snatching the baby from the fire in anger, Demeter upbraids Metaneira for her folly: her son will not now be immortal; nevertheless he will enjoy everlasting honour. Having revealed her true identity, Demeter retreats, grieving for her daughter, to a new temple built on her instructions by the Eleusinians (250–304). She then causes a dreadful famine to afflict the earth, and men till the soil without avail. When Zeus cannot persuade her through embassies from Iris and all the other gods in turn to relent, he sends Hermes to the underworld to bring back Persephone (305–41). Hades, while telling Persephone the great honours that marriage with him will bring, agrees to let her return to her mother. However he gives her the seed of a pomegranate to cat, which ensures that he will not lose her to Demeter for ever. Hermes takes Persephone back to the earth, and she is reunited with Demeter, who discusses her prospects of a complete return, and asks her to recount the story of her coercion (342–404). Persephone tells her about the recent incident of the pomegranate seed, and about the rape in the flowery meadow. The two goddesses spend the day enjoying their reunion, and they are joined by Hecate (405–40). Zeus sends Rhea to offer terms to Demeter: Persephone will spend two-thirds of the year with her mother and the gods, and the other third in the underworld. Demeter agrees, ends the famine on the earth, teaches her rites to the rulers of Eleusis, and returns with Persephone to Olympus (441–84). As the narrative closes and the timeless context of the hymn returns, that mortal whom the two goddesses love is pronounced blest, and the customary invocation and prayer for divine favour for the song is made (485–95).

ii

Richardson, in his exemplary commentary on the *Homeric Hymn to Demeter*, detects its influence in many places in subsequent Greek literature, finding its popularity greatest among the Alexandrians.[1] But what concerns the present study is that he considers, albeit very briefly, the two versions of the rape of Persephone in Ovid's *Metamorphoses* and *Fasti*. Listing a number of parallels, he asserts, against the strong current of modern opinion, that 'there is no reason to doubt that Ovid knew and imitated [the *Hymn*] directly'.[2]

Now it is clear, as is admitted by Richardson, that the

Homeric Hymn to Demeter cannot be Ovid's *only* major source. In both of his accounts, Persephone is abducted not from the Nysian plain but from Enna, and local Sicilian colour is central to much of the action. Ovid is here following the tradition which prevailed in later Greek and in Roman writings, making its first definite appearance in extant literature in the fourth century B.C.[3] This Sicilian version of the rape survives for us in two substantial pre-Ovidian accounts, Diodorus 5.2–5 and Cicero, *Verr.* 2.4.106ff. These two accounts are evidently related to each other, and are generally thought to depend on the Sicilian historian Timaeus of the late fourth and early third centuries B.C.[4]

An examination of Diodorus' account strongly suggests some affinity with Ovid's two versions: the correspondences, many of them quite substantial, are studied by Malten in his 1910 article 'Ein alexandrinisches Gedicht vom Raube der Kore'.[5] The approach taken by Malten to the question of Ovid's sources for the rape of Persephone in the *Metamorphoses* and in the *Fasti* has heavily influenced all subsequent discussions of the topic. Starting with the links between Ovid and Diodorus, he argues that it would be absurd to suppose that the Roman poet took his inspiration from a source like the Greek historian Timaeus, of whose version he takes Diodorus' to be a near-verbatim report. To explain the links, he finds it necessary to postulate a '*Mittelsmann*', who *would* have been inclined to use Timaeus and whom in turn Ovid would have been likely to use as a source for *Metamorphoses* 5 and *Fasti* 4. A learned Alexandrian poet writing a Sicily-based account of the rape of Persephone seems to be what fits the bill.[6]

It is to this hypothesis that the failure of Malten and his successors to study properly the relationship between the *Homeric Hymn to Demeter* and Ovid's two Persephones can be traced; for, following the pattern whereby all the similarities between Ovid and Timaeus (as represented by Diodorus) are explained by the postulation of an Alexandrian poetic intermediary, so this same intermediary, rather than any idea of direct influence, is invoked by Malten to explain a number of similarities which he notes between Ovid's accounts and the

Homeric Hymn.[7] The lost Hellenistic poem, then, uses Timaeus for the actual rape and other Sicilian details, and the *Homeric Hymn* for the Eleusinian action and the end of the story; and Ovid, for his part, simply follows the Hellenistic poem throughout.

Malten ends by considering some actual references to the rape of Persephone, mostly fragmentary, in Hellenistic poetry; and these lead him to suggest an identity for his '*Mittelsmann*'.[8] The opening section of Callimachus' *Hymn to Demeter* (*h.* 6.8–21), with its short, allusive discussion of Demeter's search for Persephone, is taken to be evidence for the existence of a fuller, more explicit treatment of the rape elsewhere in the *œuvre* of Callimachus, now lost; the single line of fr. 611 is argued to be a vestige of that treatment, and to be ascribable to the *Aetia*. To Malten, then, the '*Mittelsmann*' is Callimachus, writing in the *Aetia*. Barwick, however, in 1925, though acquiescing (as do all the later contributors to the *Quellenfrage*) in the critical assumptions underlying Malten's article, counter-proposes as '*Mittelsmann*' Nicander of Colophon. Drawing on an earlier article by Bethe, he is able to adduce in Nicander's support three undoubted coincidences of subject-matter between *Metamorphoses* 5 and the fourth book of the *Heteroioumena*, as attested at Antoninus Liberalis 9, 24 and 28.[9] The next move comes from Herter, in 1941, who rejects Malten's (and Barwick's) single-source theory for *Metamorphoses* 5 and *Fasti* 4, and suggests that Ovid used *both* Nicander *and* Callimachus, preferring the former poet in the *Metamorphoses*, and the latter in the *Fasti*.[10]

Now it is indeed probable that some details at least of the two Ovidian accounts of the rape are coloured by the influence of lost Hellenistic poetry. The claims of Callimachus are tenuous enough;[11] but those of Nicander must be taken seriously. As we saw in chapter 1, pp. 14–15, Ovid evidently owes to the fourth book of Nicander's *Heteroioumena* the basic idea for his Heliconian song-contest at *Met*. 5.300ff. The evidence for this is Antoninus Liberalis 9; and the two other brief Antonine epitomes mentioned above seem to indicate that Ovid underpinned this allusion by working into *Metamorphoses* 5 two stories from elsewhere in *Heteroioumena* 4. An account of the attack of Typhon on the gods (reported at Antoninus Liberalis 28) looks as if it is the model for the Pierid song at *Met.* 5.319–31;[12] and an account of Demeter's transformation of an insolent boy into a lizard (reported at Antoninus Liberalis 24) must surely lie behind the similar episode in Ceres' search for Persephone as narrated by Calliope at *Met.* 5.447–61.[13] However, it also seems clear from the epitomes that the stories of the song-contest, of Typhon, and of the lizard were wholly discrete in *Heteroioumena* 4: the efforts of the reconstructors to establish that Ovid's integrated conception of *Met.* 5.250–678 is lifted in its entirety from the *Heteroioumena*, and, more particularly, their thesis that Nicander treated in that poem the *complete* myth of Persephone and not just the lizard incident, appear both to be grounded in little more than speculation. The most recent attempt to substantiate the latter position, Montanari's in 1974, is also the most ingenious; but the net result of his scrupulous enumeration of alternative patterns of reconstruction available (or in his view unavailable) is to reveal just how few are the data on which the entire *Quellenfrage* from Malten on has been based.[14]

It seems to me that by this point the merits of the above inquiry have been rather outweighed by its disadvantages. To be reminded from time to time of the existence of gaps in our literary historical picture has been salutary; but we have probably gleaned by now everything that we are going to glean about the nature of any Hellenistic influences on Ovid which may belong in those gaps. More important, the obsessive concern with the reconstruction of lost poetry has led to the undervaluing of the more accessible parts of the literary tradition. Even the first and apparently most secure stage in Malten's original theory is open to criticism on this count, viz. his assumption that rather than putting the similarities between Ovid and Timaeus down to direct influence one must postulate a Hellenistic poetic intermediary (the prior assumption that Diodorus is equivalent to Timaeus being, of course, already taken as read). If Hellenistic poets could use Timaeus, and the learned Roman orator Cicero too (see the discussion above), is it really certain that the *doctus poeta* Ovid was incapable of doing the same? Mention of Cicero serves as a reminder that *his* prose account of the rape, brought up in previous discussions of Ovid's sources only as a chance witness to the Sicilian tradition, has already in this investigation had to be promoted to the rank of direct source (chapter 2, section vi above).

However, more than these highly problematical Sicily-based accounts of the rape, it is the *Homeric Hymn to Demeter* which has suffered serious neglect as a result of the pursuit of buried Hellenistic poetry. Most of the contributors to the *Quellenfrage* do not even pause to consider the possibility that Ovid used the *Hymn* directly: they adduce it only as an aid to the reconstruction of supposed intermediaries. Herter does bring up the idea of direct influence in his discussion of the Eleusinian action in the *Fasti*, only to dismiss it immediately: 'Ovid selber wird man die Neuformung der homerischen Szene um so weniger zutrauen, als er sonst keine eigene Kenntnis des Hymnos verrät.'[15] This is an extraordinary statement; for the fact is that it is in no small measure through the perception of close similarities between Ovid and the *Homeric Hymn* that Malten and his successors, including Herter, have built up their picture of a Hellenistic '*Mittelsmann*' in the first place.

Accordingly, resisting the assumptions of the debate thus far, I hope to demonstrate in the ensuing pages that there are more correspondences between the *Homeric Hymn* and Ovid's two accounts, both in general structure and in detail, than has been realised; and that many of these are in fact suggestive of direct, unmediated influence. In any case, even if Ovid *does* make extensive use of lost Hellenistic poetic intermediaries, there are strong *a priori* grounds to expect that, as a learned poet, he will not only be aware of the ultimate source of his borrowing, but will demonstrate his awareness by alluding directly to that source as well as to its Hellenistic progeny.[16] Thus, even without the encouragement already given by that likely allusion in *Met.* 5.386–7 to *carmina* from the plain of

Nysa (chapter 2, section viii), there is every reason for us to begin a detailed examination of Ovid's relationship to the *Homeric Hymn to Demeter* in a positive frame of mind.

iii

Let the *Fasti* 4 account of the rape of Persephone/Proserpina[17] be set beside the *Homeric Hymn* first. If the *Fasti*'s local Sicilian colour and detailed place-name catalogues are alien to the *Hymn*, and suggestive of other areas of literary influence on Ovid, yet the overall impression gained is one of similarity: in the circumstances of the rape itself, in the hospitality and nursing of the child at Eleusis, in the finding of Persephone and in the resolution of the crisis.

Before embarking on an ordered survey, it is worth going straight to two correspondences which should establish immediately that there is more at work here than mere participation in the same general tradition. First, there is the fact that one of the *Hymn*'s most distinctive similes crops up in the *Fasti* account.[18] Here is Demeter, at the moment of Persephone's recovery:

> ἤϊξ' ἠΰτε μαινὰς ὄρος κάτα δάσκιον ὕλη[19]
> (*H.Dem.* 386)

And here is her Latin equivalent, at the moment of Persephone's loss:

> mentis inops rapitur, quales audire solemus
> Threicias fusis maenadas ire comis
> (*Fast.* 4. 457–8)

The maenad comparison is reused, but with the moment of frenzied joy remodelled as a moment of frenzied grief: it is a classic case of echo with inversion. Both mothers rush: compare ἤϊξ' ἠΰτε with *rapitur quales*, and note that Ovid's transformation of the verb hints through word-play at a parallel between the mother's distress and that of the *filia rapta*.[20]

The detail of the *fusis ... comis* in Ovid's simile also participates in the allusion. If the maenad herself is shifted back from the moment of Persephone's recovery in the *Hymn* to the moment of her loss in Ovid, this new elaboration of her appearance derives in turn from the *Hymn*'s version of the moment of loss: behind the free-flowing hair of the maenad to whom the grief-stricken Ceres is compared in the *Fasti* lies the violent unveiling of her hair by the grief-stricken Demeter at that same early juncture in the *Hymn*'s narrative:

> ὀξὺ δέ μιν κραδίην ἄχος ἔλλαβεν, ἀμφὶ δὲ χαίταις
> ἀμβροσίαις κρήδεμνα δαΐζετο χερσὶ φίλῃσι
> (*H.Dem.* 40–1)

The Ovidian simile thus doubles its association with the Greek model.[21]

Finally, references to tradition and report in Roman poetry are often ways of talking programmatically about specifically *literary* tradition.[22] Therefore, when Ovid writes here *quales audire solemus* ..., it is tempting to discern a sly reference to the very allusion being made here: whence comes this familiarity with rushing maenads (the implication may run) but from the *Homeric Hymn to Demeter* itself?

The second correspondence may now be considered. When Demeter in the *Hymn* asks Helios for information about her daughter's whereabouts, he replies with a speech which ends in the following consolation:

> ἀλλὰ θεὰ κατάπαυε μέγαν γόον· οὐδέ τί σε χρὴ
> μὰψ αὔτως ἄπλητον ἔχειν χόλον· οὔ τοι ἀεικὴς
> γαμβρὸς ἐν ἀθανάτοις πολυσημάντωρ Ἀϊδωνεὺς
> αὐτοκασίγνητος καὶ ὁμόσπορος· ἀμφὶ δὲ τιμὴν
> ἔλλαχεν ὡς τὰ πρῶτα διάτριχα δασμὸς ἐτύχθη·
> τοῖς μεταναιετάει τῶν ἔλλαχε κοίρανος εἶναι
> (*H.Dem.* 82–7)

Hades himself later consoles Persephone in words almost identical to 83–5:

> οὔ τοι ἐν ἀθανάτοισιν ἀεικὴς ἔσσομ' ἀκοίτης
> αὐτοκασίγνητος πατρὸς Διός ...
> (*H.Dem.* 363–4)

In the *Fasti*, Sol is much more abrupt than his Greek counterpart; but his brief response to Ceres can be argued to show the *Hymn*'s influence:

Sol aditus 'quam quaeris', ait 'ne vana labores,
nupta Iovis fratri tertia regna tenet'
(*Fast*. 4.583–4)

vana seems to pick up *H.Dem*. 83 μὰψ αὔτως, and *Fast*. 4.584 succinctly to give the same positive view of the rape as Helios' consolation. Behind *Iovis fratri* one can see αὐτοκασίγνητος – not so much the occurrence in *H.Dem*. 85 (where it is Demeter who has Hades as brother) as the words in which Hades himself picks up Helios' speech: *H.Dem*. 364 αὐτοκασίγνητος πατρὸς Διός.

However, it is a passage a little later in the *Fasti* account that clinches the case for allusion to *H.Dem*. 82–7. Having consulted Sol, Ceres has recourse to Jupiter and asks for his help. The scene does not occur in the *Homeric Hymn*, but Jupiter's consoling words to Ceres look distinctly familiar:

Iuppiter hanc lenit factumque excusat amore,
'nec gener est nobis ille pudendus' ait.
'non ego nobilior: posita est mihi regia caelo,
possidet alter aquas, alter inane chaos'[23]
(*Fast*. 4.597–600)

nec gener est nobis ille pudendus is virtually a straight translation of Helios' οὔ τοι ἀεικὴς|γαμβρὸς ἐν ἀθανάτοις (*H.Dem*. 83–4; compare *H.Dem*. 363), and it is succeeded in 599–600 by a near variation of *H.Dem*. 85–7, with (again) a glance at *H.Dem*. 364 αὐτοκασίγνητος πατρὸς Διός in Jupiter's *non ego nobilior*.

Thus Helios' words of consolation in the *Hymn* are closely echoed here in *Fast*. 4.598–600, with variation imparted to the allusion by their transference in Ovid's version to Jupiter; and the debt is, as it were, underlined by the trace of a more direct line of descent from Helios in Sol's abbreviated speech at *Fast*. 4.583–4.

In these instances at least the *Fasti* seems to be very attentive to the *Homeric Hymn to Demeter*. A reading of the whole *Fasti* 4 narrative of the rape will reveal further similarities; and, if some of these can most safely be viewed as merely reproducing the common traditional stock of the myth or as having been filtered down from the *Hymn* to Ovid through intermediaries, others, like those just discussed, appear to arise from close Ovidian engagement with the text of the *Hymn* itself.

iv

Both accounts begin by stating their subject, the rape of Persephone (*H.Dem.* 2–3; *Fast.* 4.417). Then both move on, the *Fasti* after some Sicilian scene-setting, to the meadow (*H.Dem.* 7, cf. *H.Dem.* 417 in Persephone's retelling of the episode; *Fast.* 4.426) where the rape is to take place. In both there are lists of flowers (*H.Dem.* 6–8, cf. *H.Dem.* 426–8; *Fast.* 4.437–42), the *Fasti* catalogue being the fuller, in keeping with the larger scale of its treatment of the scene as a whole. In both the picking of the flowers is prompted by childish high spirits: *H.Dem.* 5 παίζουσαν (cf. *H.Dem.* 425 παίζομεν), *H.Dem.* 16 καλὸν ἄθυρμα 'pretty plaything'; *Fast.* 4.433 *praeda puellares animos prolectat inanis*. Perhaps, moreover, Ovid's verb *prolectat* 'lures' echoes the idea of the flower as a δόλον for the girl in *H.Dem.* 8. Each girl is accompanied by companions: *H.Dem.* 5 παίζουσαν κούρῃσι σὺν Ὠκεανοῦ βαθυκόλποις; *Fast.* 4.425 *filia, consuetis ut erat comitata puellis*, 431–2 '*comites, accedite*' *dixit* | '*et mecum plenos flore referte sinus*'; and it is tempting to see in the last-quoted verse, and again in 436 *haec gremium, laxos degravat illa sinus*, a couple of playful variations by Ovid on that compound epithet βαθυκόλποις attached to the companions in the *Hymn* line.[24]

The actual abduction in the *Fasti* seems to be indebted to the Greek version:

> ἁρπάξας δ' ἀέκουσαν ἐπὶ χρυσέοισιν ὄχοισιν
> ἦγ' ὀλοφυρομένην· ἰάχησε δ' ἄρ' ὄρθια φωνῇ
> κεκλομένη πατέρα Κρονίδην ὕπατον καὶ ἄριστον
> (H.Dem. 19–21)

> βῆ δὲ φέρων ὑπὸ γαῖαν ἐν ἅρμασι χρυσείοισι
> πόλλ' ἀεκαζομένην, ἐβόησα δ' ἄρ' ὄρθια φωνῇ
> (H.Dem. 431–2)

> ... patruus velociter aufert
> regnaque caeruleis in sua portat equis.
> illa quidem clamabat 'io, carissima mater,
> auferor!' ...
> (Fast. 4.445–8)

In the *Fasti* as in the *Hymn* the moment of seizure, the mention of the chariot (described by a colour-adjective evocative of the underworld[25]) and the girl's cry for help all follow closely on one another. As to the last of these, Ovid does more than simply redirect Persephone's cry from her father to her mother. The attachment to πατέρα of the stately Κρονίδην ὕπατον καὶ ἄριστον in her reported cry in the *Hymn* has the effect of suggesting a formal plea to the king of the gods as much as a cry to a father; in Ovid the affecting use of direct speech and the replacement of all the stately epithets by the intimate *carissima* relegate divine power-relations to the background and scale Persephone down to a mere frightened girl who wants her mother. The very switch of parent contributes to this change in tone: in Roman culture at least, a cry to a mother is more suggestive of a child's domestic distress than a cry to a father. In the same spirit of domestication, the abductor ceases to be thought of as the ἄναξ πολυδέγμων |... Κρόνου πολυώνυμος υἱός (*H.Dem.* 17–18) and becomes a plain *patruus* (*Fast.* 4.445). Note that Ovid's modification here of the *Hymn* is based on an idea found in the *Hymn* itself: the Greek Persephone, as we observed just above, could be childish too.

The *Fasti* account returns to the companions and, like Persephone a few lines earlier, they in their turn cry out; and their cries catch the attention of Ceres:

> ut clamata silet, montes ululatibus implent,
> et feriunt maesta pectora nuda manu.
> attonita est plangore Ceres ...
> (*Fast.* 4.453–5)

The companions' reaction to the rape is not mentioned in the *Homeric Hymn*, but Ovid is clearly varying the moment in the *Hymn*'s narrative when Demeter's attention is caught by cries from Persephone herself:

> ἤχησαν δ' ὀρέων κορυφαὶ καὶ βένθεα πόντου
> φωνῇ ὑπ' ἀθανάτῃ, τῆς δ' ἔκλυε πότνια μήτηρ
> (*H.Dem.* 38–9)

The cries still sound in the mountains, even if it is now with a different voice.

Both accounts proceed to describe the mother's grief-stricken reaction and the beginning of her search (*H.Dem.* 40–4; *Fast.* 4.455–62). This, it will be remembered, is the point where the *Fasti*, incorporating an allusion to the description here of the tearing of Demeter's head-dress (*H.Dem.* 40–1), relocates the *Hymn*'s later maenad simile. It is a relocation which can be viewed as faithful to the spirit of the model: for in describing Ceres at the beginning of her search through a pair of similes, the maenad (*Fast.* 4.457–8) and the cow (*Fast.* 4.459–60),[26] Ovid elaborates the technique of the *Hymn*, which also at this point characterises the goddess by means of simile – in its case a single, brief bird simile:

> σεύατο δ' ὥς τ' οἰωνὸς ἐπὶ τραφερήν τε καὶ ὑγρὴν
> μαιομένη ...
>
> (*H.Dem.* 43–4)

With σεύατο δ' ὥς τε perhaps compare the *rapitur quales* that introduces the first of Ovid's two comparisons.

Furthermore, if he displaces that bird simile here, Ovid finds room to make restitution shortly afterwards. The *Fasti* diverges at this point from the *Hymn* and launches into an extended catalogue of places in Sicily visited by Ceres; but in the midst of her wanderings, as at the beginning of them in the *Hymn*, the searching goddess is compared to a bird:

> quacumque ingreditur, miseris loca cuncta querellis
> implet, ut amissum cum gemit ales Ityn
>
> (*Fast.* 4.481–2)

The simile has, of course, been utterly transformed. Persephone's mother is still envisaged as a bird; but the comparison which in the *Hymn* illustrated the goddess's quick flight[27] now illustrates her sad lamentation. The οἰωνός of *H.Dem.* 43 was any bird at all; the *ales* of *Fast.* 4.482 constitutes a specific reference to a well-known myth, the metamorphosed Procne mourning her dead son Itys. Finally, following this last point through, one may see the *Fasti* as having imparted a 'boomerang' movement to the *Hymn*'s simple comparison of Demeter to a bird: the lamenting mother (Ceres) is envisaged as a lamenting bird: but the bird itself originated as a lamenting mother (Procne).

One further point of contact with the *Hymn* in these Sicilian wanderings occurs at *Fast*. 4.491–3, where Ceres lights a pair of torches from the fires spouted forth from Etna by Typhoeus. Ovid thus 'Sicilianises' the torches used by Demeter in her search at *H.Dem*. 48. Note, however, that the association of these brands with Etna is already found on the Sicilian side of the literary tradition in Diodorus 5.4.3 and Cicero, *Verr*. 4.106 and therefore, one guesses, in Timaeus: thus, while the detail fits neatly into the *Fasti*'s pattern of allusion to the *Homeric Hymn*, its literary ancestry contains other elements too.

v

Ceres leaves Sicily and makes her way via another catalogue of places to Eleusis, where the narrative again begins to move in step with the *Hymn*:

> ἕζετο δ᾽ ἐγγὺς ὁδοῖο φίλον τετιημένη ἦτορ
> Παρθενίῳ φρέατι ὅθεν ὑδρεύοντο πολῖται
> (*H.Dem*. 98–9)

> hic primum sedit gelido maestissima saxo:
> illud Cecropidae nunc quoque triste vocant
> (*Fast*. 4.503–4)

Both goddesses, newly arrived at Eleusis, sit down in their sorrow. The well Parthenion and the Agelastos Petra to which Ovid refers in *Fast*. 4.504 are closely linked in tradition;[28] and note how the *Fasti*, like the *Hymn* but in a different way, immediately associates the spot with the local inhabitants. As Ceres sits there, disguised as an old woman (*Fast*. 4.517–8; the same detail at *H.Dem*. 94, 101–4), she is encountered by Celeus, who is bringing home food and firewood, accompanied by his daughter and infant son. In the *Hymn* it is Celeus' four daughters, unaccompanied by their father, who encounter the goddess on their way to bring home water (*H.Dem*. 106–7 φέροιεν | ... φίλα πρὸς δώματα πατρός; compare *Fast*. 4.509–10 *domum* ... | *portat*). The domestic errand in the *Hymn* is integral to the immediate development of the plot, since it is the daughters' trip to the well that results in their encounter with the goddess. In Ovid's version too, the errand is bound up with the development of the plot, but in a delayed, oblique and even slightly ironic way: Celeus' fetching[29] of *arsuris arida ligna focis* (*Fast.* 4.510) foreshadows – note the signposting offered by the future participle – and in a sense makes possible the subsequent use of the *focus* by Ceres which will so alarm Celeus' wife:

> inque foco corpus pueri vivente favilla
> obruit, humanum purget ut ignis onus
> (*Fast.* 4.553–4)

In the Greek account Celeus' daughters now accost Demeter, beginning thus:

> τίς πόθεν ἐσσὶ γρῆϋ παλαιγενέων ἀνθρώπων;
> τίπτε δὲ νόσφι πόληος ἀπέστιχες οὐδὲ δόμοισι
> πίλνασαι ...
> (*H.Dem.* 113–15)

In the *Fasti* too it is Celeus' daughter who first accosts Ceres, and in similar terms:

> 'mater' aít virgo (mota est dea nomine matris),
> 'quid facis in solis incomitata locis?'
> (*Fast.* 4.513–14)

The use of *mater* permits a poignant play on the connotations of that word, such as would not have been possible with the *Hymn*'s corresponding vocative γρῆϋ. However, the Ovidian variation does appear to draw its inspiration from elsewhere in the *Hymn*: the echo here of the *first* address to Demeter by Celeus' daughters can be read as incorporating an allusion to the beginning of the *second* address a few moments later, where the appellation employed is not γρῆϋ but μαῖα:

> φῆ ῥα θεά· τὴν δ' αὐτίκ' ἀμείβετο παρθένος ἀδμής
> Καλλιδίκη Κελεοῖο θυγατρῶν εἶδος ἀρίστη·
> μαῖα ...
> (*H.Dem.* 145–7)

μαῖα, though roughly synonymous with γρῆϋ, has certain peculiar connotations. While usually (as here) a familiar form of address to old women, generally servants, it is cognate with μήτηρ, and seems, indeed, to be applicable to true mothers.[30] It is surely this μαῖα in *H.Dem.* 147, with its slight potential for ambiguity, which prompts Ovid's two-edged *mater*, etymologically cognate and in the same metrical *sedes*, at the beginning of the *Fasti* speech.

Celeus' daughters in the *Hymn* continue their initial questioning of Demeter thus:

> ... οὐδὲ δόμοισι
> πίλνασαι, ἔνθα γυναῖκες ἀνὰ μέγαρα σκιόεντα
> τηλίκαι ὡς σύ περ ὧδε καὶ ὁπλότεραι γεγάασιν,
> αἵ κέ σε φίλωνται ἠμὲν ἔπει ἠδὲ καὶ ἔργῳ;
> (*H.Dem.* 114–17)

In the *Fasti* the offer of hospitality is made by Celeus himself, taking up the questioning from his daughter:

> perstitit et senior, quamvis onus urget, et orat
> tecta suae subeat quantulacumque casae
> (*Fast.* 4.515–16)

Though parallel, the invitations reflect the different sets of social circumstances in the two versions. In the *Hymn* Celeus is a ruler (*H.Dem.* 97 κοίρανος; cf. *H.Dem.* 149–55, 294, 475) who inhabits a μέγαν δόμον (*H.Dem.* 171; cf. *H.Dem.* 164, 185–6). In the *Fasti* he has been transformed into a rustic in an *exiguae ... casae* (*Fast.* 4.526; cf. *Fast.* 4.516, 531), very much in the Hellenistic tradition of humble people who give hospitality to deities.[31] Indeed there is in one place a clear correspondence with the Ovidian *locus classicus* of this, Philemon and Baucis:

> tota domus laeta est, hoc est, materque paterque
> nataque: tres illi tota fuere domus
> (*Fast.* 4.543–4)

> nec refert, dominos illic famulosne requiras:
> tota domus duo sunt, idem parentque iubentque
> (*Met.* 8.635–6)

Note also that the meal set out by Celeus' family in the following couplet (*Fast.* 4.545–6) is similar to some of the fare offered by Philemon and Baucis (*Met.* 8.666, 674–7). It is in line with this presentation that in his offer of hospitality to Ceres at *Fast.* 4.515–16 and later, pressing his invitation, at *Fast.* 4.526 *surge, nec exiguae despice tecta casae* Celeus speaks as to a social superior; and the detail *quamvis onus urget*, besides drawing attention to his generosity, serves subtly to underline this position of disadvantage. The modification of the *Hymn* is considerable: there the daughters' invitation contains no such self-deprecation, perhaps rather verging on condescension in the way that it immediately consigns Demeter to the γυναῖκες … | τηλίκαι; and, of course, the *Hymn*'s Demeter does in the event become a servant to Celeus' family.

Ovid's version of the exchange between Demeter and her Attic benefactors differs from the *Hymn* in other respects too: the Ovidian goddess discloses that her daughter has been raped, where the Homeric Demeter tells a long and involved lie about her circumstances (*Fast.* 4.519–20; *H.Dem.* 120–34); and the discussion of the illness of the baby son subsequently nursed by Ceres in the *Fasti* (*Fast.* 4.529–30) has no equivalent in the *Hymn*, where the infant is quite healthy.

However, there is one further noteworthy point of convergence in this section. Demeter's reply to the daughters' initial questioning includes the following customary wish for their prosperity:[32]

> ἀλλ' ὑμῖν μὲν πάντες 'Ολύμπια δώματ' ἔχοντες
> δοῖεν κουριδίους ἄνδρας καὶ τέκνα τεκέσθαι
> ὡς ἐθέλουσι τοκῆς …
>
> (*H.Dem.* 135–7)

So in her brief reply to the parallel questioning in the *Fasti*, whose latter part, it will be remembered, is put in Celeus' mouth, Ovid's Ceres utters an equivalent wish; but it has been modified so as to fit Celeus' own aspirations rather than those of his daughters:

> sospes eas semperque parens …
> (*Fast.* 4.519)

Perhaps Ovid's version may be thought of in another way too. It seems to add the next stage, so to speak, to a sequence of happiness begun in the *Homeric Hymn*: if 'may you find a husband' is followed in the *Hymn* by 'may you become a parent', that in turn leads naturally to the *Fasti*'s 'may you remain a parent'. Indeed, Ovid's continuation of the life-cycle of the τοκεύς/*parens* is positively invited by the anticipatory use of τοκῆς in *H.Dem*. 137, which has the effect of giving a strong forward impulse to the end of the *Hymn*'s wish.

In whichever of these ways it is viewed, Ovid's version of the wish in *Fast*. 4.519 carries a double point in his narrative. In the first place, by reminding Ceres how her own parenthood is in jeopardy, it leads immediately to her disclosure of her daughter's rape:

> 'sospes eas semperque parens; mihi filia rapta est.
> heu, melior quanto sors tua sorte mea est!'
> (*Fast*. 4.519–20)

Incidentally, the goddess's wish for her benefactors' prosperity is followed in the *Hymn* too by a reference to her own pitiable state:

> ... καὶ τέκνα τεκέσθαι
> ὡς ἐθέλουσι τοκῆς· ἐμὲ δ' αὖτ' οἰκτίρατε κοῦραι
> (*H.Dem*. 136–7)

Note the parallelism of the juxtapositions ... *parens; mihi* ... and ... τοκῆς· ἐμὲ δ' ... In the second place, the conventional sentiments of Ceres' wish hit hard at Celeus too, whose own position as a parent, as we have already learnt (*Fast*. 4.512), is not as secure as Ceres might imagine.

When the goddess has greeted Celeus' wife Metaneira (*H.Dem*. 225; *Fast*. 4.539), she proceeds in similar fashion in each account to nurse their baby son, in the *Hymn* called Demophoon and in the *Fasti*, in accordance with a later development in the tradition, Triptolemus.[33] She takes him to her bosom (*H.Dem*. 231–2, 238; *Fast*. 4.550–1); she breathes her divine strength into him (*H.Dem*. 238; *Fast*. 4.540, 542); and his preternatural progress is observed by his family (*H.Dem*. 235, 240–1; *Fast*. 4.541–4). But, while burying him in the fire at night to make him immortal (*H.Dem*. 239, 242; *Fast*. 4.549–54), the goddess is interrupted by the dismayed mother; and the baby, snatched from the fire, loses its chance of everlasting life

(*H.Dem.* 243–62; *Fast.* 4.555–9). At this point Ovid has executed an interesting little variation on his model, in line with two characteristics of his poetry which often work with (though sometimes against) one another, viz. striking oxymoron and subtle observation of behavioural interaction:

> εἰ μὴ ἄρ' ἀφραδίῃσιν ἐΰζωνος Μετάνειρα
> νύκτ' ἐπιτηρήσασα θυώδεος ἐκ θαλάμοιο
> σκέψατο ...
>
> καί ῥ' ἄμυδις προσέειπεν ἐΰζωνον Μετάνειραν·
> νήϊδες ἄνθρωποι καὶ ἀφράδμονες οὔτ' ἀγαθοῖο
> αἶσαν ἐπερχομένου προγνώμεναι οὔτε κακοῖο·
> καὶ σὺ γὰρ ἀφραδίῃσι τεῇς νήκεστον ἀάσθης
> (*H.Dem.* 243–5, 255–8)

> excutitur somno stulte pia mater, et amens
> 'quid facis?' exclamat, membraque ab igne rapit.
> cui dea 'dum non es', dixit 'scelerata fuisti:
> irrita materno sunt mea dona metu'
> (*Fast.* 4.555–8)

Narrator and goddess in the *Fasti* show at once more wit and more judgement in their interpretation of the mother's conduct (*Fast.* 4.555 *stulte pia*, 4.557 *dum non es . . . scelerata fuisti*) than is found in the simple diagnosis of ἀφραδίῃσι by their respective Homeric forebears (*H.Dem.* 243, 258).[34]

There seems to be a further Ovidian glance at the recurrent ἀφραδίη/ἀφράδμων (*H.Dem.* 243, 256, 258) in the employment in *Fast.* 4.555 of a parallel Latin verbal formation, namely *amens*, modifying the mother's 'thoughtlessness' to 'dementedness'. The use of this word also relates in an interesting way to something earlier in the *Fasti* narrative itself. The description of Metaneira as *amens* brings out a parallel between her behaviour and the earlier maternal distraction of Ceres, *mentis inops* (*Fast.* 4.457) at the moment when she first misses her own child. Well may the goddess understand Metaneira's similar panic here, and refrain from the vehement anger (*H.Dem.* 251 τῇ δὲ χολωσαμένη, 254 θυμῷ κοτέσασα μάλ' αἰνῶς) of her Greek predecessor.

These closely corresponding nursing scenes conclude with parting promises from the goddess that the baby will receive compensation for his mortality (*H.Dem.* 263–7; *Fast.* 4.559–60). The *Fasti* now diverges from the *Hymn* to embark on a third geographical catalogue (*Fast.* 4.563–72). Eventually, having covered the whole world (*Fast.* 4.573–4), Ceres travels to the sky, where she consults the constellation of the Parrhasides about her daughter's whereabouts. With her plea

'Parrhasides stellae, namque omnia nosse potestis,
aequoreas numquam cum subeatis aquas,
Persephonen natam miserae monstrate parenti'
(*Fast.* 4.577–9)

and Helice's suggestion

'. . . Solem de virgine rapta
consule, qui late facta diurna videt'
(*Fast.* 4.581–2)

compare part of Demeter's speech to the sun-god himself in the *Homeric Hymn*:

ἀλλὰ σὺ γὰρ δὴ πᾶσαν ἐπὶ χθόνα καὶ κατὰ πόντον
αἰθέρος ἐκ δίης καταδέρκεαι ἀκτίνεσσι,
νημερτέως μοι ἔνισπε φίλον τέκος εἴ που ὄπωπας
(*H.Dem.* 69–71)

The *Hymn*'s reference to the panoramic vision of Helios is evidently picked up in both Ovidian speeches (*Fast.* 4.577–8, 582). In the latter of them, Ovid seems to underline his appropriation of the Greek motif through a covert ambiguity between two senses of *diurna*. Helice's preceding *crimine nox vacua est* (*Fast.* 4.581) shows that the word is contrasted here with an implied *nocturna* (*OLD* '*diurnus*' 1); but the phrase *facta diurna* also points to the fact that what Ovid's Sun (as opposed to the *Hymn*'s) beholds is precisely the 'day-by-day' (*OLD* '*diurnus*' 2), calendar-oriented action unique to the *Fasti* – which includes, of course, the moment of the *raptus* as written down in *Fast.* 4.445–6.[35] To turn then to the former Ovidian speech, an adoption of the panoramic motif there leads into an echo of the climax of the *Hymn*'s appeal (*Fast.* 4.579; *H.Dem.* 71); also, the same prayer-formula is on display as in *H.Dem.* 69–70, viz. the *potes namque omnia*.[36]

Following Helice's advice, Ceres next approaches the sun-god. As has already emerged in this chapter's introductory discussion, both the brief speech of Sol and Jupiter's longer consolation a few lines further on are closely dependent on Helios' words in *H.Dem.* 82–7. Note the shift in the order of events between the Greek version and the Latin: whereas in the *Hymn* the consultation with the Sun takes place before the wanderings which include the visit to Eleusis, in the *Fasti* it takes place after them. Thus at *H.Dem.* 90ff. it is purely her grief and her anger with Zeus that cause Demeter to wander over the earth, since she already knows from Helios where Persephone is; in the *Fasti*, as normally in later versions of the myth, it is in quest of her daughter that she roams.[37]

vi

The settlement of the crisis is narrated very rapidly in the final nine couplets of the *Fasti* version. Most of what is here can be paralleled in some way in the *Hymn*'s far longer conclusion at *H.Dem.* 334–484: Mercury's trip to the underworld, Persephone's eating of the pomegranate seed with its momentous consequences, Jupiter's division of the year and Ceres' restitution of agriculture are all familiar, the last constituting the only reference in the *Fasti* account to the famine which plays an important part in the *Homeric Hymn* (*H.Dem.* 305ff.). The *Fasti*'s treatment of these events might seem so summary as effectively to preclude any possibility of close engagement with the *Hymn*; but in fact one notable allusion is to be found in that final moment of agricultural rebirth. As in the *Hymn*, it is immediately in consequence of hearing about Jupiter's partition of the year (*H.Dem.* 460–6; *Fast.* 4.613–14) that the goddess ends her famine:

ὣ[ς ἔφατ', οὐ]δ' ἀπίθησεν ἐϋστέφανος Δημήτηρ,
αἶψα δὲ καρπὸν ἀνῆκεν ἀρουράων ἐριβώλων.
πᾶσα δὲ φύλλοισίν τε καὶ ἄνθεσιν εὐρεῖα χθὼν
ἔβρισ' ...

(*H.Dem.* 470–3)

70

> tum demum vultumque Ceres animumque recepit,
> imposuitque suae spicea serta comae:
> largaque provenit cessatis messis in arvis,
> et vix congestas area cepit opes
>
> (*Fast*. 4.615–18)

In *Fast*. 4.617 as in *H.Dem*. 471 the fields (*arva*, etymologically cognate with the Greek ἄρουραι[38]) produce corn again; and *Fast*. 4.618 reuses, though in a different way, the image in *H.Dem*. 472–3 πᾶσα ... | ἔβρισε of a full load caused by luxuriance. But it is what Ovid does in *Fast*. 4.616 to the words in the *Hymn* immediately preceding these correspondences that is of especial interest. The adjective ἐΰστέφανος, used to describe Demeter also at *H.Dem*. 224, 307 and 384,[39] seems in archaic poetry to be a general epithet applicable to any goddess;[40] but its attachment to Demeter at this particular moment of crop-restoration in the *Homeric Hymn* is apt to call to the later reader's mind the crown of corn that becomes a standard element of Demeter's iconography in ancient literature and art, symbolising her patronage of crops.[41] And it is precisely this association that Ovid has made in *Fast*. 4.616 *imposuitque suae spicea serta comae*: the line is not just an echo of the *Hymn*'s ἐΰστέφανος Δημήτηρ, but actually constitutes a sort of mythologist's commentary on the phrase.[42]

vii

plura recognosces:[43] it must now be regarded as established that one cannot read any part of Ovid's *Fasti* 4 account of the rape of Persephone without soon coming upon traces of the *Homeric Hymn to Demeter*, traces which do not seem to have been much obscured by the subsequent generations of poets who may have trodden the same path. Not only do the two narratives have the same overall configuration, but again and again the text of the *Fasti* makes detailed allusion to the *Homeric Hymn*, with the fineness of artistry characteristic of all Ovidian writing. However, this is no place to linger on general conclusions: half of the story of the *Homeric Hymn*'s influence on Ovid has yet to be told.

CHAPTER 4

THE *HOMERIC HYMN TO DEMETER*: *METAMORPHOSES* 5

When we turn our attention back to *Metamorphoses* 5, we immediately find a greater degree of divergence from the *Homeric Hymn to Demeter* than in *Fasti* 4. Foreign to the *Hymn* are the punishment of Typhoeus, the machinations of Venus and no fewer than six episodes involving metamorphosis, namely those of Cyane, the boy transformed into a lizard, Ascalaphus, the Sirens, Arethusa and Lyncus. Furthermore the visit to Attica, so central to the *Hymn* and to the *Fasti* version, is virtually elided here: the stress on the Sicilian locale is almost total. Yet, whatever other literary influences are operative in *Metamorphoses* 5, there is a great deal here to call the *Homeric Hymn* to mind – in the circumstances of the rape itself, in Ceres' initial searches, in the famine inflicted by her and in the concluding events of the story; and, as in the case of the *Fasti*, a closer examination will serve to reveal the intimacy of some of these connexions.

ii

Here again (cf. chapter 3, section iii) are Helios' words of consolation to Demeter in the *Homeric Hymn*

> ἀλλὰ θεὰ κατάπαυε μέγαν γόον· οὐδέ τί σε χρὴ
> μὰψ αὔτως ἄπλητον ἔχειν χόλον· οὔ τοι ἀεικὴς
> γαμβρὸς ἐν ἀθανάτοις πολυσημάντωρ Ἀϊδωνεὺς
> αὐτοκασίγνητος καὶ ὁμόσπορος· ἀμφὶ δὲ τιμὴν
> ἔλλαχεν ὡς τὰ πρῶτα διάτριχα δασμὸς ἐτύχθη·
> τοῖς μεταναιετάει τῶν ἔλλαχε κοίρανος εἶναι
>   (*H.Dem.* 82–7)

and the echo of *H.Dem.* 83–5 in Hades' own later words to Persephone:

> οὔ τοι ἐν ἀθανάτοισιν ἀεικὴς ἔσσομ' ἀκοίτης
> αὐτοκασίγνητος πατρὸς Διός...
>   (*H.Dem.* 363–4)

Once more, Ovid puts in Jupiter's mouth a distinctly similar speech of consolation to the aggrieved mother:

> '... sed si modo nomina rebus
> addere vera placet, non hoc iniuria factum,
> verum amor est; neque erit nobis gener ille pudori,
> tu modo, diva, velis. ut desint cetera, quantum est
> esse Iovis fratrem! quid, quod non cetera desunt
> nec cedit nisi sorte mihi? ...
>
> (*Met.* 5.524–9)

Met. 5.526 *neque erit nobis gener ille pudori* virtually translates *H.Dem.* 83–4 οὔ τοι ἀεικὴς | γαμβρὸς ἐν ἀθανάτοις (compare also *H.Dem.* 363), and *Met.* 5.527–8 *quantum est | esse Iovis fratrem* picks up, again not so much αὐτοκασίγνητος καὶ ὁμόσπορος in *H.Dem.* 85, as rather Hades' version in *H.Dem.* 364, αὐτοκασίγνητος πατρὸς Διός. Then the mention of Dis's exalted station in *Met.* 5.528–9 echoes *H.Dem.* 85–6, with *sorte* preserving the idea of allotment in the Greek ἔλλαχεν (nor is διάτριχα completely unrepresented in Ovid's text, inasmuch as *Met.* 5.529 calls to mind the earlier reference to Dis's lot by Venus at *Met.* 5.368 *cui triplicis cessit fortuna novissima regni*). Finally, the *diva* addressed to Ceres in the Latin passage (*Met.* 5.527) may be seen as picking up the vocative θεά in the Greek (*H.Dem.* 82).

Evidently the evocation of the *Homeric Hymn* here is very similar to that in the equivalent words of Jupiter in *Fast.* 4.597–600, discussed in the third chapter. Jupiter in the *Metamorphoses* perhaps emerges as the more energetic apologist in his use of the rhetoric of persuasion to press his points home:[1] *sed si modo nomina rebus | addere vera placet*; *tu modo, diva, velis*; *ut desint cetera, quantum est* ...; *quid, quod non cetera desunt*.... On a more minute scale there is an interesting comparison to be drawn between the use of direct quotation throughout the speech in the *Metamorphoses* and the glide from report to direct quotation which begins the speech in the *Fasti*:

> '... non hoc iniuria factum,
> verum amor est; neque erit nobis gener ille pudori'
>
> (*Met.* 5.525–6)

Iuppiter hanc lenit, factumque excusat amore,
'nec gener est nobis ille pudendus' ait
(*Fast*. 4.597–8)

The *Fasti's factumque excusat amore* reads as a succinct report
of Jupiter's *non hoc iniuria factum,* | *verum amor est* in the
Metamorphoses, the more so in that it reproduces two of his
actual words.[2] Then in the following line Jupiter's voice begins
to be heard in the *Fasti* too, uttering virtually the same words
as he does in *Met*. 5.526. It is here that a nice distinction can
be made. The *neque* which begins Jupiter's statement in the
Metamorphoses is closely reproduced in the *nec* which begins
Fast. 4.598: but it is rather less closely reproduced in what
Jupiter is represented as actually *saying* in that line. The fact
is that, despite my punctuation, the god does not say *nec* where
his counterpart says *neque*: rather *nec*, by a rapid connecting
device apparently unique to Ovid, stands for an *et* belonging
to the narrator's *ait* and a *non* uttered by Jupiter, something
which can be marked in modern texts only by what Housman
calls 'a grotesque employment of inverted commas', viz. *'ne' c
'gener est nobis ille pudendus' ait.*[3] The effect of asymmetry-
within-symmetry thus obtained is rather piquant. And, lest
anyone should lazily take the symmetry between *Met*. 5.526
and *Fast*. 4.598 at face value, Ovid ensures that the trick will
be appreciated by performing it here not once but twice: as well
as corresponding to *Met*. 5.526, within the *Fasti* narrative itself
'ne' c 'gener est nobis ille pudendus' ait answers, with exactly
the same false symmetry of *nec*, to a rhythmically identical and
verbally and assonantally close line in the immediately preceding speech of Ceres to Jupiter: *Fast*. 4.592 *nec gener hoc
nobis more parandus erat.*

The other correspondence which inaugurated my survey of
the influence of the *Homeric Hymn to Demeter* on *Fasti* 4 in
the previous chapter involved the comparison of Persephone's
mother to a maenad:

στῆσε δ' ἄγων ὅθι μίμνεν ἐϋστέφανος Δημήτηρ
νηοῖο προπάροιθε θυώδεος· ἡ δὲ ἰδοῦσα
ἤϊξ' ἠΰτε μαινὰς ὄρος κάτα δάσκιον ὕλῃ
(*H.Dem*. 384–6)

74

attonita est plangore Ceres (modo venerat Hennam)
nec mora, 'me miseram! filia' dixit 'ubi es?'
mentis inops rapitur, quales audire solemus
Threicias fusis maenadas ire comis

(*Fast.* 4.455–8)

The following passage in the *Metamorphoses* 5 account has never before been adduced in this connexion:

mater ad auditas stupuit ceu saxea voces
attonitaeque diu similis fuit, utque dolore
pulsa gravi gravis est amentia ...

(*Met.* 5.509–11)

Ceres, after learning from Arethusa the whereabouts of her daughter, is *attonitae ... similis*. The phrasing is such as to give one pause. If Ceres were described by a bare adjectival *attonita*, one might be inclined to read the word as merely implying in a loose way some kind of access of emotion.[4] But to say that Ceres is *like* an *attonita*, *attonitae ... similis*, demands a closer consideration of the implications of the word. It strongly suggests that the *attonita* to which Ceres is being compared is something quite specific: either the primary sense should strictly apply, Ceres thus being compared to someone stunned by lightning;[5] or, by the word's other specialised usage, the comparison should be with a woman smitten with divine frenzy[6] – in other words, with a maenad.

The attractiveness of this second interpretation in the light of the maenad comparisons in the *Homeric Hymn* and in the *Fasti* 4 narrative is immediately evident. And, gratifyingly, it is endorsed by the presence in the passage of verbal echoes of *Fast.* 4.455–8. Here Ceres is compared to an *attonita*; there, just before being compared to a maenad, she is described as *attonita* (*Fast.* 4.455). Here she suffers *amentia* (*Met.* 5.511); there, in connexion with the maenad simile, she is *mentis inops* (*Fast.* 4.457). Thirdly, the maenad's *fusis ... comis* in *Fast.* 4.458 may be seen as corresponding to Ceres' *passis ... capillis* just below this point in the *Metamorphoses* version (*Met.* 5.513). Final confirmation of the adumbrated maenad simile lies within the *Metamorphoses* passage itself. Two comparisons describe Ceres' state in *Met.* 5.509–10, the first of which has not yet been considered: *mater ad auditas stupuit ceu saxea voces.* Now at one level this functions as an element in one of the thematic networks which help to unify the texture of the *Metamorphoses*: it slyly recalls the petrifactions perpetrated by the Gorgon's head in the preceding Perseus episode, and it looks forward to another sorrowing *mater* literally rather than metaphorically turned to stone in the following book, Niobe at *Met.* 6.303–12.[7] However, in addition this striking *ceu saxea* image combines with the potentially Bacchic *attonitae ... similis* immediately below to evoke a simile in that celebrated neoteric hexameter narrative, Catullus 64:

> quem procul ex alga maestis Minois ocellis,
> saxea ut effigies bacchantis, prospicit, eheu,
> prospicit ...[8]

> (Catullus 64.60–2)

The richness of the *Metamorphoses* passage can now be appreciated. Just as in the *Fasti* (and, indeed, with a glance in its direction) Ovid has followed the *Homeric Hymn to Demeter* in comparing the goddess to a maenad; and he has built in, so to speak, an additional reference to the finest maenad simile in the Latin tradition.[9] The reader must work quite hard to elicit all this: the obliquity of the allusion in the *Metamorphoses* serves as a foil to the open self-declaration of its *Fasti* equivalent.

In conclusion, a number of interesting contrasts may be remarked. First, whereas the similes in the *Hymn* and in the *Fasti* are both associated with rapid movement on the goddess's part (*H.Dem.* 386 ἤϊξε; *Fast.* 4.457 *rapitur*, 461–2 *concita cursu | fertur*), the *Metamorphoses* comparison, like its other, Catullan progenitor, is associated with the total immobility of petrifaction. Second, whereas the *Hymn* passage is preceded by a chariot ride from the underworld (*H.Dem.* 375–84), the *Metamorphoses* passage is succeeded by a chariot ride to the heavens (*Met.* 5.511–12). Finally, there is the matter of the position in the order of events occupied by the simile in each case. The classic inversion has already been noted (in chapter

3) whereby the maenad comparison occurs in the *Hymn* just where Demeter recovers Persephone and in the *Fasti* just where she loses her. In the *Metamorphoses* the comparison comes at a third crucial juncture, viz. where the goddess learns from Arethusa of her daughter's whereabouts; and Ceres herself offers a characterisation of this moment a few lines later:

> en quaesita diu tandem mihi nata reperta est,
> si reperire vocas amittere certius, aut si
> scire, ubi sit, reperire vocas ...
>
> (*Met.* 5.518–20)

In other words, if the maenad comparison moves from the moment of Persephone's recovery in the *Hymn* to the moment of her loss in the *Fasti*, here in the *Metamorphoses* (in what must be read as a knowing variation on this relationship) it is associated with a moment which avowedly combines recovery and loss: the context has been modified by Ovid as teasingly as has the simile itself.

It is clear that in the passages just discussed *Metamorphoses* 5 is as intimately related to the *Homeric Hymn to Demeter* as is *Fasti* 4. It is also clear, not for the first time in these investigations, that the two Ovidian versions of the rape are meant to be compared and contrasted with each other.[10] In one place the *Fasti* seems to modify the *Metamorphoses*, and in another the current seems to flow in the opposite direction: the play with reported speech in *Fast.* 4.597–8 has to be read with the direct *Met.* 5.525–6 in mind, but the devious treatment of the maenad simile in *Met.* 5.509ff. is best appreciated with the more straightforward *Fast.* 4.455ff. as background. As in chapter 2, section vii, the picture which emerges, and which will continue to emerge as the present chapter unfolds, is one of mutual dependence between the two versions. Having evidently been conceived in parallel, Ovid's Persephones demand appreciation in parallel.[11]

iii

The survey may now start afresh from the site of the abduction. Again, the Sicilian locale is foreign to the *Homeric Hymn*; but that very circumstance leads, we have suggested (chapter 2, section viii), to a riddling evocation of the *Hymn* right at the outset of the narrative:

> ... non illo plura Caystros
> carmina cycnorum labentibus edit in undis
> (*Met.* 5.386–7)

And, even more than in the *Fasti*, the gathering of flowers at this Enna is reminiscent of the activity in the Νύσιον ... πεδίον. Persephone's childish delight as she picks the blooms in the *Hymn* is mirrored in *Met.* 5.391–4; and, as has already been noted in chapter 2, n. 33 above, the parallel is underlined by verbal echo:

> ... quo dum Proserpina luco
> ludit et aut violas aut candida lilia carpit
> (*Met.* 5.391–2)

ludit picks up *H.Dem.* 5 παίζουσαν, also at the line-beginning; but the whole echoes more closely Persephone's own version of the scene later in the *Hymn*:

> ἡμεῖς μὲν μάλα πᾶσαι ἀν' ἱμερτὸν λειμῶνα
> . . . .
> παίζομεν ἠδ' ἄνθεα δρέπομεν χείρεσσ' ἐρόεντα
> (*H.Dem.* 417, 425)

ludit, occurring at the line-beginning, completes a clause which starts above by setting out who is playing and where: these are precisely the circumstances of παίζομεν, except that in the *Hymn* a seven-line catalogue naming Persephone's companions[12] intervenes while the syntax is in suspension. Then, proceeding forward from *ludit*, *Met.* 5.392 like *H.Dem.* 425 is concerned with the plucking of flowers, and the combination *ludit et ... carpit* reproduces the *Hymn*'s παίζομεν ἠδ' ... δρέπομεν.

Persephone gathers a much less varied bunch of flowers in the *Metamorphoses* than she does in the *Hymn*. There is no sizeable catalogue here, but simply *aut violas aut candida lilia*. Now violets and white lilies are frequently found in the bouquets of Roman poetry, and the contrast of red and white, such as Bömer discerns in his commentary on the passage, is a common mannerism in the European literary tradition in general;[13] but I think a closer look will demonstrate that the young goddess's choice of flowers here is dictated by more than mere convention. What flowers does Persephone gather in the *Homeric Hymn*? We are told twice: first in the narrative at the beginning of the *Hymn*, and again near the end in Persephone's own recapitulation of the event:

> παίζουσαν κούρῃσι σὺν Ὠκεανοῦ βαθυκόλποις,
> ἄνθεά τ' αἰνυμένην ῥόδα καὶ κρόκον ἠδ' ἴα καλὰ
> λειμῶν' ἂμ μαλακὸν καὶ ἀγαλλίδας ἠδ' ὑάκινθον
> νάρκισσόν θ' ...
>
> (H.Dem. 5–8)

> παίζομεν ἠδ' ἄνθεα δρέπομεν χείρεσσ' ἐρόεντα,
> μίγδα κρόκον τ' ἀγανὸν καὶ ἀγαλλίδας ἠδ' ὑάκινθον
> καὶ ῥοδέας κάλυκας καὶ λείρια, θαῦμα ἰδέσθαι,
> νάρκισσόν θ' ...
>
> (H.Dem. 425–8)

Each list contains six flowers. Persephone gathers the rose (*H.Dem.* 6, 427), the saffron (*H.Dem.* 6, 426), the ἀγαλλίς (*H.Dem.* 7, 426), the ὑάκινθος (*H.Dem.* 7, 426),[14] the narcissus (*H.Dem.* 8, 428) and – what? According to the first version of the catalogue, she gathers also ἴα, i.e. violets (*H.Dem.* 6). But the second version disagrees: there ἴα are absent, and the bouquet is completed instead by λείρια (*H.Dem.* 427). Now the ancients were not in full accord as to what bloom was meant by λείριον; but while some took it to be a narcissus, it was most commonly identified with the flower which in Latin goes by the etymologically cognate name of *lilium candidum*.[15] Therefore, if asked what flowers are gathered by Persephone in the *Homeric Hymn*, the pedantic commentator is likely to go straight to the nub of the matter and to reply that, depending on which of the two versions is true, she plucks either violets or white lilies; and this is precisely what Ovid has answered, playing the pedantic commentator (perhaps one may invoke yet again that suggestive word *ludit*[16]), in a consummately economical allusion to the *Hymn*'s pair of flower catalogues:[17]

... quo dum Proserpina luco
ludit et aut violas aut candida lilia carpit
(*Met.* 5.391–2)

It is arguable that the *Homeric Hymn* itself invites this play by drawing attention to the discrepancy between its two catalogues. Persephone begins and ends her recapitulatory speech with strong avowals that she is telling the whole truth: *H.Dem.* 406 τοιγὰρ ἐγώ τοι μῆτερ ἐρέω νημερτέα πάντα; *H.Dem.* 433 ταῦτά τοι ἀχνυμένη περ ἀληθέα πάντ' ἀγορεύω. Assertions of this kind are common in epic. However, Richardson notes that Persephone actually seems within her speech to depart from the truth in claiming that Hades forced her to eat against her will at *H.Dem.* 413: contrast the original account of the incident at *H.Dem.* 371–3, where no mention of compulsion is made.[18] In the light of this, Richardson is tempted to see Persephone as 'protesting too much' in *H.Dem.* 406 and *H.Dem.* 433; and the temptation is strengthened by the fact that Demeter earlier in the poem uses a similar profession of veracity (*H.Dem.* 120–1) to introduce a complete tissue of lies.[19] If such a reading is admitted, it can now further be suggested that Persephone's protestations also serve despite herself to draw attention to the less consequential inconsistency in her report of the contents of the bouquet. Moreover, is it not the case that, in the language of the two catalogues themselves, after the crucial narcissus (*H.Dem.* 8–16, 428) the discrepant blooms can be felt to stand out a little from the rest, the ἴα alone being given an adjective in the first (*H.Dem.* 6 καλά) and in the second the λείρια being singled out by Persephone's fervent θαῦμα ἰδέσθαι (*H.Dem.* 427)? If such hints in the *Hymn* do lie behind *Met.* 5.391–2, the Ovidian allusion is all the more aptly made.

The condensation of the Greek model in the *Metamorphoses* contrasts with the *Fasti*'s presentation of a list which is even longer and more leisurely than those in the *Hymn* (*Fast.* 4.437–42; see chapter 3, p. 60 above). However, an acknowledgement of the *Metamorphoses* may none the less be discerned in the arrangement of the flowers in the parallel version: *violaria* are prominently placed at the end of the first, and *lilia* ...

alba at the end of the final line of the catalogue (*Fast.* 4.437, 442).

Dis now suddenly breaks into the peaceful scene and Persephone is carried off (*Met.* 5.395ff.; cf. *H.Dem.* 16ff.). As in the *Fasti*, Ovid modifies the *Hymn*'s account of the goddess's cry for help; but what is especially interesting here is the more elaborate treatment in the *Metamorphoses* of the detail associated with the cry in the *Fasti*, Persephone's tearing of her clothes:

> ἥγ' ὀλοφυρομένην· ἴαχησε δ' ἄρ' ὄρθια φωνῇ
> κεκλομένη πατέρα Κρονίδην ὕπατον καὶ ἄριστον
> (*H.Dem.* 20–1)

> illa quidem clamabat 'io, carissima mater,
> auferor!', ipsa suos abscideratque sinus
> (*Fast.* 4.447–8)

> ... dea territa maesto
> et matrem et comites, sed matrem saepius, ore
> clamat, et ut summa vestem laniarat ab ora,
> collecti flores tunicis cecidere remissis,
> tantaque simplicitas puerilibus adfuit annis,
> haec quoque virgineum movit iactura dolorem
> (*Met.* 5.396–401)

Persephone's childish reactions are beautifully observed here in the *Metamorphoses*. As in the *Fasti* (chapter 3, pp. 60–1 above), the idea of depicting Persephone as a child comes from the *Hymn* itself;[20] but Ovid, with his nice touch for characterisation, transcends the original in his exploration of the possibilities thus offered. Furthermore, a piece of verbal wit enriches the vignette. Persephone has been filling her *sinus* with flowers: *Met.* 5.393–4 *calathosque sinumque | implet.* What exactly is it that happens in *Met.* 5.398–9? The flowers are in the girl's *sinus*, i.e. in the hanging fold of her dress which serves as a pocket.[21] When the dress is torn, the fold is loosed, with the result that the flowers fall out (*tunicis cecidere remissis*): the material which was doubled over has become in the accident single. Now, given that in Latin the standard term for something doubled, and especially for cloth that is doubled, is *duplex*[22], after its accident this former *sinus* must be in the strictest sense of the word *simplex* (the *sim-* element being related to *semel*, and the *-plex* to *plico* 'fold').[23] *tantaque simplicitas puerilibus adfuit annis*: Persephone's grief at the loss of her flowers is attributed in *Met.* 5.400–1 to her childish simplicity; but there is also a sly hint at the fact that the *iactura* itself is to be attributed to a different kind of *simplicitas*, viz. that which has suddenly become the characteristic not just of Persephone but also of her dress! Note, incidentally, that if a word-play is associated here with the emptying of a *sinus*, in the corresponding part of the *Fasti* there is a play on words associated with the filling of *sinus* (chapter 3, p. 60 above).

iv

The abductor drives over Sicily with his victim and meets the nymph Cyane, an encounter in the *Metamorphoses* which seems to owe nothing to the *Homeric Hymn to Demeter*. Cyane upbraids Dis for the manner in which he is conducting his courtship of Persephone, contrasting the exemplary behaviour of her own husband Anapis; but she gets short shrift from the underworld king, and, traumatised, undergoes transformation (*Met.* 5.409–37). All this is absent in the *Fasti* too; but Cyane does earn one brief mention there, early in the first of the three great lists of places included in Ceres' quest for her daughter:

> iamque Leontinos Amenanaque flumina cursu
> praeterit et ripas, herbifer Aci, tuas:
> praeterit et Cyanen et fontes lenis Anapi
> et te, verticibus non adeunde Gela
> > (*Fast.* 4.467–70)

praeterit et Cyanen: to the reader with an eye on the *Metamorphoses* version, this item will inevitably stand out a little from the rest of the catalogue; and it is tempting, I think, to discern in it an arch programmatic cross-reference. As part of her itinerary in *Fast.* 4.469, Ceres 'goes past' Cyane. But *praeterire*, as well as meaning 'to pass by (so as to include)',[24] can also mean 'to pass by (so as to leave out)'[25] – which, at least in terms of narrative coverage, is effectively what Ceres does to Cyane in the *Fasti* as opposed to in the *Metamorphoses*: with *Fast.* 4.469 here contrast *Met.* 5.464–73, to be discussed below, especially 465 (same *sedes*) *venit et ad Cyanen*. And, to push things further still, *praeterire* in Latin rhetorical contexts commonly means 'to pass over (in speaking)' [26] – so that *Fast.* 4.469 can aptly hint at what *the poet himself* does here to the tale which he treats so fully in the other version: *praeterit et Cyanen*.

Let us return to the point where we left our survey of the *Metamorphoses* narrative. After Cyane's artfully narrated, limb-by-limb transformation into water (*Met.* 5.425–37),[27] Ceres finally makes her appearance in this version; and her entry is strongly influenced by the entry of Demeter into the *Homeric Hymn*'s narrative. The parallelism is not exact: in the *Hymn* Demeter is introduced at the moment of her first perception of and reaction to Persephone's loss (*H.Dem.* 39–42); in the *Metamorphoses* there is no coverage of this initial moment, but Ceres appears when already embarked on her quest, the *Hymn* being taken up as a model at the point where its narrative has moved on to describe Demeter's search for her daughter.

The affinity of *Met.* 5.438–47 with *H.Dem.* 43–51 is immediately established:

σεύατο δ' ὥς τ' οἰωνὸς ἐπὶ τραφερήν τε καὶ ὑγρὴν
μαιομένη ...

(*H.Dem.* 43–4)

interea pavidae nequiquam filia matri
omnibus est terris, omni quaesita profundo
(*Met.* 5.438–9)

The Latin goddess seeks her daughter *omnibus ... terris, omni ... profundo*, where her Greek counterpart seeks ἐπὶ τραφερήν τε καὶ ὑγρήν. Ceres' use of torches in her search carries on the allusion:

... κατὰ χθόνα πότνια Δηὼ
στρωφᾶτ' αἰθομένας δαΐδας μετὰ χερσὶν ἔχουσα
(*H.Dem.* 47–8)

... illa duabus
flammiferas pinus manibus succendit ab Aetna
perque pruinosas tulit irrequieta tenebras
(*Met.* 5.441–3)

As in Diodorus 5.4.3 and Cicero, *Verr.* 2.4.106, and as in the parallel *Fast.* 4.491–4, the torches have been 'Sicilianised'; but their debt to the *Homeric Hymn* is emphasised by verbal echo: *flammiferas pinus manibus* renders word for word αἰθομένας δαῖδας μετὰ χερσίν, the corresponding adjectives having, moreover, the same one-and-a-half-foot metrical pattern. Ceres has nothing to drink during her search, just like Demeter in the *Hymn*:

οὐδέ ποτ' ἀμβροσίης καὶ νέκταρος ἡδυπότοιο
πάσσατ' ἀκηχεμένη, οὐδὲ χρόα βάλλετο λουτροῖς[28]
(*H.Dem.* 49–50)

fessa labore sitim conceperat, oraque nulli
colluerant fontes ...
(*Met.* 5.446–7)

There are three aspects to the goddess's abstention in the Greek version to the one in Ovid. However, a second is adumbrated: Ovid's talk of 'rinsing out' the mouth[29] serves to evoke not just the *Hymn*'s mention of abstention from drinking (*H.Dem.* 49) but also, obliquely, its mention of abstention from washing, with *colluerant* calling to mind the cognate λουτροῖς in *H.Dem.* 50.

There are a couple of other points of similarity between the accounts of the days which the goddess spends searching. Immediately after mentioning her abstention from washing, the *Hymn* moves on to a new phase in the action by way of a ὅτε clause (*H.Dem.* 51). So too the *Metamorphoses*, immediately after its allusion to this abstention, makes a similar move through a *cum* (*Met.* 5.447–8); but it takes a short cut on its model by beginning the new scene not after the temporal clause but within it: the so-called *cum inversum* is employed. Then – the second point – one may see ἐπήλυθε φαινόλις Ἠώς in the *Hymn*'s ὅτε clause as prompting the mention of the advent of

Dawn earlier in the *Metamorphoses* version of the search: *Met.* 5.440 *udis veniens Aurora capillis*.

Ceres is received at a small cottage, and is mocked by an insolent boy, whom she transforms for his sins into a lizard (*Met.* 5.447–61). This detail in the myth, as we remarked in chapter 3, section ii, seems to derive from Nicander's *Heteroioumena*. It has no equivalent in the *Homeric Hymn*, though the idea of hospitality for the wandering goddess and, in particular, her acceptance from her host of a distinctive barley drink mark the passage as having some affinity with details in the *Hymn*'s Eleusinian episode (*H.Dem.* 96ff., esp. 208–11).[30]

However, a few lines later there occurs an allusion to the *Hymn* which deserves close attention in view of what has just been said about the manner of the goddess's entry into the narrative at *Met.* 5.438ff. Ceres, having returned after her worldwide search[31] to Sicily (*Met.* 5.464 *Sicaniam repetit*), where Persephone disappeared, is presented with the sight of her daughter's girdle floating on the waters of the metamorphosed Cyane (*Met.* 5.465–70); and her reaction to this is distinctly reminiscent of Demeter's display of grief at the earlier point in the *Hymn* when she *first* perceives and reacts to her loss:

> ... τῆς δ' ἔκλυε πότνια μήτηρ·
> ὀξὺ δέ μιν κραδίην ἄχος ἔλλαβεν, ἀμφὶ δὲ χαίταις
> ἀμβροσίαις κρήδεμνα δαΐζετο χερσὶ φίλῃσι
>
> (*H.Dem.* 39–41)

> quam simul agnovit, tamquam tum denique raptam
> scisset, inornatos laniavit diva capillos
> et repetita suis percussit pectora palmis
>
> (*Met.* 5.471–3)

In each case the goddess, perceiving an indication of Persephone's plight (*H.Dem.* 39 τῆς δ' ἔκλυε; *Met.* 5.471 *quam simul agnovit*), expresses her grief by tearing (*H.Dem.* 41 δαΐζετο; *Met.* 5.472 *laniavit*) in one case the veil on her hair (*H.Dem.* 40–1 ἀμφὶ δὲ χαίταις | ἀμβροσίαις κρήδεμνα) and in the other her hair itself (*Met.* 5.472 *inornatos ... capillos*).[32] The *Hymn*'s mention of the fact that she does this with her own hands is transferred in the *Metamorphoses* to a second violent action in the next line (*H.Dem.* 41 χερσὶ φίλῃσι; *Met.* 5.473 *suis ... palmis*).

This is rather interesting. After the demonstration above that the introduction of Ceres into the narrative at *Met.* 5.438–47 makes pervasive allusion to the introduction of Demeter into the *Hymn* at *H.Dem.* 39–51 except (p. 83 above) in its failure to echo her initial moment of perception and reaction at *H.Dem.* 39–42, here, some thirty lines later, that omission is, so to speak, made good. And the one clause in the Ovidian passage not so far considered suggests that this is indeed the way to read the allusion: *Met.* 5.471–2 *tamquam tum denique raptam | scisset*. In the first place, there is subtle observation of behaviour here: though Ceres has long been aware of the abduction of her daughter, it is only now, Ovid tells us, when she is confronted with the tangible evidence of the fallen girdle, that the calamity really strikes home. But also, at a more technical level, the *tamquam* clause, by presenting Ceres' display of grief here as a kind of delayed reaction to the abduction, points to the fact that in literary historical terms this display of grief is a kind of delayed *allusion* to the initial reaction to the abduction in the *Homeric Hymn*. That initial description in the *Hymn*, by being held over here until the moment of the mother's return to the scene of the crime,[33] gains both in fineness and in power: it is an object lesson in creative imitation.

There is another possible way of looking at the allusion. Whereas in the *Homeric Hymn* the goddess tears the veil on her hair, here in the *Metamorphoses* she goes one stage further in tearing her hair itself. Is this perhaps because she is to be thought of as having *previously* torn off her veil, like her Homeric counterpart, on first discovering the loss of her daughter? This could be the implication of the fact that her hair, before being torn, is already *inornatos*.[34] In the same spirit, one could read *repetita* in *Met.* 5.473 *et repetita suis percussit pectora palmis* as suggesting not just a 'rain' of blows but also, by an adumbrated ambiguity, a 'repetition' of blows inflicted at that earlier stage in the action.[35] In short, then, having passed over the initial grief of Ceres so as to treat it in its later moment of consummation, does Ovid now go some way towards reinstating that first moment between the lines, as it were, of his narrative?

v

After all this, Ceres is really no closer to finding her daughter. She reproaches the earth, Sicily especially, and inflicts on it a dreadful famine. This episode, all but elided in the *Fasti* version (see chapter 3, section vi), is reminiscent of Demeter's visitation of a famine on the earth after her visit to Celeus' house. In each case, men sow the fields in vain and are themselves faced with death (*H.Dem.* 305–11; *Met.* 5.477–86). Demeter's famine immediately prompts pleas from Iris (*H.Dem.* 314ff.) and then from all the other gods in turn, acting as Zeus' emissaries; that of Ceres immediately leads to a plea from the nymph Arethusa (*Met.* 5.487ff.).

Arethusa combines another role with that of suppliant. Whereas in the *Hymn* and in the *Fasti* it is the Sun who tells the goddess the whereabouts of her daughter, here it is Arethusa who gives the information;[36] and in ending her speech to Ceres with a reference to the positive side of Persephone's situation

<blockquote>
sed regina tamen, sed opaci maxima mundi,
sed tamen inferni pollens matrona tyranni!
(*Met.* 5.507–8)
</blockquote>

she appears to be echoing Helios' concluding words at *H.Dem.* 83–7 and Sol's abbreviated version of these at *Fast.* 4.584 *nupta Iovis fratri tertia regna tenet*. It is also the case that Arethusa has in her something of the *Hymn*'s Hermes: each travels under the earth – *H.Dem.* 340 ὑπὸ κεύθεα γαίης; *Met.* 5.504 *sub terris* – and finds Persephone ill at ease in her new abode: *H.Dem.* 344 πόλλ' ἀεκαζομένη μητρὸς πόθῳ; *Met.* 5.506 *illa quidem tristis neque adhuc interrita vultu*.

Ceres' shocked reaction to the news of her daughter's position alludes subtly, as analysed earlier in the chapter, to the maenad simile applied to the goddess at a comparable juncture in the *Homeric Hymn*, and also to the related simile in the parallel *Fasti* version. She repairs to Jupiter who, in response to her angry complaints, seeks to justify the rape in words which, again as discussed earlier in the chapter, draw extensively on the speeches of Helios and Hades in the *Hymn*. Jupiter concludes his reply to Ceres by saying that Persephone can return to the heavens if she has not eaten anything in the underworld (*Met*. 5.529–32): compare the conclusion of Jupiter's equivalent speech at *Fast*. 4.601–4 and Demeter's words to Persephone (partly lost to us) at *H.Dem*. 393ff. But Persephone cannot fulfil the condition for, as in the *Hymn* (*H.Dem*. 371–3, more or less – see p. 80 above – repeated by Persephone herself at *H.Dem*. 411–13), she has tasted the seed of a pomegranate.

The crucial act is the same, but the attendant circumstances have been altered. Whereas in the *Hymn* Hades gives the seed to Persephone to eat, in the *Metamorphoses* the goddess herself plucks the pomegranate from a tree in an underworld garden:[37]

> ... quoniam ieiunia virgo
> solverat et, cultis dum simplex errat in hortis,
> Puniceum curva decerpserat arbore pomum
> sumptaque pallenti septem de cortice grana
> presserat ore suo ...
>
> (*Met*. 5.534–8)

The modification in Ovid's account gives a new tightness to the myth. Persephone is again going through what she went through at Enna: once more she is in a rich landscape; once more she plucks (*Met*. 5.536 *decerpserat*; *Met*. 5.392 *carpit*); and once more her actions are characterised by childish simplicity (*Met*. 5.535 *simplex*; *Met*. 5.400 *simplicitas*). Even the *dum* construction employed to set the girl in the landscape (*Met*. 5.535) serves to evoke the earlier scene (*Met*. 5.391–2, 393–4). In fine, Persephone's loss of her rights to the upper world is represented as a kind of re-enactment of her original abduction. And perhaps this parallelism has a more than decorative function. Does it not carry the implication that Persephone has now made the same mistake twice, that she has failed to learn from her earlier experience the dangers attendant (traditionally so, one may add[38]) on culling the earth's fruits in a *locus amoenus*? The suggestion of innocence beguiled by sophistication in *Met.* 5.535 *cultis dum simplex errat in hortis* is striking; and it is Persephone's persistence in the *simplicitas* shown by her in the first crisis that brings about her downfall in the second.

In the *Fasti* the eating of the pomegranate seed is recounted by Mercury in a brief report:

> 'rapta tribus' dixit 'solvit ieiunia granis,
> Punica quae lento cortice poma tegunt'
> (*Fast.* 4.607–8)

We find here three *grana* to the *Metamorphoses*' seven;[39] but there are some verbal similarities between the two versions. *Met.* 5.534–5 *ieiunia* ... | *solverat* corresponds to the *Fasti*'s *solvit ieiunia*; *Met.* 5.536 *Puniceum* ... *pomum* corresponds to *Punica* ... *poma*; and the slightly surprising pale rind of the pomegranate in *Met.* 5.537 is to be explained not only (as Bömer acutely notes) in terms of its provenance in the *pallida regna*[40] but also by the fact that at the strictly verbal level *pallenti* ... *cortice* transforms the *Fasti*'s more predictable[41] *lento cortice* by adding, as it were, an extra syllable to the beginning of the adjective.

Incidentally, although Persephone is not seen to repeat the initial act of plucking in the *Fasti* as she is in the *Metamorphoses*, a similar phenomenon, but involving her mother rather than herself, is found in the course of the *Fasti*'s account of the events at Eleusis:

> illa soporiferum, parvos initura penates,
> colligit agresti lene papaver humo.
> dum legit, oblito fertur gustasse palato
> longamque imprudens exsoluisse famem
> (*Fast.* 4.531–4)

In gathering the poppy, Ceres echoes her daughter's culling of flowers a hundred lines earlier: with *legit* here compare *Fast.*

4.437, 441 and 442, and note that poppies are gathered by one of Persephone's companions at *Fast*. 4.438. But, more than this, in the next couplet Ceres foreshadows her daughter's *second* crucial act, viz. the breaking of her fast in the under-world at *Fast*. 4.607–8, quoted above: with *solvit ieiunia* refer-ring to Persephone in *Fast*. 4.607 compare *exsoluisse famem* referring to Ceres here in *Fast*. 4.534, and also *posuit ieiunia* in the following line. Thus, albeit in a very different way from the *Metamorphoses*, the *Fasti* too brings together Persephone's two moments of crisis; and perhaps it is not wholly by chance that a *dum* construction, whose application to Persephone at both of the critical moments in the *Metamorphoses* narrative is one of the things which draws them together, is applied to Ceres here in the *Fasti* at the moment when she obliquely effects the same association.

vi

The *Metamorphoses* now diverges completely from the *Homeric Hymn* in recounting the transformations of Ascalaphus, nota-ble for his disservice to Persephone (*Met*. 5.538–52), and of the Sirens, notable for the faithfulness of their service (*Met*. 5.552–63). After these episodes, the time comes for the pro-blems created by the rape to be resolved; and the *Hymn* once more shows the way. Like Zeus in the Greek account, Jupiter divides up the year so as to accommodate both claimants to Persephone:

> νεῦσε δέ οἱ κούρην ἔτεος περιτελλομένοιο
> τὴν τριτάτην μὲν μοῖραν ὑπὸ ζόφον ἠερόεντα,
> τὰς δὲ δύω παρὰ μητρὶ καὶ ἄλλοις ἀθανάτοισιν
> (*H.Dem*. 445–7; cf. *H.Dem*. 463–5)

> Iuppiter ex aequo volventem dividit annum:
> nunc dea, regnorum numen commune duorum,
> cum matre est totidem, totidem cum coniuge menses
> (*Met*. 5.565–7)

The Ovidian passage modifies the proportions;[42] but it re-tains the *Hymn*'s antithetical presentation, with the balance of *totidem* and *totidem* picking up the balance of μέν and δέ, and in particular the Latin half-line *cum matre est totidem* echoing the Greek τὰς δὲ δύω παρὰ μητρί. Moreover the phrase *volvens annus*, which occurs only here in 250-odd Ovidian uses of the word *annus*,[43] evidently functions as a straight translation of the *Hymn*'s ἔτος περιτελλόμενον.

Then at the very end, in the *Metamorphoses*' only overt acknowledgement of the Attic dimension which is so central to the *Hymn* and to the *Fasti* version, Ceres travels to Athens and enrols Triptolemus as her agent in spreading her divine gift of agriculture (*Met.* 5.642ff.). She thereby calls to mind the very last part of the *Hymn*'s narrative, where Demeter returns her attention to Eleusis and instructs its rulers, among whom Triptolemus is given pride of place, in the performance of her rites and mysteries (*H.Dem.* 473–82).[44]

Ovid's winding up of the story of the rape of Persephone in *Met.* 5.564–71 and 642ff. is effectively interrupted by the long inset tale of the attempted rape of Arethusa. However, the interruption itself should be recognised, I think, as something occasioned by the conclusion of the *Homeric Hymn*, no less than what precedes and what follows it.

Immediately after the recovery of her daughter, Demeter asks Persephone to recount the story of her coercion (*H.Dem.* 393–4, 404). Persephone's reply (*H.Dem.* 406–33), relating first how she ate the pomegranate seed in the underworld and then how Hades abducted her from the λειμών,[45] with minor variations repeats much of the narrative of *H.Dem.* 340–74 and *H.Dem.* 5–20, the recapitulation being expanded by a catalogue of Persephone's companions at the rape. This is by far the longest and most striking instance in the *Homeric Hymn to Demeter* of 'epic repetition': as Richardson points out ad loc., a number of shorter passages in the *Hymn* display this feature of archaic epic style, but such lengthy repetition is avoided in other places where the situation might seem to invite it.

Now in the final section of the *Metamorphoses* version, again just after the recovery of her daughter (*Met.* 5.572 *nata secura recepta*), Ceres, like Demeter in the *Hymn*, asks someone to recount the story of her coercion (*Met.* 5.572–3). However, it is not Persephone that she asks, but Arethusa; and thus, while she again hears about a rape in reply, it is not this time a recapitulation of the narrative of *Persephone*'s rape, but another story altogether – one, nevertheless, that constantly invites comparison with the main narrative. This too is a rape story which begins, like that of Persephone, with the maiden surprised by the predatory male in a *locus amoenus* (*Met.* 5.585ff.; *Met.* 5.385ff.). And the conclusion of the story is equally familiar: the distressed nymph Arethusa, like the distressed nymph Cyane in the main Persephone narrative, melts away completely into water, dissolving into streams of perspiration where the other dissolves into tears (*Met.* 5.632ff.; *Met.* 5.427ff.). Other, detailed points of similarity between the stories of Arethusa and Persephone encourage further comparison and contrast.[46]

What we have here, it seems to me, is a very clever piece of creative imitation: Ovid has capped his early Greek model by replacing the 'epic repetition' of Persephone's rape prompted by Demeter's request for information with a passage which, in response to an equivalent request in the *Metamorphoses*, offers not the same story but a closely parallel one. One can perhaps go further. The Arethusa episode exemplifies a literary technique common in Hellenistic and Roman poetry, and nowhere more common than in the *Metamorphoses*, whereby a short epic narrative has a different, but in some sense relevant, story inset.[47] It is tempting to read Ovid's allusion as a programmatic comment on the very nature of this technique. By setting one story inside another, as so often in the *Metamorphoses*, and by showing how in this particular case the inset story corresponds to a relatively straight retelling of the main story in the archaic Greek source, does not Ovid make the point that in a manner of speaking any such inset story can be viewed as a 'retelling' of its associated main story; that one of the key functions of an inset narrative is to provide a parallel treatment of an element in the outer narrative, and thus, in a way, to repeat that narrative? As with the playful exploitation of the single discrepancy between the flower-catalogues of *H.Dem.*

5–8 and 425–8, something completely new and unexpected has arisen out of that recapitulatory speech by Persephone in the *Homeric Hymn*.

The one passage in the *Metamorphoses* conclusion not so far considered describes the reaction of Persephone to her partial restoration to the upper world:

> vertitur extemplo facies et mentis et oris;
> nam modo quae poterat Diti quoque maesta videri,
> laeta deae frons est, ut sol, qui tectus aquosis
> nubibus ante fuit, victis e nubibus exit
>
> (*Met.* 5.568–71)

Note the language used in the first line to describe Persephone's change of inner mood and outward expression. Any mention of change in this poem must carry the possibility of a knowing reference to metamorphosis;[48] and the vocabulary employed in *Met.* 5.568 cannot but bring such associations to the fore. *verto(r)* is a very common verb in Latin, but in the *Metamorphoses* over half of its occurrences are concerned with the act of supernatural transformation. Bömer's observations on Ovidian usage show that, like *muto(r)* and *fio*, *verto(r)* virtually has the status of a technical term in the poem.[49] What is more, it occurs twice in the specialised sense within a hundred lines of the present passage, describing the transformations of Ascalaphus above (*Met.* 5.545) and of Alpheus below (*Met.* 5.638).[50] Also, of the four passages in the poem other than the present in which *verto(r)* and *facies* (in its own right a very common word in transformation scenes[51]) are found in a syntactical relation, three are directly, and the other indirectly, descriptive of metamorphosis: thus Periclymenus in *Metamorphoses* 12:[52]

> hic ubi nequiquam est formas variatus in omnes,
> vertitur in faciem volucris ...
>
> (*Met.* 12.559–60)

Finally, the unassuming word *modo* used in *Met.* 5.569 to point to Persephone's previous state makes a contribution to this playful use of the terminology of metamorphosis to describe a non-metamorphic change. '*modo* ist haüfig Terminus der

Metamorphose', observes Bömer ad loc.; and twice already in the Persephone story, once of Cyane and once of the boy transformed into a lizard, the word has been used in this quasi-formulaic manner, whereby it points to the state of the victim immediately prior to transformation:

> et, quarum fuerat magnum modo numen, in illas
> extenuatur aquas ...
>
> (*Met.* 5.428–9)

> ... et, quae modo bracchia gessit,
> crura gerit; cauda est mutatis addita membris
> (*Met.* 5.455–6)

Persephone's inner and outer change here has come in immediate consequence of the settlement worked out by Jupiter:

> at medius fratrisque sui maestaeque sororis
> Iuppiter ex aequo volventem dividit annum:
> nunc dea, regnorum numen commune duorum,
> cum matre est totidem, totidem cum coniuge menses.
> vertitur extemplo facies et mentis et oris
> (Met. 5.564–8)

Compare the result of the equivalent division of the year at the end of the *Fasti* account:

> et factura fuit, pactus nisi Iuppiter esset
> bis tribus ut caelo mensibus illa foret.
> tum demum vultumque Ceres animumque recepit
> (*Fast.* 4.613–15)

With their parallel contexts, and their identical distinctions between inner and outer elements in the change (*mentis/oris* in the *Metamorphoses*, *animum/vultum* in the *Fasti*), *Met.* 5.568 and *Fast.* 4.615 are evidently congruent – except in one crucial respect. The same settlement results in the same change of mood and of expression, but in different goddesses: in the *Fasti* it is not Persephone whose recovery is thus described, as in the *Metamorphoses*, but her mother Ceres. *vertitur extemplo facies et mentis et oris*: the play with terminology of supernatural transformation just discussed perhaps encourages one to see here for a moment, as well as a description of Persephone's change *within* the *Metamorphoses* narrative, a sly program-matic acknowledgement of a more radical change which she has to undergo *between* this line and the equivalent line in the parallel *Fasti* version: a metamorphosis, as it were, from Persephone into Ceres.[53]

Be this suggested nuance as it may, there is certainly a close correspondence between Persephone's recovery in the *Metamorphoses* and that of Ceres in the *Fasti*; and this is in line with a strong tendency towards a similar association within the *Metamorphoses* account itself. The description of Persephone's change in *Met.* 5.568–71 is bracketed by mentions of the state of Ceres: immediately beforehand in *Met.* 5.564 the mother is *maestae*; immediately afterwards in *Met.* 5.572 she is *secura*. Evidently, then, at the same time as her daughter undergoes her more fully advertised change, Ceres cheers up too.

Moreover, Ceres is drawn in still further by the language in which Persephone's recovery is described in *Met.* 5.568–71. First and most simply, the reference to the previous state of Persephone as *maesta* (*Met.* 5.569) recalls that description of Ceres as *maestae* just five lines above. Second, the implica-tions of a remark made some seventy lines above to Ceres by Arethusa must be considered:

> mota loco cur sim tantique per aequoris undas
> advehar Ortygiam, veniet narratibus hora
> tempestiva meis, cum tu curaque levata
> et vultus melioris eris ...
>
> (*Met.* 5.498–501)

In *Met.* 5.572–3 it is made clear that this *hora tempestiva* has now arrived: Ceres is *secura*, thus fulfilling the condition in *cum tu curaque levata*, and Arethusa is duly asked for her story:

> exigit alma Ceres, nata secura recepta,
> quae tibi causa fugae, cur sis, Arethusa, sacer fons
>
> (*Met.* 5.572–3)

But do not those words of Arethusa about Ceres' future change, with their distinction between inner mood and outward expres-sion (*Met.* 5.500–1 *cum tu curaque levata*|*et vultus melioris eris*) also seem to anticipate the description of *Persephone*'s recovery at *Met.* 5.568 with its parallel *mentis/oris* distinction? While *Met.* 5.568 picks up in a more straightforward way Arethusa's remark about Persephone herself in the underworld at *Met.* 5.506 *illa quidem tristis neque adhuc interrita vultu* – the evocation of Dis in *Met.* 5.569 ensures this recall – it is interesting in the present context that it should relate so aptly to her remark about Ceres too.[54] And still more intriguing is the way that a description of Ceres' expression soon after that first encounter with Arethusa

> ... ibi toto nubila vultu
> ante Iovem passis stetit invidiosa capillis
> (*Met.* 5.512–13)

is taken up by a simile in our passage. Now that Jupiter has resolved the rape problem (*Met.* 5.564ff.), the clouds covering the goddess's countenance can clear. And so indeed they do:

> laeta deae frons est, ut sol, qui tectus aquosis
> nubibus ante fuit, victis e nubibus exit
> (*Met.* 5.570–1)

But again one goddess has merged into the other. Whereas the clouds had gathered on the countenance of Ceres, it is not from Ceres' countenance they they figuratively disperse here, but from that of Persephone.

These 'intrusions' by the mother into the daughter's reactions in *Met.* 5.568–71 do not create any real confusion as to who is doing what at this point in the *Metamorphoses* narrative. Rather their effect is to suggest that Persephone and Ceres are so much in sympathy with each other that to describe the feelings of one at this moment of deliverance is also to describe the feelings of the other.

I have not mentioned the *Homeric Hymn to Demeter* for some time; and it may be that this investigation of the behaviour of Persephone and Ceres in *Met.* 5.568–71 and the surrounding lines should be read as a complete digression from the subject of the chapter. However, let the following passage from the conclusion of the *Hymn* be considered:

> ὣς τότε μὲν πρόπαν ἦμαρ ὁμόφρονα θυμὸν ἔχουσαι
> πολλὰ μάλ' ἀλλήλων κραδίην καὶ θυμὸν ἴαινον

ἀμφαγαπαζόμεναι, ἀχέων δ' ἀπεπαύετο θυμός.
γηθοσύνας δὲ δέχοντο παρ' ἀλλήλων ἔδιδ[όν τε]
(*H.Dem.* 434–7)

Like the *Metamorphoses* passage under discussion, these lines
tell how the two goddesses regain their happiness after the
return of Persephone. And like the *Metamorphoses* passage,
but in a much more straightforward way, they emphasise the
complete sympathy of daughter and mother at this point.
H.Dem. 434 ὁμόφρονα θυμόν, *H.Dem.* 435 ἀλλήλων κραδίην
καὶ θυμόν, *H.Dem.* 436 ἀμφαγαπαζόμεναι, *H.Dem.* 437
γηθοσύνας δὲ δέχοντο παρ' ἀλλήλων ἔδιδ[όν τε]: could it be
that the merging of Persephone's and Ceres' feelings discerned
in the conclusion of the Ovidian account is inspired by and
obliquely alludes to the remarkable concentration of vocabulary of concord and reciprocity applied to them in this passage
of the *Hymn*?

vii

The suggestion is offered tentatively; but the subtle approach
to the *Hymn* thus envisaged accords well with what has been
seen of Ovid's strategy elsewhere in *Metamorphoses* 5. The
allusion to the *Homeric Hymn to Demeter* in the *Fasti* version
is more pervasive than that in the *Metamorphoses*; but the
allusion here is perhaps the more impressive in the way that it
seems to demand, and then in turn to promote, an excep-
tionally deep appreciation of the inner workings of the model.

In his two accounts of the rape of Persephone, Ovid meas-
ures himself against a distinguished Greek predecessor. The
comparison does him no discredit: having considered the results of his engagement with the *Homeric Hymn to Demeter*,
we can hardly begrudge him that proud programmatic claim
in *Met.* 5.386–7.

It only remains to remark on the opening words of the
Muse's recitation in *Metamorphoses* 5. Before starting on the
narrative which will quickly move from the tale of Typhoeus
to the story of Persephone's rape, Calliope prefaces her song
thus:

> prima Ceres unco glaebam dimovit aratro,
> prima dedit fruges alimentaque mitia terris,
> prima dedit leges. Cereris sunt omnia munus:
> illa canenda mihi est. utinam modo dicere possim
> carmina digna dea! certe dea carmine digna est
>
> (*Met.* 5.341–5)

With its list of ἀρεταί linked by anaphora, its declaration that such-and-such a god will be sung, its stress on the richness of material thus available and its typical culmination in a prayer, this is evidently a hymn.[55] Not only that, but it is a hymn to Ceres. Could anything more appropriately introduce a narrative which is to be so strongly influenced by the most celebrated of hymns to Ceres' Greek equivalent Demeter? The hymnic format, no longer embracing the whole narrative as in the Homeric poem, is now restricted to a preface; but the hint is unmistakable. Before the appearance of Enna, before the introduction of Persephone, the Nysian plain is already coming into view.

ELEGY AND EPIC:
A TRADITIONAL APPROACH

My final investigation of the Ovidian Persephone owes much to a monograph which it has recently become fashionable to decry as having done more harm to the appreciation of the *Metamorphoses* than anything else this century. Formerly enshrined as a classic, Richard Heinze's *Ovids elegische Erzählung* now tends to be summoned up in critical discussions, if at all, only for immediate exorcism.

What Heinze argued, it will be remembered, was that the metrical distinction between the *Metamorphoses* and the *Fasti* carried with it a more fundamental distinction between the types of narrative in the two poems: the one was epic in character and the other elegiac. As will also be remembered, he began by considering in detail the two versions of the rape of Persephone in *Metamorphoses* 5 and *Fasti* 4, on the grounds that this uniquely substantial parallel in subject-matter between the *Metamorphoses* and the *Fasti* constituted an especially strong invitation to draw comparisons.[1] It is worth quoting in English his summary of what he claimed to have found there:[2]

Ovid in the two versions of his story has juxtaposed two types of poetic narrative, obviously with the explicit design of contrasting one with the other. In his *Metamorphoses* narrative the strong, active emotions are emphasised, sudden love and sudden anger; in the *Fasti* the softer feelings, sorrowful lamentation and pity. In the *Metamorphoses* the divine majesty of the characters is carefully enhanced; in the *Fasti* divinity is humanized. The descriptions of the *Metamorphoses* accent the grandiose; those of the *Fasti* the homely and idyllic. In the *Metamorphoses* the style of the narrative maintains a kind of solemn dignity; in the *Fasti* it is more lively and active. The first clings closely to the objectivity of epic; the *Fasti* gives more scope to the personality of the narrator and his own contemporary point of view.

Heinze argued at some length in the body of his monograph that these findings held good, not just for the two Persephone narratives, but for the *Metamorphoses* and the *Fasti* as a whole.

Although qualified in some respects by others, his conclusions commanded broad acceptance, and profoundly influenced Ovidian scholarship, for half a century. Magnus pronounced in 1920 'für künftige Erklärer der Fasten, aber auch der Metamorphosen, wird das schöne Buch auf lange eine reiche Fundgrube sein'; and in 1966 Otis could still write 'despite his evident failure to see many nuances ... his fundamental distinction remains as clear and self-evident as when he first propounded it in 1919'.[3]

However, it was perhaps inevitable that a formulation as extreme as Heinze's would eventually face a more radical challenge.[4] The similarities in narrative manner between the *Metamorphoses* and the *Fasti*, it began to be felt, were just as noteworthy as any difference between them. What of the fact that other epics quite evidently contain much more in the way of 'die göttliche Majestät ... geflissentlich gesteigert' and 'das Grandiose' than the *Metamorphoses*, and that other elegiac poems offer 'weichere Empfindungen' than the *Fasti*?[5] Is it really possible to distinguish between the descriptions of landscape in the two works? Has Heinze no sense of Ovid's humour?

The most concentrated (and most vehement[6]) criticism has come from D.A. Little. Little demonstrates through close analysis that the *Metamorphoses* and the *Fasti* often signally fail to conform to the epic–elegiac distinctions laid down by Heinze.[7] More seriously, he calls Heinze's very premises into question,[8] arguing that it is a 'pseudo-truism' to claim that poets like Ovid attached importance to distinctions between genres like epic and elegy. Such differences of narrative manner as really do exist between the *Metamorphoses* and the *Fasti* have nothing to do with genre, according to Little, but find their full explanation in the divergent requirements of (in the former case) a poem which tells entertaining stories for their own sake and (in the latter case) a poem concerned to offer an exposition and celebration of the Roman cult.

Now there is much good sense in the first part of this reappraisal. The reaction of recent critics against Heinze's overepic reading of the *Metamorphoses* has yielded valuable work on the poem's undoubted affinities with the elegiac tradition, notably that of Tränkle and Knox. But, as will happen, the balance has tipped a little too far the other way; and the old orthodoxy which regarded the *Metamorphoses* as fundamentally epic in character is in danger of giving way to a new orthodoxy which holds, not just that the *Metamorphoses* contains unepic elements, but that the epic criterion is not relevant to the appreciation of the poem at all.[9] The leap from the first of these propositions to the second is a large one, and has, I fear, been too lightly undertaken. The plain fact is that Ovid in the *Metamorphoses* abandons the habits of well over half a working lifetime to write in hexameters rather than in elegiac couplets;[10] and we will do well to ask ourselves whether we are prepared to regard this move as wholly without significance before we dismiss Heinze's genre-based approach completely.

Another slightly worrying tendency in recent contributions to the discussion has been a failure to recognise that the parallel Persephone narratives must constitute something of a special case in any comparison between the *Metamorphoses* and the *Fasti*. It was, after all, the very uniqueness of the opportunity for direct comparison and contrast here which first attracted Heinze's attention; and it was only after he had set out the clear generic distinctions (as he saw them) between *Met.* 5.341ff. and *Fast.* 4.417ff. that he went on to argue for an extension of these distinctions to the *Metamorphoses* and the *Fasti* as a whole.

Now in Heinze's reading the significance of the correspondence of the twin stories turned out to be simply that it rendered more observable certain contrasts in narrative technique which were found to obtain impartially throughout the *Metamorphoses* and the *Fasti*. His overall reading of the poems has been questioned; but it has not occurred to anyone to question that crucial step which produced it. The fact is that the uniqueness of the opportunity offered in *Met.* 5.341ff. and *Fast.* 4.417ff. of comparing two substantial versions of the same story could actually be viewed *a priori* as militating *against* any simple extension of conclusions drawn there to other areas of the two poems: an atypical correspondence might call for an atypical response, rather than for an especially clear version of a typical one.

The implications are important: Heinze's critics have evidently felt up to now that their strictures on his overall interpretation of the poems are automatically applicable to his interpretation of the two Persephone stories. But this is not necessarily so. The parallel accounts of the rape cannot be carelessly lumped in with the rest of the *Metamorphoses* and the *Fasti* in wholesale judgements on the genre-based approach: they must be treated first and foremost as the remarkable exercise in cross-reference which they indubitably are: and only with due care can they be viewed as part of a wider picture.

As a final preliminary, it may be remarked that, contrary to what might be expected of it, the present inquiry will not attempt an exhaustive survey of precisely how much in *Met.* 5.341ff. can be called truly epic, and how much in *Fast.* 4.417ff. truly elegiac. Clearly Heinze pushed the distinction too far; but the key to the understanding of the generic issue[11] lies not so much in asking how many degrees too far he pushed it, as rather in giving fresh consideration to the other question posed by Little, viz. whether he was justified in formulating the distinction at all.

Some measurements will indeed be offered in this chapter, in order to show on the one hand that there is more than enough potential for genre-based differentiation between the twin Persephone episodes to make Heinze's approach very attractive, yet on the other that there are sufficient weak spots to make any simple acquiescence in it impossible. But what the ensuing chapter will then attempt to demonstrate is that this untidy state of affairs is by no means the impasse which it is currently taken for. Not only when they are being observed, but also when they are being transgressed, boundaries of genre will be argued to be essential to the presentation of *Met.* 5.341ff. and *Fast.* 4.417ff. Justification for the invocation of the epic and elegiac categories in the Persephone episodes will be sought in terms new to the long-standing critical controversy, and through the use of previously unrecognised evidence; evidence, moreover, which will allow to Ovid a larger role in the discussion than heretofore.

ii

In Heinze's view, what above all else marked out the *Fasti* 4 treatment of the Persephone myth as elegiac was its stress on sorrowful lamentation and pity ('schmerzliche Klage und Mitleid'): hence his employment of 'das ἐλεεινόν' as a label for the elegiac type of narrative.[12] Heinze has sometimes been accused of imputing characteristics to genres which would not have been recognised by the poets he writes about; but here he could hardly be on firmer ground. Although elegy in Augustan Rome most famously means subjective love elegy, its supposed origins are always kept in view:

> versibus impariter iunctis querimonia primum
> (Horace, *A.P.* 75)

From the time of Aristophanes and Euripides ancient opinion is unanimous in connecting elegy with mourning. The etymology from ἔλεος is frequently offered, as are etymologies from the εὖ λέγειν, or the ἒ ἒ λέγειν, of funereal lament.[13] Lament for the dead featured at what is for us, and may well have been designed by the author as, the beginning of Catullus' sequence of elegiac poems (Catullus 65),[14] and at the very end of the first book of Propertius (1.22). Ovid himself earlier in his career had explicitly called on this traditional association in the poem on the death of Tibullus in the *Amores*,

> Memnona si mater, mater ploravit Achillem,
> et tangunt magnas tristia fata deas,
> flebilis indignos, Elegia, solve capillos:
> a, nimis ex vero nunc tibi nomen erit
> (*Am.* 3.9.1–4)

and in the elegiac output of his final decade he was to find the association with lament all too pertinent to his own living death in exile.[15] Remember also the characteristic mood of the *Heroides*, expressed again and again through the verb *queri*,[16] and note Sappho's reasons for switching from lyric to elegy in the pseudo-Ovidian *Epistula Sapphus*:

> forsitan et quare mea sint alterna requiras
> carmina, cum lyricis sim magis apta modis.

103

> flendus amor meus est – elegiae flebile carmen;
> non facit ad lacrimas barbitos ulla meas
>
> (*Ep. Sapph.* 5–8)

Plaintive lament and pity, then, are fundamental to the elegiac genre; and, whatever may be the case in the *Fasti* as a whole, these are certainly the dominant emotions in the *Fasti*'s elegiac version of the Persephone story. Even Little goes some way towards acknowledging the emphasis, though he refuses to interpret it in generic terms.[17] The lament is rendered all the more elegiac by its specifically funereal tinge: the lost Persephone is not literally dead, but abduction to the underworld constitutes a powerful metaphor for death.

Ceres' cry '*me miseram!*' on entering the narrative at *Fast.* 4.456 sets the keynote for her demeanour throughout.[18] She laments her lost daughter as a heifer does her stolen calf,

> ut vitulo mugit sua mater ab ubere rapto
> et quaerit fetus per nemus omne suos,
> sic dea nec retinet gemitus ...
>
> (*Fast.* 4.459–61)

and as the metamorphosed Procne does her dead Itys:[19]

> quacumque ingreditur, miseris loca cuncta querellis
> implet, ut amissum cum gemit ales Ityn
>
> (*Fast.* 4.481–2)

Her grief at Eleusis is so great as to infect the very rock on which she sits,

> hic primum sedit gelido maestissima saxo:
> illud Cecropidae nunc quoque triste vocant
>
> (*Fast.* 4.503–4)

and it finds expression, if not in tears, at least in the closest equivalent which a god can muster:

> dixit, et ut lacrimae (neque enim lacrimare deorum est)
> decidit in tepidos lucida gutta sinus
>
> (*Fast.* 4.521–2)

Her plaint is long and deep at the information given to her by the Sun about her daughter's whereabouts,

> questa diu secum, sic est adfata Tonantem
> (maximaque in vultu signa dolentis erant)
> *(Fast.* 4.585–6)

and long and deep again at the news that Persephone has
forfeited her rights to the world of the living by breaking her
fast:

> non secus indoluit quam si modo rapta fuisset
> maesta parens, longa vixque refecta mora est
> *(Fast.* 4.609–10)

This has been a great load of grief: at *Fast.* 4.615 *tum demum
vultumque Ceres animumque recepit* the stress falls firmly on
demum.

Nor is it Ceres alone who gives way to *querimonia.* When
Persephone fails to answer them, the young goddess's companions fill *(Fast.* 4.453 *implent)* the mountains with their
ululatibus, just as Ceres a little later will fill *(Fast.* 4.482 *implet)*
all places with her *miseris . . . querellis.* So too at Eleusis Celeus
and his daughter add their tears to Ceres' tear-like drops: *Fast.*
4.523 *flent pariter molles animis virgoque senexque.* The stress
on lament here emerges all the more clearly for a contrast,
already mentioned in chapter 3, section v, which can be drawn
with the episode's literary source. In the *Homeric Hymn to
Demeter,* Celeus' baby son appears to be perfectly healthy; here
in the *Fasti,* he is ill and close to death. This, and not just their
sympathy for Ceres, is surely to be thought of as prompting
the tears of the two Eleusinians at *Fast.* 4.523: Ceres' conventional wish to Celeus at 519 'sospes eas semperque parens' has,
unknown to her, hit a sensitive spot. And it is as a result of the
same modification that when Ceres crosses Celeus' threshold
in the *Fasti* account she sees the whole place full of grief: *Fast.*
4.537 *limen ut intravit, luctus videt omnia plena.* Note for the
third time in less than a hundred lines the vocabulary of full-
ness *(Fast.* 4.453 *implent,* 482 *implet,* 537 *plena)* employed to
describe a scene of lamentation: the narrative seems thus to
draw attention to its own plenitude of grief and mourning.

There is nothing like the same emphasis on *querimonia* in
the *Metamorphoses*' hexameter version of the rape. The Eleu-

sinian episode, which in the *Fasti* is so generous in tears both for Persephone and for Celeus' son, is virtually elided here; and the brief lizard story (*Met.* 5.447–61), which is in one sense an equivalent, describing as it does another instance of hospitality offered to Ceres on her travels (cf. chapter 4, p. 85 and n. 30), shows the goddess not lamenting, but angrily meting out punishment. Similarly, there is no place in the *Metamorphoses* narrative for the expressions of sorrow by Persephone's companions and by her mother at *Fast.* 4.453–62: that part of the action is passed over altogether here.

And on the two occasions when Ceres *does* display grief in this version, the emotion is not dwelt on, as Heinze notes,[20] but hardens at once to active anger. In the first case, gestures of mourning in *Met.* 5.471–3 give way in 474ff. to the more savage action of the infliction of the famine.[21] Similarly, whereas in the narrated time[22] of the *Fasti* 4 episode an unbroken mood of plaintive grief reigns from Ceres' receipt of the news of her daughter's whereabouts until her address to Jupiter,

> questa diu secum, sic est adfata Tonantem
> (maximaque in vultu signa dolentis erant)
> (*Fast.* 4.585–6)

in the corresponding time-space in the *Metamorphoses* 5 episode the emotions are more complex, and the grief, as such, more fugitive:

> mater ad auditas stupuit ceu saxea voces
> attonitaeque diu similis fuit, utque dolore
> pulsa gravi gravis est amentia, curribus oras
> exit in aetherias. ibi toto nubila vultu
> ante Iovem passis stetit invidiosa capillis
> (*Met.* 5.509–13)

The predominant feeling here, the feeling associated in this version with the word *diu*, is not grief but stupefaction; and, although stupefaction does eventually give way to grief (*Met.* 5.510–11 *utque dolore | pulsa gravi gravis est amentia ...*), when Ceres stands before Jupiter at *Met.* 5.512–13 her mood seems to have hardened again to something more awful.

106

However, let us not be seduced too much by special pleading. The Ceres of the *Metamorphoses* laments much less, or much less obtrusively, than does the Ceres of the *Fasti*; but, despite her hexametric environment, she does not, as we have just seen, eschew elegiac grief altogether. Moreover her daughter here gives expression to *virgineum ... dolorem* (*Met.* 5.401) as she is abducted; at *Met.* 5.549 Ascalaphus becomes a *venturi nuntia luctus*; and, most spectacularly, at *Met.* 5.425ff. Cyane dissolves utterly into tears. Heinze has little to say about these exceptions to his rule; but, even if they are few beside that weight of grief in the *Fasti* version, it will be well to bear them in mind when general conclusions are attempted later.

iii

It is, I think, symptomatic of a broader tendency that not one, but two of the *Metamorphoses* passages cited in the above discussion find the Ceres of the hexameter version engaged in the angry exercise of supernatural power. In the scene of hospitality at *Met.* 5.447–61 she inflicts a change of shape on the insolent boy who mocks her as she drinks; and in *Met.* 5.474ff. she exacts a powerful revenge for the loss of Persephone by inflicting a terrible famine on the earth.

The savage might which informs the latter action is stressed, both in the narrative itself

> ... ergo illic saeva vertentia glaebas
> fregit aratra manu, parilique irata colonos
> ruricolasque boves leto dedit arvaque iussit
> fallere depositum vitiataque semina fecit
> (*Met.* 5.477–80)

and in the plea uttered by the nymph Arethusa just below:

> '... immensos siste labores,
> neve tibi fidae violenta irascere terrae'
> (*Met.* 5.490–1)

This supernatural destructiveness is absent from the *Fasti* version. There the famine, while not actually omitted, is relegated to the margins of the narrative (chapter 3, section vi). Only at the very end, and in rather an oblique manner, are we told of Ceres' interference with the crop:

> imposuitque suae spicea serta comae:
> largaque provenit cessatis messis in arvis,
> et vix congestas area cepit opes
> (*Fast.* 4.616–18)

Cannot this concentration on the exercise of supernatural power in the hexameter version and its qualified rejection in the elegiac version be read, in Heinze's terms, as reflecting in the one case an alignment with, and in the other a renunciation of, pretensions characteristic of the hexameters of heroic epic?

There is evidence elsewhere to suggest that the contrast *should* be read in these terms. Consider the presentation of the rape itself. In the *Fasti* it appears as a simple erotic incident, a spontaneous act of lust:

> carpendi studio paulatim longius itur,
> et dominam casu nulla secuta comes.
> hanc videt et visam patruus velociter aufert
> (*Fast.* 4.443–5)

The act itself is just as speedy in the *Metamorphoses*,

> paene simul visa est dilectaque raptaque Diti:
> usque adeo est properatus amor ...
> (*Met.* 5.395–6)

but in this version it constitutes the realisation of what is presented as a grand design to alter the balance of power in the whole universe. In *Met.* 5.365ff. Venus plots with her son both to annex the kingdom of Pluto to her empire, so that it may be added to the other two-thirds of the universe, already under her sway,

> tu superos ipsumque Iovem, tu numina ponti
> victa domas ipsumque, regit qui numina ponti:
> Tartara quid cessant? cur non matrisque tuumque
> imperium profers? agitur pars tertia mundi
> (*Met.* 5.369–72)

and, by making an example of Persephone, to put a stop to the revolts which have become a problem in her heavenly sphere

108

of influence:

> et tamen in caelo, quae iam patientia nostra est,
> spernimur, ac mecum vires minuuntur amoris.
> Pallada nonne vides iaculatricemque Dianam
> abscessisse mihi? Cereris quoque filia virgo,
> si patiemur, erit; nam spes adfectat easdem
>
> (*Met.* 5.373–7)

The rape, then, will be the master-stroke by which her realm will be at once expanded and secured:

> at tu pro socio, siqua est ea gratia, regno
> iunge deam patruo ...
>
> (*Met.* 5.378–9)

The elegiacs of the *Fasti* are innocent of this pretension to cosmic significance: and the hexameter version's superstructure of power-politics overarching the act of lust in the pleasance of Enna seems once more indicative, as Otis suggests,[23] of an alignment with the epic tradition from Homer to Virgil, with its characteristic determination of action on the ground by action on another, higher plane. And the epic pretension can be felt to be further increased by the fact that in this case it is not just the latter set of actors who are gods, but also the former set: on a scale of noble themes, the divine clearly outranks the heroic and the human.[24]

The vocabulary used by Venus as she hatches her plot serves to drive the point home: *Met.* 5.365 *arma*; 366 *tela*; 368, 378 *regnum*; 370 *regere*; 372 *imperium*. Her preoccupations here are evidently those of grand hexametric epic, at least in the stereotype propounded by the *docti poetae* of Augustan Rome:

> res gestae regumque ducumque et tristia bella
> quo scribi possent numero, monstravit Homerus
>
> (Horace, *A.P.* 73–4)

Compare *inter alia* the *reges et proelia* denied to the young Virgil by Apollo at *Ecl.* 6.3; the *arma virumque* to which he eventually graduates (*Aen.* 1.1); and Ovid's own earlier plans for hexametric composition, frustrated at the beginning of the *Amores*:

arma gravi numero violentaque bella parabam
edere, materia conveniente modis.
par erat inferior versus; risisse Cupido
dicitur atque unum surripuisse pedem
(*Am.* 1.1.1–4)

Note that while *Ecl.* 6 and *Am.* 1.1 both renounce weighty
epic poetry for a slighter alternative (*Ecl.* 6.8 *tenui ... harun-
dine*; *Am.* 1.1.19 *numeris levioribus*), in one case the alternative
is the *agrestem ... Musam* (*Ecl.* 6.8) of bucolic,[25] and in the
other the *Musa per undenos emodulanda pedes* (*Am.* 1.1.30) of
the elegiac rhythm: elegy is one of a number of approaches
which are felt to involve in quite general terms an avoidance
of epic grandeur, and the espousal of a humbler level in a hier-
archy of poetic categories.

It is interesting to set the emphases just noted in *Met.* 5.341ff.
and *Fast.* 4.417ff. against that common source of theirs, the
Homeric Hymn to Demeter. In the *Hymn*'s version of events,
the guiding hand of Zeus lurks behind his brother's abduction
of Persephone. The preface states this,

... ἠδὲ θύγατρα τανίσφυρον ἣν Ἀϊδωνεὺς
ἥρπαξεν, δῶκεν δὲ βαρύκτυπος εὐρύοπα Ζεύς
(*H. Dem.* 2–3)

and Helios later confirms it:

... οὐδέ τις ἄλλος
αἴτιος ἀθανάτων εἰ μὴ νεφεληγερέτα Ζεύς,
ὅς μιν ἔδωκ' Ἀΐδῃ θαλερὴν κεκλῆσθαι ἄκοιτιν
αὐτοκασιγνήτῳ ...
(*H.Dem.* 77–80)

The only further detail vouchsafed to us of Zeus' πυκινὴν ...
μῆτιν (*H.Dem.* 414) is that it was he who caused Earth to set
the trap of the blooming narcissus for Persephone:

νάρκισσόν θ', ὃν φῦσε δόλον καλυκώπιδι κούρῃ
Γαῖα Διὸς βουλῆσι χαριζομένη πολυδέκτῃ
(*H.Dem.* 8–9)

Διὸς βουλή, it may be remarked, is something of a catchphrase
in archaic Greek epic for the grand designs of the king of the
immortals.[26] Thus Ovid in the *Metamorphoses* version can be

felt to inherit from the *Homeric Hymn* the idea of higher manipulation; and to give added emphasis to it, replacing as he does a family plot with a more grandiose scheme of imperial expansionism. Conversely, in the *Fasti* he opts out of such epic motivation altogether.

Similarly, Ovid's treatment of the famine in the elegiac version can be read as a qualified rejection, and that in the hexameter version as an acceptance, or even an intensification, of Demeter's role as awful goddess in the *Hymn*: cf. (again) chapter 3, section vi, and chapter 4, p. 87 above.

The only occasion on which the Ceres of the *Fasti* obtrusively exercises supernatural power is in her attempt at Eleusis to purge the mortality of Celeus' baby son (*Fast.* 4.549ff.). The whole Eleusinian episode is absent from the *Metamorphoses* version; but the comparison with *H.Dem.* 239ff. is instructive. As I pointed out in chapter 3, section v, when Metaneira interrupts Ceres the mildness of the goddess's reaction contrasts with the vehement anger of her Greek predecessor: *Fast.* 4.557 *cui dea 'dum non es', dixit 'scelerata fuisti'*; *H.Dem.* 251 τῇ δὲ χολωσαμένη, *H.Dem.* 254 θυμῷ κοτέσασα μάλ' αἰνῶς. The *Hymn*'s Demeter is very much the powerful goddess chastising an erring mortal:

> νήϊδες ἄνθρωποι καὶ ἀφράδμονες οὔτ' ἀγαθοῖο
> αἶσαν ἐπερχομένου προγνώμεναι οὔτε κακοῖο·
> καὶ σὺ γὰρ ἀφραδίῃσι τεῇς νήκεστον ἀάσθης
> (*H.Dem.* 256–8)

And whereas she goes on to announce before her departure

> εἰμὶ δὲ Δημήτηρ τιμάοχος, ἥ τε μέγιστον
> ἀθανάτοις θνητοῖσί τ' ὄνεαρ καὶ χάρμα τέτυκται
> (*H.Dem.* 268–9)

to demand that a temple and altar be built for her, and to stage an epiphany (throwing off her old woman's disguise) in all her hugeness, beauty, fragrance and brightness (*H.Dem.* 270–81), the only manifestation of divinity given by Ovid's parting Ceres lies in the brief phrase *nubem trahit* (*Fast.* 4.561). It is the image of Ceres as gently sorrowing mother that continues to dominate the *Fasti* narrative.

The Eleusinian action offers another, more substantial contrast between the *Fasti* version and its Greek model, already mentioned in the chapter 3 discussion. In the *Homeric Hymn* Celeus is represented as a ruler, one of those

> ... οἷσιν ἔπεστι μέγα κράτος ἐνθάδε τιμῆς,
> δήμου τε προὔχουσιν, ἰδὲ κρήδεμνα πόληος
> εἰρύαται βουλῇσι καὶ ἰθείῃσι δίκῃσιν
> *(H.Dem.* 150–2)

and the owner of a μέγαν δόμον (*H.Dem.* 171; cf. 164, 185–6). In the elegiacs of the *Fasti* he has been transformed into a humble rustic, living in no palace now, but in an *exiguae ... casae* (*Fast.* 4.526; cf. 516, and also 531 *parvos ... penates*). One could hardly ask for a clearer instance of avoidance of epic values.[27] Ovid turns down a chance here to write of kings, and instead tells the Eleusinian story as a tale of lowly country folk. One may perhaps cite in this connexion a contrast between the humble and the grand dwelling in *Amores* 3.1, where it serves as an *overtly* programmatic metaphor for the difference in generic level between elegy and, not epic, but that other elevated literary category, tragedy.[28] The personified Elegia speaks to the personified Tragoedia:

> non ego contulerim sublimia carmina nostris:
> obruit exiguas regia vestra fores
> *(Am.* 3.1.39–40)

However, once more, as with the question of the presence or absence of lament, we should beware of giving to tendencies the status of absolute rules. The *Fasti* narrative does seem in many ways to eschew epic grandeur; but it still contains the odd reminder that its principal actors are powerful gods, as in the words of the Sun:

> Sol aditus 'quam quaeris', ait 'ne vana labores,
> nupta Iovis fratri tertia regna tenet'
> *(Fast.* 4.583–4)

And, conversely, the cottage at which Ceres stops on her travels in the *Metamorphoses* narrative is quite as humble as is Celeus' dwelling in the *Fasti*

... cum tectam stramine vidit
forte casam parvasque fores pulsavit ...
(*Met*. 5.447–8)

even if the point is not dwelt on in the same way.[29]

So too the erotic intrigue may be loaded up in the *Metamorphoses* version with the weighty machinery of grand epic; but, for all that, it remains on one level an erotic intrigue more suited to the world of elegy. In seeking to establish 'das δεινόν' as an epic label to set against 'das ἐλεεινόν', Heinze went much too far, treating the divine power-struggles of *Met*. 5.341ff. as if they really were awe-inspiring.[30] The fact is that there are no bloody battlefields here, no real wars: the epic machinery is slightly at odds with the rather unepic character of much of the action. Otis offers an engaging demonstration of this;[31] and we should, I think, have more qualms than does Otis about accepting such a qualification of Heinze's view of the episode on one hand, and yet continuing on the other to see Heinze's fundamental distinction as 'clear and self-evident'.[32]

iv

So where does all this leave us? The differences in emphasis between the two versions of the rape noted in the main body of this chapter, if clear-cut, would strongly suggest that the metrical distinction between the hexameters of the *Metamorphoses* account and the elegiac couplets of the *Fasti* account should indeed be viewed as carrying with it a definite tendency in the one case towards an epic, and in the other towards a less grand, and specifically elegiac type of narrative. The problem is that the differences are *not* completely clear-cut. My discussion, though finding more to agree with in Heinze's analysis of the twin stories than does most recent criticism, nevertheless reveals grey areas too substantial to be ignored.

The same problem crops up to a greater or lesser extent with other details which I have not found space to discuss in this chapter. Thus, for instance, Heinze's attempt to extend his generic contrast to the landscape descriptions of *Met*. 5.385–91 and *Fast*. 4.427–30 shows admirable sensitivity to the numinousness in the former landscape of the *perpetuum ver* (cf. chapter 2, section ii), but no less insensitivity to the essential affinity of the two as *loca amoena*.[33]

The fact is that the labels of 'epic' and 'elegiac' work often enough as descriptions of the respective versions of the myth to ensure that Heinze's approach will always be tempting; but they fail often enough to call, for many, its basic validity into question. If *Met.* 5.341ff. will never be vindicated as a perfect paradigm of epic, nor *Fast.* 4.417ff. as a perfect paradigm of elegy, what is the point of continuing an attempt to distinguish generically between them? Is it really telling us anything about them? I think that it is; but we will not come any closer to finding out what by simply continuing (as we could) to catalogue further observances and infringements of Heinze's distinctions. It is time to view the question from a different point of view altogether, one more sympathetic to the nuances of Ovidian poetry, and of Ovidian poetics.

CHAPTER 6

ELEGY AND EPIC: A NEW APPROACH

What has led recent critics to see an impasse in the situation outlined at the end of the previous chapter, and to seek escape by jettisoning epic and elegiac criteria altogether, is a simple and apparently commonsensical assumption: namely, that to prove generic inconsistency in a piece of poetry is to prove the irrelevance of genre to it.

Nobody should know better than the reader of Ovid's *Fasti* that this assumption is a false one. The *Fasti* is a poem programmatically obsessed, not just with its elegiac form, but with the strains put on that form by the epic weightiness of much of its subject-matter.[1] This is most openly seen in Ovid's self-questioning in *Fasti* 2 when he sets out to deal with Augustus' assumption of the title *Pater Patriae*:

> deficit ingenium, maioraque viribus urgent:
>   haec mihi praecipuo est ore canenda dies.
> quid volui demens elegis imponere tantum
>   ponderis? heroi res erat ista pedis[2]
>   (*Fast.* 2.123–6)

Ovid has already discussed this question of generic identity in the programmatic preface to the second book:

> nunc primum velis, elegi, maioribus itis:
>   exiguum, memini, nuper eratis opus.
> ipse ego vos habui faciles in amore ministros,
>   cum lusit numeris prima iuventa suis.
> idem sacra cano signataque tempora fastis:
>   ecquis ad haec illinc crederet esse viam?
>   (*Fast.* 2.3–8)

It is implicit in his request to the war-god Mars in the Book 3 preface to disarm before entering the poem, and in his assurance to Venus in the Book 4 preface that he has not abandoned his roots in erotic elegy;[3] and it is once more explicit in Juno's address to him at the beginning of Book 6:

namque ait 'o vates, Romani conditor anni,
ause per exiguos magna referre modos'
(*Fast.* 6.21–2)

These passages are strangely cited by Little as evidence for
the *irrelevance* of elegiac norms to the *Fasti*:[4] for him, the
synthesis of the slight and the grand to which they bear witness
demonstrates Ovid's lack of interest in distinctions between
genres. What the passages actually show is, of course, almost
exactly the opposite of this. The fact that the accommodation
of grand subject-matter to the elegiac metre has to be discussed
at so many key points in the poem, the fact that it is stated by
the poet to be so daring and problematic, bears witness not to
a blunting but to a sharpening of generic sensibilities: Ovid
insists on making the issue of its elegiac status absolutely
central to a reading of the *Fasti*.

There is a lesson here which can be applied to Augustan
poetry in general, viz. that the undoubted tendency of writers
in these years to mix and exchange topics between the generic
categories must not be taken to imply a lack of interest in or
awareness of what constitutes the norm in each genre. The
Augustans are heirs to a tradition of Alexandrian learning one
of whose specialties is εἰδογραφία, research on poetic genres.
The well-known passage on genres defined by metre and subject
in the *Ars Poetica* (Horace, *A.P.* 73–85), mentioned twice in the
previous chapter (pp. 103 and 109), shows the influence of this
tradition; and, whilst Horace's words may be no literal guide
to the practice of Augustan poetry, they are a very important
witness to the theory which lies behind that practice.[5] In Ovid
himself, this same consciousness of a normative poetics based
on the genres comes out in a passage in the *Remedia Amoris*:

at tu, quicumque es, quem nostra licentia laedit,
si sapis, ad numeros exige quidque suos.
fortia Maeonio gaudent pede bella referri:
deliciis illic quis locus esse potest?
grande sonant tragici: tragicos decet ira cothurnos;
usibus e mediis soccus habendus erit.
liber in adversos hostes stringatur iambus,
seu celer, extremum seu trahat ille pedem.

116

blanda pharetratos Elegia cantet Amores
   et levis arbitrio ludat amica suo.
Callimachi numeris non est dicendus Achilles;
   Cydippe non est oris, Homere, tui
                                                    (*Rem.* 371–82)

In reality, of course, Ovid does not always adhere to such *dicta*. However, appreciation of, say, the *Remedia* itself does depend on an awareness of the fact that it represents a bold marriage of elegiac norms on the one hand and norms of didactic epos on the other. Whether they are being kept or broken, generic rules are always relevant to an Augustan poem.

Thus in the *Fasti*, where this universal interest in genre manifests itself with unusual explicitness, any tendencies which *can* be read as elegiac *will* be read as elegiac, whatever other, non-generic lines of interpretation they may admit too.[6] And, equally importantly, the presence in the *Fasti* of elements which tend to epic rather than to elegiac norms does not undermine the genre-based approach, but actually constitutes an important part of it: the poem's generic self-consciousness is expressed not just in observance but also in creative transgression of the expected bounds of elegy.

ii

These remarks apply to the *Fasti* as a whole. What of *Fast.* 4.417ff. in particular? In the previous chapter, strong tendencies towards what looked like a distinctively elegiac treatment there of Persephone's rape were discerned; but the generic reading was felt to be threatened by traces of apparently epic pretension (chapter 5, pp. 112–14). It can now be affirmed that what appears to be markedly elegiac is indeed to be read as markedly elegiac, and that any traces of grander pretension are also to be read as such: the discussion above has shown that both elements are covered by the *Fasti*'s genre-based poetics.

However, as also emerged from chapter 5, the discrepant traces in *Fast.* 4.417ff. are relatively few (fewer, for instance, than in that encomium of Augustus in *Fast.* 2.119–44): the balance in the Persephone episode is unmistakably weighted in favour of elegiac norms. Is this perhaps because the *Fasti* is trying to stay on its best elegiac behaviour here, the better to cope with the unique challenge presented in this episode to its generic identity, viz. the availability for direct comparison of a hexameter version of the same story in the contemporary *Metamorphoses*? I stressed at the outset the necessity of bearing in mind the special status of this episode.

Moreover there is another reason, internal to the poem, why elegiac decorum should be more of a *desideratum* here in the fourth book than elsewhere in the *Fasti*. After the perilously unelegiac preoccupation of Book 3 (March) with its eponymous deity Mars, god of war, the programmatic preface to Book 4 (April) reveals the poet at some pains to demonstrate to Venus, goddess of love and dedicatee of this book, that, despite any appearance to the contrary,

> 'alma, fave', dixi 'geminorum mater Amorum';
> ad vatem vultus rettulit illa suos;
> 'quid tibi' ait 'mecum? certe maiora canebas.
> num vetus in molli pectore vulnus habes?'
> (*Fast*. 4.1–4)

and despite, one may add, his earlier final farewell to this same *mater Amorum* at the end of his love elegies, he has by no means abandoned his roots in light erotic poetry:[7]

> 'saucius an sanus numquid tua signa reliqui?
> tu mihi propositum, tu mihi semper opus.
> quae decuit primis sine crimine lusimus annis;
> nunc teritur nostris area maior equis.
> tempora cum causis, annalibus eruta priscis,
> lapsaque sub terras ortaque signa cano.
> venimus ad quartum, quo tu celeberrima mense:
> et vatem et mensem scis, Venus, esse tuos'
> (*Fast*. 4.7–14)

There are good reasons, then, for the Persephone episode to strive to be one of the most elegiac in this frequently unelegiac poem; and, before leaving the *Fasti* for the last time, I would like to suggest that Ovid actually includes in the middle of the episode a notable programmatic assertion of its distinctively elegiac character.

Ceres, we read, wanders all over Sicily:

> quacumque ingreditur, miseris loca cuncta querellis
>   implet, ut amissum cum gemit ales Ityn.
> perque vices modo 'Persephone!' modo 'filia!' clamat,
>   clamat et alternis nomen utrumque ciet;
> sed neque Persephone Cererem nec filia matrem
>   audit, et alternis nomen utrumque perit
> <div align="right">(<i>Fast.</i> 4.481–6)</div>

Now the first thing which strikes one about these lines is their highly mannered use of balance and responsion: no better example could be offered of the way in which the form of the elegiac couplet can impose its personality on the rhetoric of a passage, encouraging in it neat patterns of variation and antithesis, releasing and checking its flow by turns, and denying to it the freedom of range allowed by continuous hexameters with their greater flexibility of caesura, end-stop and enjambment.[8] There is antithesis between couplets, with (483–4, 485–6) *modo 'Persephone!'* picked up by *neque Persephone, modo 'filia!'* by *nec filia, clamat* by *audit,* and *et alternis nomen utrumque ciet* by *et alternis nomen utrumque perit*; there is antithesis between hexameter and pentameter, with (483, 484) *perque vices* varied by *et alternis, modo 'Persephone!' modo 'filia!'* by *nomen utrumque,* and *clamat* both picked up by *clamat* and varied by *ciet*; and there is even antithesis within the individual line, with (483) *modo 'Persephone!'* balanced by *modo 'filia!'* and (485) *neque Persephone Cererem* by *nec filia matrem.*

Moreover, as well as being quintessentially elegiac in their rhetorical structure, these verses are also quintessentially elegiac in their subject-matter. Elegy, remember, is the genre of the *querimonia*, especially of the *querimonia* for the dead. There is much lament in the *Fasti* version of the Persephone myth; but nowhere is there more than in these six lines. *Fast.* 4.481–6 are self-proclaimedly given over to the *miseris ... querellis* of Ceres for Persephone; and not only that, but the goddess's grief for her lost daughter is compared in 482 to the grief of another mother who mourns an actual death. Furthermore, even if Persephone, unlike Itys, is not truly dead, there is a suggestion of symbolic death (cf. chapter 5, p. 104) in the fate of her uttered name in 486 *et alternis nomen utrumque perit*.

Thus Ovid produces in these lines what is in effect a display-piece in elegiac narrative; and, I think, ever the virtuoso, he cannot resist pointing out just what he has done. *Alternis* in 484, and again in 486, describes (like *per ... vices* in 483) the 'alternation' of the cries *'Persephone!'* and *'filia!'* uttered by Ceres; but can one not also read the two occurrences of the word as drawing attention to the very shape of the verses in which they stand? The adjective *alternus* has a technical prosodic sense used overtly by Ovid at *Fast.* 2.121 ... *canimus sacras alterno carmine Nonas, Trist.* 3.1.11 *alterno ... versu,* and *Trist.* 3.1.56, 3.7.10 *alternos ... pedes*. What each of these passages refers to is, of course, the elegiac couplet.[9] Is it not rather tempting to read that redoubled *alternis* in *Fast.* 4.484 and 486 as containing an arch programmatic hint that Ceres' cries of lamentation here, indeed that all the scenes of mourning in this episode, are to be read in full consciousness of the fact that they are written in the 'alternating' hexameters and pentameters of the elegiac rhythm?[10] One could hardly ask for a more remarkable vindication of the generic approach.[11]

iii

When we turn from the *Fasti* to the *Metamorphoses*, the principle of the universal relevance of genre in Augustan poetry will continue to stand us in good stead. The long discussion of whether or not the *Metamorphoses* is a proper epic cannot be cut short by claiming the question itself to be an idle one, as some have tried to do (see chapter 5, p. 101 and n. 9). In Augustan Rome, a hexameter work of fifteen books and nearly 12,000 lines, recounting events which span the whole of world history from the creation down to the poet's own day, cannot avoid being assessed as in some sense a contribution to the tradition of grand epic, especially when placed in the context of a predominantly elegiac *œuvre*. The problems involved in such an assessment are, of course, legion: but far from being irrelevant, they constitute an essential element in the poem's make-up.

Ovid, indeed, hints at these tensions in the brief programmatic proem to the *Metamorphoses*, where not one, as was formerly thought, but two technical terms of poetics are invoked (see chapter 1, section v):

> ... primaque ab origine mundi
> ad mea perpetuum deducite tempora carmen
> (*Met.* 1.3–4)

The *Metamorphoses* aspires to be a *perpetuum carmen*, one of those continuous epic poems of many thousands of lines on kings and heroes deplored in the preface to Callimachus' *Aetia*; but the aspiration is at once rendered problematic by the word *deducite*, which hints that the poem will also seek to align itself with the opposing, unepic tradition of the *deductum carmen*, the slender Muse preferred by the *Aetia* preface.

Thus, in the opening lines of the poem, the epic criterion is immediately established as relevant, even if only as a point of reference for generic conflict. Now whereas in the case of the *Fasti* the strains put on its elegiac form tend to come from a single direction, viz. from the more elevated world of epic, as the *Metamorphoses* progresses a more complex set of tensions emerges. Boundaries are crossed and recrossed as in no poem before. Elements characteristic of elegy, bucolic, didactic, tragedy, comedy and oratory mingle with elements variously characteristic of the grand epic tradition and with each other. Occasionally the poem parodies a particular style; more often its play between literary forms is a matter of nuance within a remarkably unified narrative idiom. However, wherever its shifts may take it, the metre, bulk and scope of the poem ensure that the question implied in that opening paradox will never be completely eclipsed: namely, in what sense is the *Metamorphoses* an epic?

iv

The question will never be completely eclipsed; and nowhere, surely, is it more likely to be kept in view than in the one place in the *Metamorphoses* where direct comparison on a large scale is invited with Ovid's contemporary elegiac poem, the *Fasti*.

We have just seen how the elegiac couplets of the *Fasti* version of the Persephone story assert their elegiac character in the face of this challenge. Do the hexameters of the *Metamorphoses* version show themselves correspondingly epic?

Well, the previous chapter suggested that the generic status of *Met.* 5.341ff. was far from unambiguous: this chapter too will have to take notice of that fact. However, it is fair to say that we discerned many tendencies in the *Metamorphoses* version of the rape which beside *Fast.* 4.417ff. could indeed be viewed, and therefore almost certainly *should* be viewed, as markedly epic. Let us now consider these tendencies in a new perspective.

Here once more (cf. chapter 4, section vii) is the hymnic preface to Calliope's narrative:

> prima Ceres unco glaebam dimovit aratro,
> prima dedit fruges alimentaque mitia terris,
> prima dedit leges. Cereris sunt omnia munus:
> illa canenda mihi est. utinam modo dicere possim
> carmina digna dea! certe dea carmine digna est
>
> *(Met.* 5.341–5)

What is the point of that aspiration in 344–5? On one level, there is a simple answer, viz. that the wish to treat the subject (in this case the goddess Ceres) worthily is conventional in hymnic contexts.[12] However, Ovid is not one to let a sleeping cliché lie; and, in the preface to this particular narrative, under unique pressure as it seems to be to assert its epic status, there is surely something peculiarly apposite about a wish to utter poetry of divine grandeur, *carmina digna dea*.

If such a reading of the wish has always been available, what makes it newly impossible to ignore is the rediscovery in the past decade of a 'missing link' in the literary history of *Met.* 5.344–5 by the Egypt Exploration Society.[13]

> . . . . .] . . . . . taṇdem fecerunt ç[ar]mina Musae
> quae poṣsem domina deicere digna mea
> (Gallus, *P. Qaṣr Ibrîm* 6–7)

It has by now become clear that this part of the papyrus from Qaṣr Ibrîm captures an important programmatic moment in the elegies of Cornelius Gallus. Virgil echoes these lines, probably more than once, in the *Eclogues*; Propertius alludes to them in his fourth book;[14] and, more pertinently here, Ovid redeploys them in the sequence of programmatic poems which opens his *Amores*:

> te mihi materiem felicem in carmina praebe:
> provenient causa carmina digna sua
> (*Am.* 1.3.19–20)

The contextual affinities between Gallus' and Ovid's *carmina digna* here could hardly be closer:[15] the merits of a collection of elegiac poems are assessed with reference to the poet's mistress, by the one in what seems to be a closing programme[16] and by the other in an opening programme. The *carmina* which in Gallus are *domina ... digna mea* become in Ovid's elegant variation, in the same line-positions, *causa ... digna sua*, the *causa* being the mistress addressed in the line above.

Such, briefly recounted, is Ovid's first encounter with the *carmina digna* of Gallus, *P. Qaṣr Ibrîm* 6–7; and it is in the preface to the Persephone story in *Metamorphoses* 5 that he renews his acquaintance, for reasons which this time will need some teasing out, but in words which could not more explicitly acknowledge their model.[17]

Met. 5.344–5 *utinam modo dicere possim | carmina digna dea* – seven words, with four of them straight from the Gallan sentence, namely *dicere, possim* (from *possem*), *carmina* and *digna*. What of the other three? The *carmina* that Gallus can utter must be worthy of *domina ... mea*, whereas Ovid's must be worthy of a *dea. dea* echoes *domina* in that it comes immediately before the main caesura of its line and participates in strong alliteration of 'd'; but *dea* also evokes *mea*, in that the first half of Ovid's hexameter, a dactylic word followed by *digna dea* (and a strong pause) echoes, in the natural position for such an effect, the second half of Gallus' pentameter, a dactylic word followed by *digna mea*. Thus, in a manner of speaking, Gallus' *domina ... mea* becomes Ovid's *dea* by a process of assonantal and metrical conflation. This leaves only *utinam modo* in Ovid's sentence which, in accordance with the difference between Gallus' retrospective and Ovid's prospective viewpoints, one may set off against *tandem*. As for the 'd' alliteration mentioned above, Ovid, a second-generation Augustan, has only two in a row to Gallus' three;[18] but he gives ample reinforcement to these with two more initial 'd's later in the line.

The two sides of this attempted equation between the Gallan and Ovidian sentences fail to balance in one major respect: the word-for-word correspondence of the rest focuses attention on the fact that the *Metamorphoses* lacks a reference to the first stage in the Gallan poetic process, whereby the Muses make the *carmina* for the poet to utter: *fecerunt* (*carmina*) *Musae* | *quae*. There is a very good reason for the imbalance. The *carmina* in *Met.* 5.341ff., remember, are not uttered by Ovid *in propria persona*: the speaker is none other than Calliope, representing her eight sisters in a poetry contest on Mount Helicon against the daughters of Pieros. The lack in Ovid's sentence of a reference to Gallus' song-supplying Muses is not fortuitous, but makes a piquant and very Ovidian comment on the Gallan passage: namely, that the one poet who does not have to worry about getting *carmina* from the Muses is a poet who is a Muse herself.

This is a neat variation; but the real force of the allusion is to be found elsewhere. It resides, surely, in that switch from Gallan *domina* to Ovidian *dea*. I suggested at the outset that *carmina digna dea* could be felt to fit in peculiarly well with an epic pretension. It can now be seen just how close the fit is. When Gallus makes his programmatic claim to have produced (with his Muses) *carmina* worthy of a *domina*, he means that he has written good love elegy. When Ovid's Calliope recalls this but says that she wants *her carmina* to be worthy of a *dea*, she evidently has something more ambitious in mind for her hexameters: a specifically elegiac programme is being upgraded into an epic one.[19]

It may also be relevant to recall Ovid's own use of the mistress as a criterion in the *causa carmina digna sua* at *Am.* 1.3.19–20. If in reading *Met.* 5.344–5 one is reminded of this earlier echo of the Gallan couplet as well as of the Gallan couplet itself, then Calliope's epic programme caps not only Gallus', but also Ovid's own Gallus-derived elegiac programme.[20]

Calliope's wish thus emerges quite clearly as a generically specific one. However, if the implications of the allusion may be pursued a little further, it is not equally clear that she has faced up to *exactly* what it is that she is taking on. To surpass elegy in *dignitas* is one thing if elegy means the *Amores* of Gallus or Ovid: but how will the hexameters of *Met.* 5.341ff. cope with their task of asserting generic superiority over the new kind of elegy which they face in *Fast.* 4.417ff., an elegy which on Ovid's own admission is at the best of times rather weightier than any *Amores* (see the introduction to *Fasti* 4, discussed earlier in the chapter, and especially 4.9–12)? The specifically epic aspiration is present; but it is not altogether unproblematic.

One might add that it is not just the allusion in the last two lines of Calliope's hymnic preface which is indicative of epic aspiration: the very fact that such a hymn to a deity precedes the main account at all points in the same direction. Calliope's performance thus takes on the traditional shape of the epic recitation, perhaps especially familiar to later ages from the evidence of the *Homeric Hymns* and from the beginnings of Hesiod's *Theogony* and *Works and Days*.[21]

There is yet another hint to be picked up here. Who is the singer of *Met.* 5.341ff.? As the Gallan allusion rather cleverly emphasises, it is not Ovid *in propria persona*, but a Muse. And what of the particular choice of Muse? Calliope, as her sister reminds Pallas at the end of the recital, is the eldest of the nine:[22]

> finierat doctos e nobis maxima cantus
> (*Met.* 5.662)

She is also (as *maxima* can equally imply) their chief, and already recognised as such in Hesiod:

> Καλλιόπη θ᾽· ἡ δὲ προφερεστάτη ἐστὶν ἁπασέων.
> ἡ γὰρ καὶ βασιλεῦσιν ἅμ᾽ αἰδοίοισιν ὀπηδεῖ
> (Hesiod, *Theog.* 79–80)

This primacy in age and in importance finds expression from early times in two noticeable tendencies. One is that Calliope can represent synecdochically the entire family of Muses; and the other is that she tends to be associated with what is grandest in literature.[23] We are frequently reminded that in Augustan Rome the Muses had not yet been strictly assigned their separate provinces; but it is hard not to see some significance in the fact that *Met.* 5.341ff., with its generically-charged preface, is represented as being composed and sung by the Muse who, later to be confirmed more explicitly as the Muse of epic, is already something of a special patron of elevated poetry.[24] As in the case of Uranie eighty lines earlier (chapter 1, pp. 15–16 and n. 41), Ovid reflects here an ever-growing interest among poets in differentiating the Muses by function.

Consider, finally, the circumstances in which Calliope sings. In the *Metamorphoses* it is always important to pay attention to the dramatic 'frame' of an inset narrative; and nowhere is it likely to be more important than when that 'frame' places us in the mythical home of poetic inspiration itself. Calliope sings the rape of Persephone on Mount Helicon, as the Muses' entry in a momentous poetry contest (the whole of which is in turn recounted by another Muse to Pallas as an inset narrative in the story of Pallas' visit to Helicon).[25] The Muses' challengers are a group of would-be usurpers, the daughters of Pieros: what Calliope is defending in this contest is nothing less than her own and her sisters' right to control the fountain of poetry, the Hippocrene:

> '... nobiscum, siqua est fiducia vobis,
> Thespiades, certate, deae ...
> > ... vel cedite victae
> fonte Medusaeo et Hyantea Aganippe'
> (*Met.* 5.309–10, 311–12)

It is in this connexion that the results of the present inquiry can be seen to tie in rather neatly with a small but tendentious point made in my first chapter (section vi). I remarked there on the fact that whereas the Hippocrene in the *Fasti* discussion of the Pegasus myth is made to flow by a hoof which is *levis* (*Fast.* 3.456 *cum levis Aonias ungula fodit aquas*), in a parallel *Metamorphoses* reference, set right here in Book 5 on Mount Helicon, the hoof which performs this same action is not *levis*, but its programmatic 'opposite' *dura* (*Met.* 5.256–7 *novi fontis*

... | *dura Medusaei quem praepetis ungula rupit*). We have now seen rather more action on Mount Helicon than we had then. A song has been sung here with marked epic tendencies which are in contrast with elegiac tendencies in a parallel treatment of the same theme in the *Fasti*. Its preface, moreover, has been seen to make programmatic advertisement of its epic aims; and its 'author' has been seen to be a Muse with an ingrained preference for poetic grandeur. It now makes a great deal of sense that the waters of the Hippocrene in defence of which this song is sung have an origin, recounted less than a hundred lines earlier, which serves to associate them with 'weighty' poetry, to distance them from 'slight' poetry; and, specifically, to encourage contrast with the 'slight' poetry of the *Fasti*.

v

That might appear to be the end of the story; but there is a little more to be told. The last chapter did indeed reveal marked epic tendencies in *Met.* 5.341ff.; but it also acknowledged that the episode was no paradigm of epic, that in certain respects it was quite as unepic as *Fast.* 4.417ff. If Ovid's Calliope is really aiming for epic *dignitas*, as she claims at the beginning of her recital, why, it may be asked, does she not put some more distance between herself and that elegiac version of the Persephone myth in the *Fasti*?

I have already hinted at one possible response, viz. to say that one can hardly expect her to be able to pull generic rank with complete consistency on an unorthodox elegy like the *Fasti*, which is itself, even in its most elegiac moments, engaged in something of a flirtation with the grandeur of epic. However, this is only half an answer. The fact is that, just as *Fast.* 4.417ff. is no orthodox piece of elegiac writing, so – or even more – *Met.* 5.341ff. is no orthodox piece of epic writing: Calliope would certainly have come up with something more unambiguously stern than this, if her sole concern had been to produce the weightiest hexameter narrative possible.

As it is, I think Ovid hints strongly that that is *not* Calliope's sole concern. The ambiguities of generic level in her narrative are matched, I suggest, by a certain ambiguity in her program-matic stance.

The *Metamorphoses* 5 version of the Persephone myth is actually involved, remember, in *two* exercises in poetic con-trast. As well as its covert but immensely detailed opposition with the parallel *Fast.* 4.417ff., it is also in competition, more overtly but in a much more limited way, with a piece in *Meta-morphoses* 5 itself: namely, the rival effort of the Pierids in the Heliconian poetry contest. This song is represented as getting extremely short shrift from the Muse-narrator on whom we depend for the story of the contest: whereas she reproduces all 321 verses of her own sister's recital, she offers only the last 5 verses of the Pierid's, condensing the rest into a meagre 8-line précis.[26] However, enough information is given to invite us to draw some conclusions about what this song was, and why it failed to convince the judges of its superiority to Calliope's subsequent performance:

> tunc sine sorte prior, quae se certare professa est,
> bella canit superum falsoque in honore Gigantas
> ponit et extenuat magnorum facta deorum
> *(Met.* 5.318–20)

The Pierid, we go on to learn (*Met.* 5.321ff.), tells in particular of Typhoeus, of the panic that he caused among the gods, and of their flight from him to Egypt.

Such is the poetic work which is so resoundingly voted down in the contest on Mount Helicon:

> at nymphae vicisse deas Helicona colentes
> concordi dixere sono ...[27]
> *(Met.* 5.663–4)

Its great fault is evidently its moral reprehensibility. The pious five-line hymn with which Calliope's response opens, and espe-cially that wish to utter *carmina digna dea* in *Met.* 5.344–5, stands in strong moral contrast to and delivers an implicit rebuke to her rival's impious attitude towards the gods, em-phasised in the Muse's précis above, and attested also in the insolence which the challengers are said to bring to their whole conduct of the contest (*Met.* 5.305–18; cf. *Met.* 5.664–71). The

implicit rebuke is strengthened when Calliope, after her preface, gets her narrative under way by capping the Pierid tale
with a brief account (*Met.* 5.346–55) of how Typhoeus' pre-
sumption meets with its appropriate punishment:

> vasta Giganteis ingesta est insula membris
> Trinacris et magnis subiectum molibus urget
> aetherias ausum sperare Typhoea sedes
> (*Met.* 5.346–8)

There is a hint here for the daughters of Pieros of what lies
in store for themselves: the Muses will give the impious challengers the same short shrift (*Met.* 5.664ff.) as they give their
impious stories.[28]

The Muses, then, disapprove of the Pierid challenge on
moral grounds. However, it is tempting to see their disapproval
working in another way too.[29]

Consider the character of the Pierid song. Interestingly, it
appears to be precisely what circumstances might have led us
to expect, but what we evidently do not get, from Calliope: viz.
an extremely weighty piece of hexameter narrative. The battle
of Giants with gods, or Gigantomachy,[30] is an epic subject;
but it is more than simply that. Concerning as it does the
warring of the Olympians themselves (*Met.* 5.319 *bella canit
superum*), it is conventionally regarded as the very sternest kind
of martial epic that there is.[31] There are a curiously large
number of references in Augustan poetry to the Gigantomachy
as a possible literary project; but almost always it is spoken
of as something to be rejected, abandoned, or firmly set in
the future.[32] The fact is that to any writer with an ounce of
Callimacheanism in his make-up this theme more than any
other stands for the sort of unacceptable pomposity repudiated
in the *Aetia* preface:

> μηδ' ἀπ' ἐμεῦ διφᾶτε μέγα ψοφέουσαν ἀοιδήν
> τίκτεσθαι· βρονταν οὐκ ἐμόν, ἀλλὰ Διός
> (Callimachus, *Aet.* fr. 1.19–20)

Thus in Propertius 2.1 the Gigantomachy not only comes at
the head of a list of epic themes rejected by the poet,

quod mihi si tantum, Maecenas, fata dedissent,
ut possem manus ducere in arma manus,
non ego Titanas canerem, non Ossan Olympo
impositam, ut caeli Pelion esset iter
(Propertius 2.1.17–20)

but it reappears later on in what looks like a direct reference (*intonet*; cf. βροντᾶν) to the very dictum of Callimachus just quoted:[33]

sed neque Phlegraeos Iovis Enceladique tumultus
intonet angusto pectore Callimachus
(Propertius 2.1.39–40)

The circumstantial evidence, I suggest, leads one to suspect rather strongly that the Muses here in *Metamorphoses* 5 are in some sympathy with this prevailing literary-critical fastidiousness about Gigantomachies. The Pierid song fails to break the Muses' hold on the Hippocrene; its authors are represented by the Muse-narrator as impious and impolite; and, I think, they are also represented as rank bad poets.

In the very last lines of the book (*Met.* 5.677–8), after they have been punished with the loss of their human form, the Pierids are said to have retained as *picae* their *facundia prisca . . . | raucaque garrulitas studiumque immane loquendi*. This disparaging comment by the Muse on the long-windedness of her unsuccessful literary rivals is surely reminiscent of nothing so much as the standard Callimachean criticism of poetry marred by undiscriminating prolixity.[34] Moreover, the *picae* into which the Pierids are transformed have the characteristic of *imitantes omnia* (*Met.* 5.299). If this too is thought of as a continuation of their human tendencies, another literary judgement by the Muses seems to be intended: the punishment which they inflict on their rivals brands those rivals as having been, like (for instance) Horace's *imitatores, servum pecus* (*Ep.* 1.19.19), the sort of unlearned poets in whom the subtle art of literary *imitatio* is reduced to slavish copying of tradition.[35] Finally, consider the account by the Muse of the Pierids' earlier history:

Pieros has genuit Pellaeis dives in arvis;
Paeonis Euippe mater fuit: illa potentem

130

> Lucinam noviens, noviens paritura, vocavit.
> intumuit numero stolidarum turba sororum
> perque tot Haemonias et per tot Achaidas urbes
> huc venit et tali committit proelia voce
>
> (*Met*. 5.302–7)

In 305 the brutish Pierids are said to 'swell up' with arrogance; but may not the Muse's *intumuit* also hint, through allusion to a widespread literary-critical metaphor in words like *tumidus* and *turgidus*, at the 'inflated' pomposity which is shortly going to characterise their contribution to the Heliconian poetry contest?[36] Once more, her own implied standards are those of *non inflati . . . Callimachi* (Propertius 2.34.32).[37] An ambiguity available in *numero* promotes the implication: the Pierids' overweening pride in their number will find expression in the swollen bombast of their 'numbers'.[38] To the challengers themselves, of course, the size of their family is a rather more favourable portent of poetic ability:

> '. . . nobiscum, siqua est fiducia vobis,
> Thespiades, certate, deae. nec voce, nec arte
> vincemur totidemque sumus . . .'
>
> (*Met*. 5.309–11)

Thus there is some reason to think that the Pierid Gigantomachy incurs the Muses' displeasure not just because it is impious, but because it is the 'wrong kind' of poetry. And this, I would suggest, is what complicates the poetic aims of the Calliope into whose mouth Ovid puts the *Metamorphoses* version of the Persephone story, and what leads her to produce in *Met*. 5.341ff. a piece of narrative which is at the same time epic and slightly less than epic in character. If she is thought of as shrinking fastidiously from the extreme of epic represented by the Pierid Gigantomachy, the failure of her hexameters to maintain in every respect their generic distance from the elegiac couplets of *Fast*. 4.417ff. (themselves, remember, not wholly without pretension to epic elevation) at once finds its explanation: Calliope is a half-hearted epicist.

Ultimately, *Met*. 5.341ff. resists neat generic classification, just as recent critics have tended to feel. However, through the enactment in the story's programmatically-charged Heliconian

setting of a finely-nuanced drama of literary aspiration, pre-
judice and conflict centred on the internal narrator Calliope,
our attention is drawn (albeit less explicitly than it was by some
of the *Fasti*'s elegiac identity crises) to the fundamental importance here too of generic criteria.

We have a Calliope, then, who simultaneously embraces and
undermines her epic pretensions. The drama should not be an
altogether unfamiliar one to the reader of the *Metamorphoses*.
The pressures on Calliope are, of course, specific to the circumstances of the fifth book. But do they not also evoke in
their individual way the tension alluded to by Ovid back in the
proem to the *Metamorphoses*, the tension which in some sense
informs his whole enterprise?

> ad mea perpetuum deducite tempora carmen
> (*Met.* 1.4)

How can the *Metamorphoses* aspire to the grand epic tradition
of the *perpetuum carmen*, if it also seeks to align itself with the
opposing, unepic *deductum carmen*? In what way is a poem
founded on such a generic paradox to be classified?

These are questions which are still being posed here in *Metamorphoses* 5. It is possible to map out the main currents of
literary programme, as I have been attempting to do in this
chapter; but on the ground, as it were, the constant flux of
programmatic nuance in this area of the poem is, and should
be, a slightly disorientating experience for the reader. The
Hippocrene is produced by a *dura ungula* (*Met.* 5.257): so why
does Uranie lead Pallas there (as noted in chapter 1, section v)
by means of the oppositely-charged word *deduxit* (*Met.* 5.263)?
Calliope, a Muse of grand poetry, begins her song with an
aspiration to grandeur and, one may perhaps even add, rises
to sing (*Met.* 5.338) in a grand sort of way:[39] so why is it
that the strings of the lyre which she tunes are *querulas* (*Met.*
5.339) – more suited, one would think, to the humbler strains
of elegy? The Pierid Gigantomachy is for the Muses a representative of what is despicable in poetry: but should one necessarily accept at face value their biased view of their rivals'
performance?[40] Points of view subtly change, answers turn

into questions: the terms of reference of the programmatic debate on Mount Helicon are in constant shift. It is precisely because it is made so problematic by Ovid that genre is important to the account of Persephone's rape. Much of the poetic energy of this part of the *Metamorphoses* comes from the play of definition and counter-definition, of qualification and requalification, involved in the endless deferral here of final generic classification.

vi

The most appropriate way to conclude the chapter, therefore, will be to add on just one more instance of the elusiveness of Calliope's poetic idiom. What above all else gives an epic flavour to the *Metamorphoses* 5 account of the rape is perhaps, as discussed earlier (chapter 5, pp. 107–11), its background of Olympian power-politics. That flavour, we may now add, is actually enhanced by specific evocation of divine machinery in the very epic with which more than any other Ovid's *Metamorphoses* is concerned to come to terms, viz. Virgil's *Aeneid*.[41] Venus' speech to Cupid, with its grand designs on Dis and Persephone, recalls nothing so much as that other speech of a Venus to a Cupid in the first book of the Virgilian epic, where the victims are Aeneas and Dido.

Heinze noted the parallel; and he also noted how it is underlined by an allusion in the opening words of the speech:[42]

> nate, meae vires, mea magna potentia ...
> (Virgil, *Aen.* 1.664)

> arma manusque meae, mea, nate, potentia ...
> (*Met.* 5.365)

mea ... potentia is reproduced in the same metrical *sedes*; the initial *nate* moves to the fourth trochee, where it supplants *magna*; and *meae vires* is varied (and metrically lightened) by *manusque meae*. The initial position in the line, formerly occupied by *nate*, now goes to the new arrival *arma*. This choice of opening word for Venus' speech could even be read as reinforcing the generic point of the Virgilian allusion: *arma* is both

the opening, titular word of the *Aeneid* and, like *bella*, something of a catchword in programmatic discussions of epic.[43]

Thus the literary origin of the power-politics of *Met.* 5.365ff.
in the first book of the *Aeneid*[44] spells out all the more clearly
their quintessentially epic character. Or does it? Is there not a
certain element of paradox in the allusion?

The *arma* here are not, after all, the grim swords and spears
of martial epic: they are the darts of Cupid, more at home in
the world of love elegy. The Ovidian speech does indeed allude
to the divine machinery of the *Aeneid*; but it alludes to precisely
that turn of the *Aeneid*'s divine machinery which introduces
into the grand epic of *arma virumque* an element of eroticism
reminiscent, not just of Apollonian epic,[45] but also of the intimacy of personal love poetry. Later in the train of events set
in motion by Venus and Cupid at *Aen.* 1.664ff. lies Dido's
famous diminutive: *Aen.* 4.328–9 *si quis mihi parvulus aula|
luderet Aeneas.*[46] The fact is that, far from being a paradigm
of epic, in its own way the love-affair of Dido and Aeneas in
Aeneid 1 and 4 raises as many problems about generic classification as does Calliope's recital here in *Metamorphoses* 5.

It is worth noting that Ovid shows himself well aware of this
aspect of Virgil's Dido episode elsewhere. His own epistle of
Dido to Aeneas (*Heroides* 7) explores not just the gulf between Virgil's epic (and tragic) heroine and the familiar elegiac
domina, but also the real affinity between them;[47] and that
same affinity lies behind our poet's rather disingenuous attempt
later in his career to bracket the *Aeneid* with the *Ars Amatoria*:

> et tamen ille tuae felix Aeneidos auctor
> contulit in Tyrios arma virumque toros,
> nec legitur pars ulla magis de corpore toto,
> quam non legitimo foedere iunctus amor
> (*Trist.* 2.533–6)

The evocation of Virgilian epic in *Met.* 5.365ff. evidently
raises as many questions as it answers: the subject of genre
continues to tease.

EPILOGUE

At the beginning of *Metamorphoses* 10, the bard Orpheus descends to the underworld in quest of Eurydice. There he encounters the king of the dead, Dis, and Persephone, now his wife and queen. It is Love, Orpheus tells the royal couple, that has compelled him to make the fearful journey:

> vicit Amor. supera deus hic bene notus in ora est;
> an sit et hic, dubito. sed et hic tamen auguror esse,
> famaque si veteris non est mentita rapinae,
> vos quoque iunxit Amor ...
>
> (*Met.* 10.26–9)

We, the readers of the *Metamorphoses*, are well acquainted with the story of which he speaks. By drawing on every last minute of recorded time, and by interpreting its brief to treat of transformation in the broadest possible way, Ovid's poem renders itself coextensive with the history of the world; and the myth of the rape of Persephone is thus simultaneously part of the universe of our experience, and part of our experience (as the suggestive *fama* here serves to remind us[1]) of the *Metamorphoses*.

And, if *we* recall the Persephone myth most sharply from the hexameters of *Met.* 5.341–661, Orpheus too, interestingly, can be thought of as having precisely this version in *his* mind. Orpheus' mother, remember (Ovid himself draws our attention to the fact below at *Met.* 10.148), at whose knee he will first have learnt the great stories of the world, is the Muse Calliope; and Calliope it was who sang for us in the fifth book of the *Metamorphoses*.

Therefore, in pondering here the plausibility of the Persephone myth, Orpheus in effect scrutinises for a moment, by the criteria of poetic truth and falsehood, an earlier portion of the very work of literature in which he himself stands.[2] The story of the rape has not yet left Ovid's study; but the story of its reception has already begun.

NOTES

1 *Metamorphoses* 5.256–64: the Heliconian fount

1 Unless otherwise stated, my quotations throughout of the *Metamorphoses* are taken from the text of Anderson (1977), and those of the *Fasti* from Alton, Wormell and Courtney (1978). A few changes in orthography and punctuation have been made.

2 The Muses' association with Helicon does not appear in Homer: see West (1966) on Hesiod, *Theog.* 1.

3 Riley (1869), 166; cf. *OLD* s.v. *origo* 3b, citing this line.

4 See e.g. Ross (1975), 31, for the suggestion of Alexandrian aetiology in *Ecl.* 6.72 (and the difficulties thereby raised); and compare e.g. Ovid, *Fast.* 2.269, 4.783.

5 The name is first attested at Hesiod, *Theog.* 6; its derivation from the Ἵππος of the present myth is set out explicitly at Aratus, *Phaen.* 216–21 (quoted on p. 7).

6 See *TLL* 9.2.958.35ff. and 986.33ff., *OLD* s.v. *origo* 4b; and e.g. *Fast.* 1.611, 5.445–6.

7 See in general, and on Tibullus, Cairns (1979a), 90–9; on Lucretius, Snyder (1980) *passim*. Ovid's *penchant* for etymology will be discussed in the introduction to Dr J.C. McKeown's forthcoming commentary on the *Amores*.

8 See also Cornutus, *N.D.* 22 τὸν Πήγασον, ἀπὸ τῶν πηγῶν ὠνομασμένον.

9 This second etymology implicit in *Met.* 5.262–3 lays bare what is probably a fundamental truth about the mythology of Pegasus, viz. that it was precisely the linking of his name with the word πηγή (which may or may not be the correct etymology: see Chantraine s.v. Πήγασος) which caused stories of spring-creation to accrete about him. Besides the Heliconian Hippocrene, Pegasus is associated with a spring in Troezen (Pausanias 2.31.9), and with another near Corinth (Statius, *Theb.* 4.60–1, *Silv.* 2.7.2–4): see *RE* 19.58.58ff.

10 See *TLL* 9.2.985.50ff.

11 It was Professor E.J. Kenney who pointed out to me the suggestiveness of *vera* in this connexion.

12 The phrase is first attested in the second century A.D.: see *TLL* 9.2.990.54ff.

13 In the Varronian instances, the metaphor in *fons* is sometimes more and sometimes less alive: see variously *L.L.* 8.5, 8.62, 5.92. For the metaphor upheld in Horace, *A.P.* 53 by *cadent* and *parce detorta*, see Brink (1971) on *A.P.* 53.

14 Note that Pallas' and Uranie's conversation has already become pre-occupied with *origines* at *Met.* 5.256–9 above, where the origin of the Hippocrene in Pegasus' action is mentioned in the same breath as the origin of Pegasus himself in Medusa's blood.

15 One or two further verbal similarities between the passages may be noted. Though Germanicus has *pedis ictibus hausit* where Ovid has *pedis ictibus undas*, the word directly above *hausit* in the sixth foot of Germanicus 219 is *unda*. More trivially, compare *fontes* in Germanicus 222 with *fontis* in *Met.* 5.263, both in first-foot position; and *Pegasus* in Germanicus 222 with *Pegasus* in *Met.* 5.262, both in fourth-foot position and both second word in a sentence begun by a monosyllable.

16 See *RE* 8.1854.63ff. for a survey of the extant tradition.

17 See Le Boeuffle (1975), xv–xvi, for the high standing of Aratus' *Phaenomena* in Roman times. It was partly or wholly translated by Cicero, Varro of Atax (who probably rendered only the *Prognostica*), Germanicus, Avienius (in the fourth century A.D.) – and by Ovid (see pp. 13–14).

18 See Ernout–Meillet s.vv. *pes* and *unda* for these cognates.

19 On the use of formulae like φασί, *ferunt fama, fertur* etc. by ancient poets to stress the traditional nature of their stories and to disclaim invention, see Norden (1926) on Virgil, *Aen.* 6.14; also Nisbet and Hubbard (1970) on Horace, *Carm.* 1.7.23. Cf. esp. chapter 3, p. 58 and n. 22.

20 *LSJ* s.v. διαφημίζω II flattens the sense of διεφήμισαν here to 'call, name'. However, there is no reason not to keep the full etymological implication of the word (cf. *LSJ* s.v. διαφημίζω I), rendering it 'make known, spread abroad [as]': thus the *TGL* definition *vulgo fama aliquid*.

21 See Chantraine s.v. φημί for the etymological link.

22 Remember too the additional coincidences of phraseology which would be involved: see n. 15 above.

23 Plausible motives can be suggested for each of these Ovidian distortions, in the former case literary and in the latter political. An incomplete *Metamorphoses* is essential to the story told in *Trist.* 1.7 of Ovid's attempt to burn his poem before departing to a living death in exile, since that story is clearly designed to evoke the perfectionism of the dying Virgil: see Grisart (1959); Evans (1983), 43–4; and cf. now Hinds (1985), 21–7. And the claim in *Tristia* 2 that not just six, but all twelve books of the *Fasti* have already been drafted – for the Latin of *Trist.* 2.549 does indeed specify that number, despite some desperate attempts in the past to translate otherwise – may be designed to hold out a promise to Augustus that clemency for the poet will result almost immediately in the completion of the one Ovidian work which should really appeal to him. The prospect of a *Fasti* 8, dealing with the anniversaries of the month *Sextilis* or *Augustus*, should be especially enticing: see Syme (1978), 34, for the potential cluster of 'Augustan dates' in that book; also Ovid himself at *Fast.* 5.145–8.

24 Thus Fränkel (1945), 143 and n. 2.

25 Thus Syme (1978), 21–36.

26 See e.g. Heinze (1919), 1 = (1960), 308; Wilkinson (1955), 241; Otis (1970), 21–2; Kenney in *OCD*, 764; and Wormell (1979), 40–1, with a remark which will prove especially pertinent to the present study: '... each [poem] is a kind of commentary on the other'.

27 For illustration of this in the present study, see chapter 2, section vii; chapter 4, section ii.

28 For Callimachus' *Aetia* and Aratus' *Phaenomena* as the main Greek models of the *Fasti*, see Wilkinson (1955), 242. On one occasion in the poem, Ovid spells out his debt to Aratus with the utmost clarity. In Book 5, after a preliminary consultation with the Muses about the etymology of the month of May, he opens his account of the Kalends with a piece of astronomy which he introduces with the words *ab Iove surgat opus* (*Fast.* 5.111): the evocation of the opening phrase of Aratus' *Phaenomena*, ἐκ Διὸς ἀρχώμεσθα, is unmistakable. For the celebrity of these Aratean words in antiquity, see Gow (1952) on Theocritus, *Id.* 17.1; for other Latin imitations, see Soubiran (1972) on Cicero, *Arat.* I.

29 *OLD* s.v. *fruor* 2.

30 Both of these items belong distinctively to the iconography of Pegasus – the wings obviously so, and the bridle because of the myth of his taming by Bellerophon – and only enter the Aratean tradition, apparently, when its Ἵππος becomes identified with Pegasus. For the history of the identification of the Hippocrene Horse and Pegasus, see *RE* 8.1854.63ff., Le Boeuffle (1975) on Germanicus 207.

31 See Owen (1915) for the ancient citations, which yield one two-line and one three-line fragment.

32 Mr I.M. Le M. Du Quesnay, remarking especially on the fact that Ovid exercises here his hexametric skills, prefers (in conversation with me) to envisage the translation of Aratus' didactic *epos* as something undertaken by our poet by way of *immediate* preparation for the great works of his middle period, when most of the early amatory poetry has already been written. The present point at issue is not affected.

33 See e.g. Lueneburg (1888); Kenney (1969), 4 and n. 7.

34 One of the two extant fragments of Ovid's *Phaenomena*, concerning the *Pleiades*, may lend a little support to the idea that Ovid was apt to draw on the language of his own version of Aratus for the astronomy of the *Fasti*. Compare Aratus 257–8 ἑπτάποροι δὴ ταί γε μετ' ἀνθρώπους | ὑδέονται | ἐξ οἷαί περ ἐοῦσαι ἐπόψιαι ὀφθαλμοῖσιν; what seems to be Ovid's version of this in his *Phaenomena*, *Pliades ante genus septem radiare feruntur*, | *sex tamen apparent, sub opaca septima nube est*; and part of a discussion of the Pleiades at *Fast.* 4.170 *quae septem dici, sex tamen esse solent*. The two Ovidian passages could be independent of each other; but it is tempting to see the *Fasti* pentameter-end *sex tamen esse solent* as influenced by the *Phaenomena* hexameter-beginning *sex tamen apparent* – if, that is, one accepts with Heinsius (and Owen) against the MSS that this is what Ovid wrote in the *Phaenomena*, rather than *sed tamen apparet*

(codd. Vaticanus and Parisinus *apparent*: see Hagen (1902), 357) *sub opaca septima nube*. One may contrast the slightly different verbal approaches to the *sex tamen* ... detail in the versions of Cicero, *Arat.* fr. 33.29–30 *hae septem vulgo perhibentur more vetusto | stellae, cernuntur vero sex undique parvae* and Germanicus 259–60 *septem traduntur numero, sed carpitur una, | deficiente oculo distinguere corpora parva*.

35 For the Nicandrian approach to *Met.* 5.256–64, see e.g. Haupt, Ehwald and von Albrecht (1966) on *Met.* 5.257 and 294ff.; Papathomopoulos (1968) on Antoninus Liberalis 9.2 (his n. 15).

36 For the general importance of Nicander as a source for Ovid's *Metamorphoses*, see Plaehn (1982); and e.g. Otis (1970), index s.v. Nicander. On *Heteroioumena* 4 and *Metamorphoses* 5, see further chapter 3, section ii.

37 See Bömer (1969–) on *Met.* 5.294ff. Pausanias 9.29.2ff. preserves a story which is not wholly dissimilar.

38 In a generation less sympathetic than our own to the Hellenistic spirit, Rose (1928), 174 n. 34, offered the following acerbic comment on the Nicandrian version: 'This may be cited as an example of the rubbish which an Alexandrian sometimes produced when he tried to improve on a myth.'

39 '... a second, distinct literary tradition', I write, thus envisaging Ovid as combining two *independent* sources, Aratus and Nicander, in his conception of Pegasus' hoof-blow: for this technique of allusion, see chapter 4, n. 9 below. However, as Mr I.M.Le M. Du Quesnay suggests to me, a more elaborate piece of speculation is also possible. Nicander might *himself* have taken something from the Aratus passage for *his* version of the hoof-blow, in which case Ovid's combined allusion would be of the two-tier type characterised in chapter 3, n. 16 below. In support of this conjecture, one might adduce apparent Nicandrian debts to Aratus in the *Theriaca*: see Gow and Scholfield (1953), 7 n. 1.

40 In deference to what seems to be almost universal critical practice among Latinists, I retain the term 'programmatic' to describe any poetic allusion to the 'making' of poetry, whether it comes at the beginning of a work (where the phenomenon does indeed tend to be especially pronounced), in the middle or at the end, and whether it refers to the work in hand, to another work or to poetry in general.

41 Poets were certainly interested by this date in the idea that different Muses had different provinces: see Propertius 3.3.33 *diversaeque novem sortitae iura puellae*, and the slightly grudging concessions of Nisbet and Hubbard (1970) on Horace, *Carm.* 1.24.3. An obvious way to determine a Muse's province was by etymologising on her name: so perhaps at *Carm.* 1.24.3 Melpomene is the Muse who μέλπεται (as well as Nisbet and Hubbard, see Fraenkel (1957), 306 n. 2). Ovid explicitly shows himself interested in such an approach in designating Erato as the appropriate Muse to deal with matters of love (Greek ἔρως) at *A.A.* 2.15–16

nunc mihi, si quando, puer et Cytherea, favete; | *nunc Erato, nam tu nomen Amoris habes*; cf. *Fast.* 4.195–6 and, earlier, Plato, *Phaedr.* 259c–d, Apollonius Rhodius 3.1–5. Uranie's name could not but mark her out for astronomy: see Grube (1965), 5 n. 3; and, for what looks like an earlier exploitation of the association, Cicero, *Div.* 1.11.17 with Pease (1920–3) ad loc. Cf. also chapter 6, pp. 125–6, on Calliope. Interestingly, at a later date the mosaic of Monnus at Trier (end of third century to beginning of fourth century A.D.) includes amongst other pictures of Muses and writers a group, set in an octagon, of Uranie and Aratus: a photograph of this will be found in Maass (1898), 173.

42 I owe this rather neat point to Mr I.M.Le M. Du Quesnay.

43 *OLD* s.v. *pes* 1 and 11 respectively.

44 See *TLL* 7.1.165.23ff., *OLD* s.v. *ictus* 4c.

45 The suggested ambiguity involves the *collective* sense of metrical *pes*: see *OLD* s.v. *pes* 11b 'the feet of a line, etc., considered together, rhythm, or metre'.

46 I owe this nuance to Professor E.J. Kenney.

47 See Beare (1957), 58ff.; Allen (1973), 100.

48 For the echo here of Callimachus, *Aet.* fr. 1.23–4 . . . .] . . . ἀοιδέ, τὸ μὲν θύος ὅττι πάχιστον | θρέψαι, τὴ] γ Μοῦσαν δ᾽ ὠγαθὲ λεπταλέην, see Pfeiffer (1949–53) ad loc.

49 For discussions of programmatic *deducere*, see Eisenhut (1961) = (1975), 247–63; Ross (1975), 134–5; and Kennedy (1980) on *Culex* 2.

50 See the examples at *TLL* 5.1.282.55ff., *OLD* s.v. *deduco* 4b.

51 See e.g. Herter (1948), 139–45 = von Albrecht and Zinn (1968), 351–8; Wimmel (1960), 76 n. 1 and 331 n. 1; and cf. Horace, *Carm.* 1.7.6 with Nisbet and Hubbard (1970) ad loc.

52 The force of *deducite* in *Met.* 1.4 struck no fewer than three scholars writing independently of each other in the mid-1970s: Due (1974), 95 and n. 8; Gilbert (1976); and Kenney (1976), 51–2.

53 With the oblique uses of programmatic *deducere* suggested below, compare Ross (1975), 26–7 and 65–6, on Virgil, *Ecl.* 6.69–71 and Propertius 1.1.19–24 respectively; also Putnam (1979), 167, on Virgil, *Geo.* 3.10–11.

54 For the influence at Rome of Callimachean polemic against tragedy, most apparent in Ovid, see Thomas (1979), 180–95, esp. 190 and n. 41; also Thomas (1978). See further p. 22 and chapter 5, p. 112.

55 Dr Duncan Kennedy (in personal correspondence) suggests, attractively, that the specifically Callimachean connotations of the sense 'to compose' can again be pressed. The Callimachean *deductum carmen* eschews as subject-matter *tristia bella* (see e.g. Virgil, *Ecl.* 6.3–8). How appropriate, then, that when Ovid's poem 'takes him over' in this way, it leads him to the *ara PACIS*.

56 *OLD* s.v. *deduco* 2b.

57 Cf. Hollis (1970) on *Met.* 8.789, pointing out the echo of that line in *Trist.* 3.10.75; Hinds (1985), 26–7; and also chapter 2, n. 1 below.

58 On programmatic *durus*, see Rothstein (1920–4) on Propertius 1.7.19; on *levis*, see Nisbet and Hubbard (1978) on Horace, *Carm.* 2.1.40. *durus* and *levis* are members of two opposed 'families' of adjectives more or less closely associated with Callimachean literary debate at Rome, the one including also such terms as *gravis, magnus, maior, grandis, inflatus*, and the other such terms as *mollis, tenuis, gracilis, parvus, exiguus, angustus*. There is a particularly notable cluster of oppositions between the two groups at *Trist.* 2.327–40: with that passage, see Wimmel (1960), 297–8.

59 For the common ground between Ovid's polemical discussions of tragedy and of epic, see chapter 5, p. 112 and n. 28.

60 The suggested contrast between the two springs, expressed as it is in terms of the water-producing hoof rather than in terms of the flow of water itself, constitutes an interesting extension of the water-symbolism so characteristic (see Wimmel (1960), 222–33) of Callimachean programmatic discussion.

61 For *cavus/cavare* used to describe teeth hollowed by decay, see Propertius 4.5.68, Pliny, *Nat.* 7.70, 22.121, 23.148, 25.170 and 171, 30.22; to describe ulcers, Celsus 6.6.23, Pliny, *Nat.* 26.143.

62 Ten lines earlier in the poem under discussion here, Ovid addresses the following compliment to Germanicus Caesar: *Pont.* 4.8.69–70 *quod nisi te nomen tantum ad maiora vocasset, | gloria Pieridum summa futurus eras*. This surely constitutes a recall of the almost identical compliment addressed by one of the Muses to Pallas just after the *Metamorphoses* 5 mention of the Hippocrene: 5.269–70 *o, nisi te virtus opera ad maiora tulisset, | in partem ventura chori Tritonia nostri*. This allusion, if such it is, lends gratifying support to the case for reading the *cava ungula* of *Pont.* 4.8.80 as carrying a reference to the *dura ungula* of *Met.* 5.257.

2 *Metamorphoses* 5.385–91: the landscape of Enna

1 It was on a 'grand tour' in his youth taking in Asia as well as Sicily that Ovid visited Enna. On his friend Pompeius Macer see Syme (1978), 73–4. There are many echoes in *Pont.* 2.10.21ff. of the subject-matter and words of *Met.* 5.341ff.: with *Pont.* 2.10.24 compare *Met.* 5.353; with 25 compare *Met.* 5.405–6 and 385 (noting how *lacus* in the *Ex Ponto* line effects a sort of conflation of the two *Metamorphoses* passages); and with 26 compare *Met.* 5.638 (noting the subtle shift whereby a detail which in the *Metamorphoses* refers to Arethusa is applied in *Pont.* 2.10 not to Arethusa, despite her presence in 27–8 below, but to her *Metamorphoses* 5 'foil' Cyane: cf. *Met.* 5.417–18). One might perhaps read Ovid's insistent allusion to *Metamorphoses* 5 here in *Pont.* 2.10.21ff. as a hint (which need not, of course, be taken at face value) that it was from his experience of Sicily on this early trip with Macer that he drew the main inspiration for the narrative of this part of the *Metamorphoses*.

To the present-day visitor the landscape of Enna is lost. By laying a motor-racing track around Lago di Pergusa the twentieth-century Sicilians have ensured that now, at least, there is no danger of confusing literary convention with the reality of the place.

2 See Curtius (1953), 195, for this definition of the pattern; and 192 for the history of '*locus amoenus*' as a technical term, suggesting that it is already alluded to by Horace at *A.P.* 17. For further discussion of the *locus amoenus* pattern, see Nisbet and Hubbard (1978) on Horace, *Carm.* 2.3, intro. and line 6; also, more extensively, Schönbeck (1962).

3 For *loca amoena* in the *Metamorphoses*, see Wilkinson (1955), 180ff., Segal (1969), *passim*. In the fifth book, note (besides the present passage) 263–6, 336, 587–91. For the particular importance to the *Metamorphoses* of the pastoral landscape, see Segal (1969), 71–85.

4 Compare Virgil's evocation of this passage at *Aen.* 7.699–702; also at *Geo.* 1.383–4 where, however, swans are not specified. In Ovid, see already *Her.* 7.1–2 ... *udis abiectus in herbis | ad vada Maeandri concinit albus olor* (for the lower reaches of the Maeander as part of the Ἄσιος λειμών, see Fordyce (1977) on Virgil, *Aen.* 7.701–2); *Met.* 2.252–3.

5 See Gatz (1967), *conspectus locorum* s.vv. *ver aeternum, terra abundantem victum ferens.*

6 See Curtius (1953), 185–6, for Homeric milieux like the gardens of Alcinous (*Od.* 7.117–18 τάων οὔ ποτε καρπὸς ἀπόλλυται οὐδ' ἀπολείπει | χείματος οὐδὲ θέρευς, ἐπετήσιος) as a common ancestor of later 'everyday' pleasances and of supernatural places of the heart's desire.

7 For the use in educated Roman circles of this un-Latin sound, see Allen (1978), 52–3.

8 The 'oe' in *Phoebeos* reinforces the sound-pattern: for its true diphthongal value, see Allen (1978), 62.

9 The goddess's 'insertion' into the grove here (*quo ... Proserpina luco*), coming as it does just after the mention of its ever-blooming flowers, perhaps has the effect of calling to mind a traditional etymology of *Proserpina*: Varro, fr. 140 Fun. *tellurem putant esse ... Proserpinam quod ex ea proserpant fruges.* Nor is this, incidentally, the only etymology which seems to be hinted at in 391. The designation here of the landscape as a *lucus* is associated with a marked stress in 388–9 on the exclusion of the sun's rays (on which see further below): the effect is perhaps to evoke the well-known derivation *lucus a non lucendo* (Quintilian, *Inst.* 1.6.34 *etiamne a contrariis aliqua sinemus trahi, ut 'lucus' quia umbra opacus parum luceat ... ?*; *TLL* 7.2.1750.74–8).

10 The correspondence here of object to object and of subject to subject can perhaps be felt to criss-cross interestingly with the natural sense-pairs in the line, viz. 'coolness' and 'dampness' on one hand, and 'branches' and 'flowers' on the other. This was remarked by an anonymous reader of an earlier version of this chapter presented in Cambridge Fellowship competitions.

11 On Ovid's fondness for syllepsis, see Kenney (1973), 125 and n. 76.

12 Segal (1969). Cf. Parry (1964).

13 Segal (1969), 54. Like him, and like most modern editors, I prefer *ictus* (cod. Neapolitanus: see Anderson (1977) ad loc.) to *ignes*, the prevalent MSS reading.

14 For *ictus* of the male sexual act, see Adams (1982), 148–9; for the question of the authenticity of Juvenal 6.126, see Courtney (1980) ad loc.

15 See Segal (1969), 50; but the defence here of his interpretation is mine.

16 At the end of Lucretius 4, imagery of both blood (1036, 1045–56 and elsewhere) and water (1035–6) is overtly applied to the ejaculation of semen. Note especially the parallels of diction with the present passage in 1049–53 ... *et illam | emicat in partem sanguis unde icimur ictu, | et si comminus est, hostem ruber occupat umor. | sic igitur Veneris qui telis accipit ictus, | sive puer membris mulieribus hunc iaculatur.* Also, the phrase *emicat ... alte* is used of blood at Lucretius 2.195 (see Bömer (1969–) on *Met.* 4.121); and *foramen* is a favourite term of Lucretian physics.

17 See chapter 4, p. 89 and n. 38 for the traditional suggestiveness of this motif.

18 For the sexual possibilities in the words, see Adams (1982), 90, 207.

19 As well as the passage quoted here, see *Od.* 19.440–3.

20 For the beam of light as a missile, see Barrett (1964) on Euripides, *Hippolytus* 530–4; and, for the 'arrow' image as a development of the 'striking' one, see Diggle (1970) on Euripides, *Phaethon* 3.

21 Apollo was, while Helios was not, traditionally an archer. The earliest certain literary identification of the two is at Euripides, *Phaethon* 225: see Diggle (1970) ad loc. for the later history of the identification in Greek literature and thought. Farnell (1896–1909), 4.136ff., claims that 'the ordinary Greek did not identify or associate Apollo and Helios in cult or habitual conception'. Cf. n. 24 below.

22 For *ictus* as the Latin equivalent of βολή in this sense, see Nisbet and Hubbard (1978) on Horace, *Carm.* 2.15.10. For examples of *icio* so used, see *TLL* 7.1.160.29ff., *OLD* s.v. *icio* 2b; for *ictus*, *TLL* 7.1.166.29ff., *OLD* s.v. *ictus* 5. Two qualifications to these lexical articles are worth making. The first (and only pre-Lucretian) instance given of *icio* in the sense under discussion is Ennius, *Ann.* 85 Sk. *exin candida se radiis dedit icta foras lux.* However, this is not quite on all fours with the succeeding examples or with the Greek usage: see Steuart (1925) ad loc. (Bk 1, fr. 33.15 in her ed.) 'the actual form of the expression may be due to an imperfectly conceived metaphor, as if the Far Darter smote Lux with the rays that are his arrows'; also G. Williams (1968), 686, who likewise sees a visual aberration, and suggests an explanation. Again, the first (and only pre-Lucretian) instance given of *ictus* in the sense under discussion is Tubero, *Hist.* 9. However, this is almost certainly post-Lucretian: see Ogilvie (1970), 16–17, for the confusion concerning various Tuberones.

23 The case of Lucretius is interesting here. While he will have had the poetic

tradition of 'striking' imagery in mind, *icio* and *ictus* for him describe quite scientifically the impact of the atomic particles of which the rays of his non-anthropomorphised sun, like everything else in his universe, consist: see Lucretius 2.808, 5.607 and 613, 6.514 and 1102.

His importance in the tradition should not be minimised. I would suggest that, by using the long-established (in Greek; for Lucretius' position in the Latin history see n. 22 above) image in a novel, scientifically precise way, Lucretius hands it back to his poetic but non-scientific successors charged with new life. This sort of thing cannot be measured: but it is, I think, partly the revivifying influence of Lucretius which gives rise to the equal but different precision of Ovid's use of the 'striking' image here in *Met.* 5.389.

24 For the history of the name Phoebus, see Bömer (1969–) on *Met.* 2.24. Full surveys of its use by Ovid and his Latin poetic predecessors may be found in Fontenrose (1939) and (1940). However, the contention in these two articles that the sun and Apollo, despite sharing the appellation Phoebus, are always kept entirely distinct from one another is unacceptable. First, it flies in the face of common sense; second, the precedent afforded by the limited Greek tradition of sun–Apollo identification (n. 21 above: it includes, significantly, Callimachus, at fr. 302 and perhaps fr. 273) is more important than Fontenrose (1940), 440, allows; and finally, in Ovid's case, the identifications at *Met.* 2.454 and *Fast.* 3.346 and 353 cannot, for all Fontenrose's efforts at (1940), 436–40, be explained away.

25 Cf. *OLD* s.v. *velum* 3, and, for a full discussion, Graefe (1979).

26 See Segal (1969), 17 and n. 40.

27 The terms in which Haupt, Ehwald and von Albrecht (1966) on *Met.* 5.389 define *vela* indicate that they have taken the point: 'über das römische Amphitheater wurden bei den Schauspielen grosse Tücher (*vela*) zum Schutze gegen die Sonne gespannt'.

28 For the supporting masts of theatrical and amphitheatrical awnings, see Lucretius' earlier imaginative use of the *velum*: 4.75ff. *et volgo faciunt id lutea russaque vela | et ferrugina, cum magnis intenta theatris | per malos volgata trabesque trementia flutant*; cf. 6.108ff. The brackets which carried the masts of the *velum* in the Flavian amphitheatre, the Colosseum, are still visible: see Ward-Perkins (1981), 70.

29 A tension between the natural and the artificial is likewise essential to the design of the *actual* gardens of the Italian Renaissance. The parallel is no idle one: Professor John Dixon Hunt shows that Ovid's *Metamorphoses* had a considerable influence on the conception of the Renaissance garden, felt not only in mythological sculptures, sometimes containing explicit Ovidian allusions, in its pools and grottoes, but also in its 'metamorphic' play with water, rock and vegetation, and in the whole idea of the garden as a wonderful and numinous place. This material comes from a talk given to the Shirley Society of St Catharine's

College, Cambridge, in March 1982, entitled 'Ovid, metamorphosis and the Renaissance garden': some of it is to be found in Hunt (1983), and fuller publication is promised.

Another important element in the Renaissance garden – see Hunt (1980) – is a sense of landscape as theatre, both in terms of physical configuration and as a 'stage' for spectacle: in this too, my discussion here and below tends to suggest, it displays a fundamentally Ovidian character.

30 Ovid alludes in these lines to Propertius' discussion of primitive Rome at 4.1.15–16 *nec sinuosa cavo pendebant vela theatro,|pulpita sollemnis non oluere crocos.*

31 See *OLD* s.v. *theatrum* 1c.

32 See Segal (1969), 74–5; and e.g. Theocritus, *Id.* 1.1–23, 5.31–4; Virgil, *Ecl.* 1.1–5, 7.1–20. Here in *Metamorphoses* 5, note in this connexion 333–7.

33 *OLD* s.v. *ludo* 1. To anticipate a subject which will be investigated thoroughly later in this study, Ovid's Persephone surely inherits her sportive mood whilst gathering flowers from her predecessor in the *Homeric Hymn to Demeter*: compare especially *Met.* 5.392 *ludit et ... carpit* with *H.Dem.* 425 παίζομεν ἠδ' ... δρέπομεν.

34 *TLL* 7.2.1773.61ff.; *OLD* s.v. *ludo* 6 'to take part in a public entertainment or show'; and *OCD*, 624–5 s.v. *ludi.*

35 It may or may not be relevant to note that, at least under Nero, mythological stories were quite literally, and gruesomely, acted out in the amphitheatrical arena: see Suetonius, *Nero* 12.2; Martial, *Sp.* 5–8; and Auguet (1972), 100–4.

36 The technical term 'ἔκφρασις' is used of the set-piece description of works of art, landscapes and other items. The term is first attested in the first century A.D.; but the phenomenon which it describes is well-established in literature long before this: see Cairns (1984), 155 n. 116.

37 Besides Austin (1955) on Virgil, *Aen.* 4.480ff. and 483, and Austin (1971) on *Aen.* 1.12, for discussions of this pattern in Greek and Latin see Vahlen (1903), cl n.; Fraenkel (1912), 46ff.; von Albrecht (1964), 182–4; and G. Williams (1968), 640ff.

38 In the *Aeneid, est locus* occurs at 1.159 (words separated), 1.530, 3.163, 7.563; *locus est* at 4.481 (quoted in text). In Ovid, *est locus* occurs at *Her.* 16.53, *Met.* 2.195, 4.773 (actually *esse locum: oratio obliqua*), 8.788 (quoted in text), 15.332, *Fast.* 2.491, 4.337, *Pont.* 3.2.45; *locus est* at *Met.* 12.39 (words separated), *Fast.* 4.427, 5.707, *Trist.* 4.4.63. In prose, note *est locus* at Sallust, *Cat.* 55.3 (words separated); *locus est* at [Caesar], *B.Alex.* 27.1.

39 That *locus* was felt to have a special position over the alternatives in this descriptive mannerism, whereby *est*, or sometimes *erat* or *fuit*, is coupled with a 'place or object' noun – something which tends simply to be taken for granted in modern discussions – is shown first by the fact that *locus*

is general whereas the alternatives are particular; then by the fact that the *locus* opening is associated with an especial strictness of phrasing in the formula (the separation of the verbal element in the formula from the noun, comparatively rare with *locus* itself, is common with the alternatives; and the use of a past tense of *esse* rather than the present is never, so far as I know, found in the *locus* opening, but is common in the alternatives); by the fact that *locus* tends to occur more frequently in an author than any alternative; that the sole surviving instance of the mannerism in Ennius is a *locus* opening (*Ann.* 20 Sk., quoted in the text above); and finally, much later, that both instances of the mannerism in the 295-line epic *tour de force* in the *Satyricon* are *locus* openings (Petronius, *Bell. Civ.* 67, 146). I am fortunate here to have had access to a long list of instances of the formula in Latin literature compiled by Dr Stephen Oakley in an unpublished paper entitled '*est locus*, ἦν δέ τις and related expressions'. I am grateful to him, as also to Dr Neil Hopkinson, for discussion of this section.

40 For Lucretius' philosophical interest in etymologies, see Snyder (1980), *passim*; for his suggestive placings of related elements in successive lines, Snyder (1980), 67–8 with 90–108.

41 I have not found any instances of *lacus* in the descriptive formula in pre-Ovidian poetry; but in Ovid cf. *Met.* 9.334 and *Fast.* 3.264. Is an ecphrastic *locus* pun active in these passages too? It is perhaps suggestive that in the latter one there is substantial disagreement in the MSS between *lacus* and *locus*. Note too that in *Met.* 15.332, cited above as an instance of *est locus*, the overwhelming reading of the MSS is actually *lacus*. In the present passage, the case for a pun is rendered uniquely strong by what happens at the point of return to narrative (see text below).

42 Austin (1971) on Virgil, *Aen.* 1.12. My concern here is with this final pick-up that marks the return to narrative, and not with the internal pick-ups that frequently articulate the description. This distinction is blurred by Austin himself: with the present note compare (1955) on *Aen.* 4.483, and especially the example common to both discussions, viz. *Aen.* 1.441, whose 'pick-up' is 450 in one discussion, and 446 in the other. So too in von Albrecht's (1964), 183–4, useful 'Grundform der ekphrastischen Topothesie', the final item, 'Verknüpfung mit dem Folgenden durch Relativ- oder Demonstrativ-pronomen', fails to distinguish (as his examples show) between linkage with narrative proper and linkage with more ecphrasis. Admittedly, it is not possible in some cases to draw a clear line of demarcation.

43 Cf. e.g. Virgil, *Aen.* 7.563–70 *est locus – fauces – quis*; *Met.* 2.195–8 *est locus – Scorpius – hunc*; and note that a closing *hic, illic* vel sim. may sometimes be ambiguous in its reference.

44 For paronomasia between *lucus* and *lacus*, cf. *Fast.* 6.755–6, *TLL* 7.2.865.52–4; and (on Lucretius 5.75) Snyder (1980), 100.

45 See e.g. *Am.* 3.13.7–8, *Met.* 15.791–3; and *TLL* 7.2.1754.36–7.

46 Kenney (1970), 418. The writers on rhetoric furnish ample evidence of the celebrity of the *Verrines* in general (Seneca, *Suas.* 2.19; Quintilian, *Inst. passim*) and of this passage in particular (*Inst.* 4.2.19, 4.3.13, 9.4.127, 11.3.164).

47 What follows is a slightly altered and augmented version of Hinds (1982).

48 I am tempted to suggest that *edam* at the end of *Fast.* 4.417 may react with this fleetingly geographical *locus* before the caesura to produce a pun on the opening words of Cicero's ecphrasis: the demand in the Ovidian line would come very aptly from a *loco perexcelso atque edito*.

49 Ovid's alteration of the meaning of *locus* perhaps contains a further element of conscious wilfulness: the *locus* which as a Ciceronian 'site' owed its peculiar distinctiveness to the endurance of its floral aspect throughout the year, ... *omni tempore anni*, is now forced by Ovid to denote a *single* 'occasion' in his calendar year/poem.

50 Merkel (1841), cclvi.

51 Diodorus, at the corresponding point in his treatment of Enna (5.3.3), writes ἄλση καὶ περὶ ταῦτα ἕλη. Cicero's and Diodorus' versions of the rape are believed to go back to a common source, Timaeus of Tauromenium: see chapter 3, n. 4 below. Is it not, then, tempting to infer that this Diodoran assonance derives from Timaeus, and that what Cicero is offering in *lacus lucique* is a felicitous Latinisation of an original Timaean paronomasia?

52 At the beginning of his Punic episode at Enna, Livy evokes the *Fourth Verrine* ecphrasis directly, with Livy 24.37.2 *Henna, excelso loco ac praerupto* echoing Cicero's opening *Henna ... est loco perexcelso atque edito*. And the presentation of Pinarius' action as sacrilege (Livy 24.38.8– 9) must, I think (the commentators, who note the other parallels, are silent here), owe something to Cicero's denunciation of the religious crimes of Verres at *Verr.* 2.4.110–12. In particular, compare Livy's description of Enna as *non hominum tantum sed etiam deorum sedem* with Cicero's more elaborate conceit in the same vein beginning *etenim urbs illa non urbs videtur, sed fanum Cereris esse*. The number and nature of these similarities seems to overrule any doubts arising from our ignorance of what was in Livy's main source for the episode (presumably Polybius: see Klotz (1940–1), 113), and to guarantee Ciceronian influence.

53 For *ludo* in this sense see *TLL* 7.2.1774.36ff., 1776.4ff.

54 The starting-point of the rape story is not openly advertised in the *Metamorphoses* as it is in the *Fasti*, something illustrative of the fundamental difference between the formats of the two poems. Calliope stated in her preface at *Met.* 5.341–5 that she would sing of Ceres, and since then the narrative has been moving from the story of Typhoeus' fate (prompted by the rival Pierid song at 319–31) to the enactment of this aim, by means of the kind of ingenious and seamless transition characteristic of the *Metamorphoses*. It is only in the course of Venus' scheming speech in 365–79 that the reader begins to realise that the

promised story concerning Ceres is at hand, and that its precise subject is the rape of Persephone. Thus, the new 'paragraph' at 385, with the immediate clarification of setting and subject offered in the opening *haud procul Hennaeis* ..., is perhaps the obvious juncture for programmatic reflection.

55 Note, by the way, that the *locus* in *Fast.* 4.427, mentioned earlier in connexion with the *Fasti*'s allusive pun on the word, actually states in its description of Enna the standard ecphrastic formula which the *Metamorphoses* description has been argued to hint at: compare *Met.* 5.385 *haud procul Hennaeis lacus est a moenibus* ... with *Fast.* 4.427 *valle sub umbrosa locus est aspergine* .... I suspect that this highly instructive cross-reference is quite deliberate: it is underlined by the identical line-positions of *lacus est* and *locus est*, the former followed by a *moenibus* and the latter by aspergine (similar vowels underlined).

56 For the importance of the *Homeric Hymn to Demeter* in antiquity, see chapter 3, n. 1. To call it an 'old *Attic* hymn', incidentally, may be a mistake: see Richardson (1974), 52–6.

57 On the history of the Sicilian version of the rape, see chapter 3, p. 53. For a full survey of attested locations of the rape other than Nysa, see Richardson (1974) on *H.Dem.* 17.

58 Stephanus Byzantinus, *Ethn.* s.v. lists no fewer than ten.

59 See Richardson (1974) on *H.Dem.* 17. There is some inscriptional evidence to confirm the special position in Carian Nysa of Pluto and Core: see *RE* 17.1638.11ff.

60 The surgery necessary for the text at this point must be along the lines of Groskurd's ὑπερβᾶσι τὴν Μεσωγίδα ἐπὶ τὰ πρὸς τὸν νότον μέρη Τμώλου τοῦ ὄρους. The town of Nysa itself lay on the southern slopes of the Mesogis range, i.e. on the slopes facing the plain of the Maeander. Thus a λειμών thirty stadia away (i.e. *c.* $3\frac{1}{2}$ miles) and watered by a stream of the Cayster must lie to the north, over the ridge of the Mesogis, i.e. facing the plain of the Cayster, which is itself bounded on the far, north side by the Tmolus range. Jones's (1917–32) solution to the crux, to insert καί before τὸ ὄρος, produces intelligible Greek but geographical gibberish.

61 The remark comes in *Geog.* 13.14.12 where, lamenting the confusing nature of the boundaries in this area of Asia Minor, Strabo writes οὐδ' ἡμῖν ἴσως ἐπὶ τοσοῦτον φροντιστέον, ὡς ἀναγκαῖον χωρομετροῦσιν, ἀλλὰ τοσοῦτον μονον ὑπογραπτέον, ὅσον καὶ οἱ πρὸ ἡμῶν παραδεδώκασιν.

62 For the interest of the Callimachean school in rivers, see F. Williams (1978) on Callimachus, *h.* 2.108. At *Geog.* 9.1.19, Strabo refers disparagingly to a comment about the Eridanus in Callimachus' river treatise.

63 Nisbet and Hubbard (1978) on Horace, *Carm.* 2.20.10. There is further discussion ad loc. and in their introductory note to the poem.

64 For *cycnus*, see *TLL* 4.1585.16ff., *OLD* s.v. *cycnus* b; for *olor*, *TLL*

9.2.572.15ff., *OLD* s.v. *olor* a. 'Poets and other literary men' do not seem to be evoked at *Aen.* 7.699 or 11.458; but they are at Lucretius 3.7, 4.181, 4.910; Virgil, *Ecl.* 8.55, 9.29, 9.36; Propertius 2.34.84; and Horace, *Carm.* 4.2.25, 4.3.20. For the nature of the evocation in the *Ecl.* 9.29 passage, see Coleman (1977) ad loc.; the other instances stand in no need of explanation.

65 At *Her.* 7.1–2, the *olor* is associated with Dido, as 'authoress' of her dying epistle; at *Met.* 14.429–30 *cycnus* is associated with the poetess Canens, at *Fast.* 2.108–10 *olor* with the minstrel Arion, and at *Trist.* 5.1.11–12 *olor* with Ovid himself as author of his exile poetry.

Finally, note the subtle evocation of literary production in *Met.* 2.252–3 *et quae Maeonias celebrabant carmine ripas|flumineae volucres, medio caluere Caystro. celebrabant* here is generally rendered 'thronged', like the compound *concelebrant* in its model (see, I think, Bömer (1969–   ) ad loc.) Lucretius 2.344–5 *et variae volucres, laetantia quae loca aquarum| concelebrant circum ripas fontisque lacusque* (discussed in another connexion in section vi of this chapter). But Ovid has a *carmine* where Lucretius had none, and this causes a number of other possible meanings to be felt: 'which filled the Maeonian banks with song' (so Loers (1843) ad loc.); 'for whose singing the Maeonian banks were famous' (so M.M. Innes (1955), 56; Riley (1869), 56, ambiguously); and, most interestingly, 'who celebrated the Maeonian banks in their song' (so Riley (1869), 56, ambiguously; for the widespread use of the verb *celebro* of poets and the fame that they confer by their work, see *TLL* 3.746.52ff., *OLD* s.v. *celebro* 6). It is through this last nuance, surely, that Ovid has truly transformed his Lucretian model. As has been noted more than once in this chapter, poets from Homer on had made the Cayster and its swans famous: here, by a bold conceit, the birds themselves join the ranks of the celebrants.

66 It is perhaps worth noting at this point that Ovid seems to be responsible for the introduction of swans to Enna: neither Cicero nor Diodorus mentions any.

67 See *TLL* 5.2.88.16ff., *OLD* s.v. *edo* 9. Modern editors are evenly split in their preferences between *edit* and the unexceptionable MSS alternative *audit*. I have aligned myself in my argument here with the *edit* camp; but the essential point in my paragraph is unaffected if *audit* is read.

68 The *labentibus . . . undis* of *Met.* 5.387 readily assimilate themselves to the programmatic landscape: for the symbolic association of water with poetry in Alexandrian and Roman writing, see Nisbet and Hubbard (1970) on Horace, *Carm.* 1.26.6; Wimmel (1960), 222–33.

3 The *Homeric Hymn to Demeter*: *Fasti* 4

1 Richardson (1974). See not only his excellent section on the influence of the *Homeric Hymn* on later literature (68–73; cf. 67–8 for direct

quotations), but also his survey of other versions of the Persephone myth
in antiquity (74–86); and cf. Frazer (1921), 34–41.

2 See Richardson (1974), 72. He lists the following parallels in the *Fasti*:
4.437ff. ~ *H.Dem.* 6ff., 425ff.; 447–8 ~ *H.Dem.* 20ff. etc.; 453 ~
H.Dem. 38; 455 ~ *H.Dem.* 39; 457–8 ~ *H.Dem.* 41ff., 386; 498ff. ~
H.Dem. 43; 502ff. ~ *H.Dem.* 96ff.; 503–4 ~ *H.Dem.* 98, 201–2;
513–14 ~ *H.Dem.* 113ff., 147; 517–18 ~ *H.Dem.* 101ff., 42, 182, 197;
540ff. ~ *H.Dem.* 233–41; 550 ~ *H.Dem.* 231, 238; 553ff. ~ *H.Dem.*
239ff.; 557ff. ~ *H.Dem.* 256ff.; 561–2 ~ *H.Dem.* 275–81; 577ff. ~
H.Dem. 69ff.; 581ff. ~ *H.Dem.* 62–3, 69–70, 76ff.; 584 ~ *H.Dem.* 85–7;
591–2 ~ *H.Dem.* 83–5, 363–4; 598–600 ~ *H.Dem.* 83–7, 363ff.; 603–4,
607–8 ~ *H.Dem.* 372–4, 393ff. etc.; 605 ~ *H.Dem.* 335; 613–14 ~
H.Dem. 445ff., 463ff.; 615–16 ~ *H.Dem.* 470ff. In the *Metamorphoses*
he lists 5.391ff. ~ *H.Dem.* 6ff., 16–20; 438ff. ~ *H.Dem.* 43ff.; 446–7 ~
H.Dem. 49–50; 449ff. ~ *H.Dem.* 202–11; 471–2 ~ *H.Dem.* 40–1,
90; 477–86 ~ *H.Dem.* 305ff.; 506–8 ~ *H.Dem.* 83ff., 363–9; 521–2,
526–9 ~ *H.Dem.* 83ff., 363–4; 530–2, 564ff. ~ *H.Dem.* 393ff., 445–7,
463–5. From here on, I shall refer to these lists only on the few occasions
when Richardson enlarges on a parallel in the body of his commentary;
but their pertinence, especially in the case of the *Fasti*, will be evident
throughout the ensuing discussion.

3 See Richardson (1974), 76–7, for the early history of this Sicilian version
in literature; and note Zuntz (1971), 70–1, who remarks also on coins of
c. 450 B.C. from Enna which already seem to show Demeter on her
chariot seeking her daughter: these are illustrated in Hill (1903), 91.

4 See Richardson (1974), 77. Jacoby (1950–5), comm. 593 with n. 585,
though reporting some dissentient views, is himself in no doubt that
Diodorus' account is closely dependent on Timaeus. I discuss one of the
points of similarity between Diodorus and Cicero in chapter 2, n. 51
above; others are conveniently listed by Hall (1897) on Cicero, *Verr.*
2.4.106.

5 Malten (1910), 521–4, presents the main correspondences in tabular
form; see also Haupt, Ehwald and von Albrecht (1966) on *Met.* 5.375 for
a correspondence not included by Malten.

6 Malten (1910), 526–7.

7 Malten (1910), 527–32.

8 Malten (1910), 540–53.

9 Barwick (1925) argues for Nicandrian influence on both Ovidian versions; Bethe (1904) had concerned himself only with the *Metamorphoses*.

10 Herter (1941), reviving the earlier view of Förster (1874), 74–88 and
293ff.

11 The tenuousness of the claim that Callimachus' *Aetia* included a substantial Persephone episode is well demonstrated by Montanari (1974),
esp. 113–15. To argue that the obliquity of Callimachus' reference to the
rape of Persephone at *h.* 6.8–21 implies a full and explicit treatment of

the rape elsewhere in his *œuvre* is to misunderstand a fundamental point about Alexandrian poetry, viz. its cultivation of obliquity for its own sake. Fr. 611, which has an undoubted affinity with *h.* 6.15 (and, I think, with *h.* 6.9), is designated by Pfeiffer (1949–53) as '*incertae sedis*': he reports ad loc. Malten's idea of a Persephone episode in the *Aetia*, but concludes '*at ne minima quidem ex parte confirmatum est*'. For fuller discussion of the Callimachean claim, see Montanari's article. For another thought about the obliquity of *h.* 6.8–21, see chapter 4, n. 28 below.

12 The detailed correspondences are discussed by Bethe (1904), 9–11; and by Papathomopoulos (1968) on Antoninus Liberalis 28.

13 On the detailed correspondences, see Pressler (1903), 17.

14 Montanari (1974) surveys the previous history of the *Quellenfrage* lucidly and judiciously. However, his own ingenious attempt to see traces of a major Nicandrian Persephone narrative buried in a *scholium* on *Theriaca* 483–7 – Montanari (1974), 117ff. – is at least as conjectural as the views that he himself dismisses.

15 Herter (1941), 253.

16 This principle of two-tier allusion is enunciated by Cairns (1979), 121. In most instances noted, information in the passage under consideration (A) is such as to allow both the nearer source (B) and the farther one (C) to be identified at once: see e.g. Kenney (1979), 106–12 with n. 31, on the sources of Virgil, *Aen.* 2.471–5 and 496–9; also chapter 6, n. 45 below. The mannerism may also take a more abstruse form where the direct allusion in A to C depends for its recognition on a contextual link present in B, and not in A itself: see Du Quesnay (1977), 55, on Virgil, *Ecl.* 4, Theocritus, *Id.* 17, and Callimachus, *h.* 4.260ff. I am indebted to Dr J.C. McKeown for discussion of this point.

17 In the *Fasti* version the goddess is called 'Persephone' five times and 'Proserpina' once; contrariwise, in the *Metamorphoses* version she is called by the Latinised name four times and by the Greek name once.

18 Malten (1910), 531, himself remarks on it as a striking correspondence.

19 My quotations of the *Homeric Hymn to Demeter* are taken throughout from the text of Richardson (1974).

20 The association of Persephone in the *Fasti* account with *rapere* and its cognates is established in the very first line: *Fast.* 4.417 *exigit ipse locus raptus ut virginis edam*. Cf. later *rapere* at *Fast.* 4.519, 525, 581, 607 and 609; also *raptor* of Dis at 590. Note also that in the cow simile which immediately follows the maenad one in *Fast.* 4.459–60 Persephone is represented by a *vitulo ... ab ubere rapto*.

21 This twofold debt to the *Hymn* in *Fast.* 4.457–8 is noted by Richardson (1974) on *H.Dem.* 41.

22 On this kind of 'Alexandrian footnote' (thus described in Ross (1975), 78), see earlier chapter 1, pp. 8–9, and chapter 2, p. 40; also, at the end, my epilogue.

23 The text here is that of Frazer (1929).

24 I owe this suggestion to one of the participants (I cannot remember which) in a Cambridge research seminar devoted to an earlier, abbreviated version of this and the following chapter in March 1983.

25 For the Stygian connotations of the gold of Hades' chariot, see Richardson (1974) on *H.Dem.* 19, comparing e.g. the Golden Bough; for those of the *caeruleis ... equis* see *TLL* 3.106.74ff., *OLD* '*caeruleus*' 9d.

26 The cow simile is indebted to Lucretius 2.355ff.: see Bömer (1957–8) on *Fast.* 4.459.

27 Gods flying or moving are often compared to birds in epic: see Richardson (1974) on *H.Dem.* 43.

28 See Richardson (1974) on *H.Dem.* 200 with Appendix I for this association.

29 Note that there is a certain aptness not just in the firewood but also in the kind of food carried home by Celeus. We learn from the passage which introduces the narrative of the rape that before the advent of Ceres men lived on *glandes*: *Fast.* 4.399–402 *postmodo glans nota est: bene erat iam glande reperta,|duraque magnificas quercus habebat opes.|prima Ceres homine ad meliora alimenta vocato|mutavit glandes utiliore cibo.* Thus it is rather appropriate that Celeus should have been gathering *glandes* (*Fast.* 4.509–10) just before *he* becomes personally acquainted with Ceres.

30 For the word's etymology and meaning, see Chantraine s.v. μαῖα; also, for its being used of true mothers, Dale (1954) on Euripides, *Alc.* 393–415.

31 See Malten (1910), 531–3, and Richardson (1974) on *H.Dem.* 96, who also note that there may be an echo here of the Orphic version of the myth in which the people who receive Ceres are poor herdsmen (*Orphica* fr. 52 K.).

32 For such a wish as typical in an epic scene of meeting, see Richardson (1974) on *H.Dem.* 135ff.

33 Triptolemus in the *Homeric Hymn* is one of the rulers of Eleusis (*H.Dem.* 153, 474). As the tradition of the myth develops, he becomes younger in representations, emerges as Demeter's special favourite, and thus (it seems) comes to supplant Demophoon in the role of nursling: see Richardson (1974) on *H.Dem.* 153.

34 For Demeter's lack of sympathy with Metaneira in this part of the *Homeric Hymn*, see now Thalmann (1984), 93, who relates it to a broader concern in the *Hymn* with the disjunction between immortal and mortal.

35 In a society where *Acta Diurna* is a 'household name' for a day-by-day record, this play on the sense of *facta diurna* perhaps arises all the more naturally: on the widely read journal of Roman events thus entitled, whose publication dates from 59 B.C., see *OCD* s.v. Acta ad fin.; Suetonius, *Iul.* 20.

36 On the δύνασαι γάρ form of the prayer in *H.Dem.* 69–70, see Richardson

(1974) ad loc.; on this formula in Greek and Latin in general, see Norden (1926) on Virgil, *Aen.* 6.117 and (1913), 154.

37 See Richardson (1974) on *H.Dem.* 90–7.

38 On the relationship between the two words, see Ernout–Meillet s.v. *arvom*.

39 Note also καλλιστέφανος Δημήτηρ at *H.Dem.* 251 and 295.

40 See Richardson (1974) on *H.Dem.* 224. Homer and Hesiod attach the epithet to a number of goddesses and heroines.

41 See Frazer (1912), I, 43; Bömer (1957–8) on *Fast.* 4.616.

42 It is characteristic of Hellenistic poetry to use imitation to comment on and interpret the model: see Du Quesnay (1979), 68 and n. 234. Cf. also chapter 4, pp. 79–80.

43 For the wealth of suggestion in these words, cf. chapter 2, p. 40.

4 The *Homeric Hymn to Demeter*: *Metamorphoses* 5

1 Cf. Heinze (1919), 5–6 = (1960), 311.

2 With *Met.* 5.525 compare also *Fast.* 4.589 *iniuria facti* in Ceres' immediately preceding speech: see Bömer (1969–) on *Met.* 5.525–6.

3 See Housman (1897), 426–7 = (1972), 413–14, who collects examples of the device. My punctuation for *Fast.* 4.598 is that of Frazer (1929). Alton, Wormell and Courtney (1978) have recourse to the opposite expedient of omitting all inverted commas until the following line. Interestingly, in the revised Loeb *Metamorphoses*, Miller and Goold (1977–84), Goold actually uses the method of punctuation put forward by Housman.

4 See *OLD* s.v. *attonitus* 2. M.M. Innes' (1955) translation takes this approach to *Met.* 5.510: '... and for a long time seemed to be dazed'.

5 See *TLL* 2.1154.44ff., *OLD* s.v. *attonitus* 1: the latter includes the present passage among its examples. Watts (1954) renders *Met.* 5.509–10 thus: 'The mother heard, and stood for long like one | Transfixed by lightning or transformed to stone.'

6 Cf. e.g. *Trist.* 5.3.37–8 *sic tibi cum Bacchis Satyrorum gnava iuventus | adsit, et attonito non taceare sono*, and see *TLL* 2.1157.30ff., *OLD* s.v. *attonitus* 3.

7 For such networks in the *Metamorphoses*, see e.g. Galinsky (1975), 79–109 (his Chapter 2). For a more detailed approach, see Crabbe (1981) on *Metamorphoses* 8. Prominent mentions of stone in the *Metamorphoses* are usefully listed (though sometimes bizarrely analysed) by Bauer (1962), 3–9.

8 Note that Ovid had already alluded to these lines of Catullus, showing especial interest in the idea of the *saxea effigies*, in the verse epistle of Ariadne to Theseus: *Her.* 10.47–50 *aut ego diffusis erravi sola capillis, | qualis ab Ogygio concita Baccha deo, | aut mare prospiciens in saxo frigida sedi, | quamque lapis sedes, tam lapis ipsa fui.* Ovid divides here into two

pictures the single image of Catullus 64.61, as Palmer (1898) on *Her.*
10.50 observes.

9 Such '*contaminatio*' is a standard technique of allusion: see e.g. Cairns
(1979), 121 and n. 4; Du Quesnay (1979), 43–4 and n. 86.

10 Cf. chapter 2, sections vii and viii ad fin. Two seminal studies compare
the Ovidian Persephones: Malten (1910) is under consideration here in
chapters 3 and 4; and Richard Heinze's monograph, avowedly different
in its interests – see Heinze (1919), 2 = (1960), 308–9 – receives due attention in chapters 5 and 6.

11 For the simultaneity of the *Metamorphoses* and *Fasti* as a whole, see (as
well as chapter 2, section vii) chapter 1, pp. 10–11.

12 There appears to be a verbal echo in the *Metamorphoses* version of the
last line of that catalogue, viz. *H.Dem.* 424 Παλλάς τ' ἐγρεμάχη καὶ
Ἄρτεμις ἰοχέαιρα, in the rather different context of Venus' remarks to
Cupid about the spread of virginity: *Met.* 5.375–6 *Pallada nonne vides
iaculatricemque Dianam | abscessisse mihi?* In both cases Pallas occupies
the beginning, and Diana/Artemis with her weapon-epithet the second
half, of a line. Now Malten (1910), 520, traces *Met.* 5.375–6 to a
discussion of the virginity of the same two goddesses in lines 7–20 of the
Homeric Hymn to Aphrodite, a passage completely unconnected with the
rape of Persephone. He may be right; but it seems to me that the line in
the *Homeric Hymn to Demeter* must be relevant too: it is highly appropriate that, in a discussion of the virginity of Pallas and Diana which
occurs in the *context* of the rape of Persephone, Ovid should show his
awareness of the fact that these two goddesses were famously supposed
to have been actually *present* at the rape by a verbal allusion to the line
of the *Homeric Hymn to Demeter* in which they are listed among Persephone's companions. The two motifs involved here, viz. the virginity of
the goddesses and their presence at Persephone's rape (see further Bömer
(1969–   ) on *Met.* 5.375), are overtly combined earlier in the tradition:
see Diodorus 5.3.4 μυθολογοῦσι δὲ μετὰ τῆς Κόρης τὰς τῆς ὁμοίας
παρθενίας ἠξιωμένας Ἀθηνᾶν τε καὶ Ἄρτεμιν συντρεφομένας συνάγειν
μετ' αὐτῆς τὰ ἄνθη.

13 For contrasts of red and white in Roman poetry, see Du Quesnay (1973),
14 and n. 48; also Bömer (1969–   ) on *Met.* 6.46–7. For the opposition
of these two colours in general, see Lodge (1977), 19 and n., who argues
that as well as the opposition of white to black, the opposition of red to
white or black is quite fundamental too. It has indeed been argued that,
as languages with only two 'basic colour terms' have words for black and
white, so languages with only three 'basic colour terms' have words for
black, white and red: see Berlin and Kay (1969), cited in Lodge's note,
esp. 1–14.

14 It is not certain what flowers are meant by the names ἀγαλλίς and
ὑάκινθος. The former may be a kind of iris, and the latter has been identified with many flowers, including the modern hyacinth: see Richardson
(1974) on *H.Dem.* 7.

15 For the meaning of the word, see Richardson (1974) on *H.Dem*. 427 and Chantraine s.v. λείριον, the latter of whom notes the etymological link with Latin *lilium*.

16 For reflexive twists in the word *ludit* here, cf. chapter 2, pp. 35 and 41–2.

17 For allusion functioning as commentary, cf. chapter 3, section vi and n. 42.

18 Richardson (1974) on *H.Dem*. 413. Allen, Halliday and Sikes (1936) ad loc. also note the discrepancy.

19 See Richardson (1974) on *H.Dem*. 406 and 120–1.

20 See Richardson (1974) on *H.Dem*. 16, quoting *Met*. 5.400–1; also the beginning of the present section.

21 See *OLD* s.v. *sinus* 4a.

22 See *TLL* 5.1.2258.68ff., *OLD* s.v. *duplex* 1.

23 See *OLD* s.vv. *simplex* and *-plex* for the formation of the word.

24 See *OLD* s.v. *praetereo* 2a.

25 See *OLD* s.v. *praetereo* 2c; and note in this connexion *Fast*. 4.574, discussed in n. 31 below.

26 See *OLD* s.v. *praetereo* 5.

27 Two thoughtful, and differently troubled, discussions of this passage are worth looking at: Kenney (1973), 142–5, and Davie (1983), 'The Fountain of Cyanë', a poem in the 1982 trilogy 'Three for Water Music' (from the latter comes the barbed compliment, with its own built-in word-play, which stands as an epigraph to the present study).

28 Callimachus echoes these two verses in line 12 of his *Hymn to Demeter*: οὐ πίες οὔτ' ἄρ' ἔδες τῆνον χρόνον οὐδὲ λοέσσα. Cf. also line 16; with *H.Dem*. 200 as well as 49–50. Callimachus' obliquity in the opening section of his *Hymn* (chapter 3, p. 54 with n. 11) finds here, I suspect, something like a true explanation: it is not the theme of some putative *Aetia* episode which is first allusively referred to and then dismissed (*h*. 6.17 μὴ μὴ ταῦτα λέγωμες ...) in this preface, but the theme of the *Homeric Hymn to Demeter* itself.

29 See *OLD* s.v. *colluo* 1.

30 On *Met*. 5.447–61 as a 'delocalised' Eleusinian episode see most elaborately Montanari (1974); on the constitution and purpose in the Eleusinian mysteries of the drink known as 'Cyceon', see Richardson (1974), Appendix 4.

31 The two lines which deal with Ceres' worldwide search merit some discussion: *Met*. 5.462–3 *quas dea per terras et quas erraverit undas,* | *dicere longa mora est: quaerenti defuit orbis*. These correspond to a similar 'editorial' comment in the *Fasti* account: *Fast*. 4.573–4 *quo feror? immensum est erratas dicere terras:* | *praeteritus Cereri nullus in orbe locus*. The *Fasti* couplet brings to an end the last of the three great geographical lists in that version of the story; and it is surely at the avoidance of such catalogues in the *Metamorphoses* version that Ovid's *dicere longa mora est* in *Met*. 5.463 knowingly glances. In the *Fasti*, *praeteritus Cereri nullus in orbe locus*: no place has been 'left out' by Ceres (*OLD* s.v. *praetereo*

2c) – or indeed, one may feel, by her poet (*OLD* s.v. *praetereo* 5; cf. p. 83 on *Fast.* 4.469). Dr Denis Feeney helped me to pursue some of the nuances in Ovid's wilfully unstable use of the verb *praetereo* in *Fasti* 4. Ovid's liking for self-reference, incidentally, is manifested as archly in the second *Fasti* 4 geographical catalogue as it is in the first (pp. 82–3) and third: see Hinds (1984) for a reflexive twist, rather different from the other two, in *Fast.* 4.500.

32 See Richardson (1974) on *H.Dem.* 41 for the variation.
33 The feeling that this is a return to the starting-point is enhanced by the verbal echo in *Met.* 5.462 *quas dea per terras et quas erraverit undas*, just before Ceres goes back to Sicily, of the beginning of the description of her search at *Met.* 5.439 *omnibus est terris, omni quaesita profundo*.
34 I owe this suggestion to another (regrettably anonymous) participant in the Cambridge seminar mentioned in chapter 3, n. 24 above. One might choose, I suppose, to take *inornatos* proleptically: but to do so would be a little odd after Ovid's earlier emphasis on Ceres' travel-weariness.
35 In *Met.* 5.464 Ceres *Sicaniam repetit*; now in 473, one may say, as part of that return, it is her own *pectora* which is *repetita*.
36 See Richardson (1974) on *H.Dem.* 75ff. for the various informants in the myth's tradition.
37 See Richardson (1974) on *H.Dem.* 372 and Bömer (1969–) on *Met.* 5.533 for this variation, which may well be wholly Ovid's own invention.
38 See Bühler (1960) on Moschus, *Eur.* 30–2, 63–71; and compare the myth of the Garden of Eden.
39 The *Fasti*'s specification of *three* seeds has its literary point. As Mr I.M. Le M. Du Quesnay remarks to me, the *tribus ... granis* of *Fast.* 4.607 are echoed just below in the *bis tribus ... mensibus* of 614, so that Jupiter can be felt to have used the number of seeds eaten as the basis for his numerical calculation of Persephone's consequent obligations to each world.
40 Bömer (1969–) on *Met.* 5.537. He is right to insist that the natural colour of a pomegranate's rind is darker than *pallens*, though one cannot agree with his implication that it is as red as is the centre.
41 See Bömer (1969–) on *Met.* 5.537 ad fin.
42 See Bömer (1969–) on *Met.* 5.564–71, Richardson (1974) on *H.Dem.* 399ff.
43 Bömer (1969–) on *Met.* 5.565 notes two parallels in Virgil, viz. *Aen.* 1.234 *volventibus annis* and, perhaps more appositely as describing the passage of time within a single year rather than the passage of many years, *Geo.* 2.402 *atque in se sua per vestigia volvitur annus*.
44 Here in the *Metamorphoses* Triptolemus is a *iuvenis* (*Met.* 5.649, 661); in the *Fasti* version he is a baby, equivalent not to the *Homeric Hymn*'s Triptolemus but to its Demophoon. The difference in treatment shows Ovid's awareness of Triptolemus' changing role in the myth: see chapter 3, p. 67 and n. 33.

45 Whereas Demeter's first question in *H.Dem.* 393–4 (which survives only in fragments) refers to Persephone's having eaten in the underworld, the question in *H.Dem.* 404 refers to the moment of abduction itself: see Richardson (1974) on *H.Dem.* 403–4.

46 While being pursued by Alpheus, Arethusa appeals to Diana: *Met.* 5.618–20 *'fer opem, deprendimur,' inquam | 'armigerae, Diana, tuae, cui saepe dedisti | ferre tuos arcus inclusaque tela pharetra!'* This detail calls to mind the bow, arrows and quiver of the main story which, however, far from being associated with the salvation of the victim, are actually the cause of all her troubles (*Met.* 5.365–84). The cloud which plays such a prominent part in Arethusa's story (*Met.* 5.621ff.) slyly recalls a piece of verbal play with clouds in the main story, to be discussed later in this section of my chapter. Alpheus fails to locate any futher *vestigia* of Arethusa at *Met.* 5.630–1 *neque enim vestigia cernit | longius ulla pedum.* The main story too is concerned with locating the traces of a lost girl at *Met.* 5.468ff. (see esp. 476 *vestigia damni*); and so is the parallel account of Persephone's rape in the *Fasti* which, interestingly, offers something even closer to the present passage: *Fast.* 4.463 *inde puellaris nacta est vestigia plantae.* Note the paradoxical twist to the motif in Arethusa's case, whereby it is an *absence* of *vestigia* which is telling. The liquefied nymph finally escapes when Diana breaks open the ground for her: *Met.* 5.639 *Delia rupit humum.* In the main story, the breaking open of the ground by Dis at *Met.* 5.423 *icta viam tellus in Tartara fecit*, far from bringing salvation to the nymph Cyane, is a *cause* of the distress which ends in her liquefaction. Arethusa's story ends with a subterranean trip from Greece to Sicily; immediately after the return to the main narrative Ceres makes an airborne trip from Sicily to Greece.

Further observations can be made about each of the two parallels mentioned in my discussion in the text. While both stories begin with a maiden surprised by a predatory male in a landscape, in Arethusa's case the situation is given a neat twist by the fact that the predatory male is actually *part* of the landscape: Alpheus is both peaceful water and lustful river-god. In Persephone's story there are elements in the *locus amoenus* which hint imagistically at the violence which threatens (see chapter 2 above), but in Arethusa's the threat of violence is quite literally immanent in the *locus amoenus* itself. As for the second parallel, when, eleven lines having been devoted to a limb-by-limb description of Cyane's liquefaction, Arethusa's is broken off after only four lines with the words *et citius, quam nunc tibi facta renarro, | in latices mutor* (*Met.* 5.635–6), one can see in the comment, besides another instance of Arethusa's concern with the timing of narrative acts (cf. *Met.* 5.498–501), a knowing glance by Ovid at the fact that he must cut short his description so as to avoid repeating what he has written in the main story.

Segal (1969), 56, notes the 'general parallelism between the two episodes'. Incidentally, in the wider context of the whole poem, the pursuit of Arethusa especially calls to mind that of Daphne in *Met.* 1: Ludwig (1965), 35 and n. 40, remarks on this; and discussion with Dr Anna Wilson persuades me that the correspondence would bear further study.

47 See Crump (1931), 23–4; also Wilkinson (1982), 329. It is a little misleading to use, as do many, the label 'epyllion technique' for this: see Lyne (1978), 34. The inset story is one of the principal features of the construction of the *Metamorphoses*: see e.g. Crump (1931), 195–216. Ovid's virtuosity in it is nowhere more apparent than here in *Metamorphoses* 5: not only is Arethusa's story set into Persephone's, but Persephone's is set into the story of the contest between the Muses and the daughters of Pieros, which in turn is set into the story of Pallas' visit to Mount Helicon. For some further observations on the insets of *Metamorphoses* 5, see chapter 6, pp. 126ff. and n. 25.

48 For a stimulating exploration of this idea, see Anderson (1963).

49 Bömer (1969–   ) on *Met.* 3.674 and 5.568.

50 *Met.* 5.637–8 *positoque viri, quod sumpserat, ore | vertitur in proprias, ut se mihi misceat, undas* may even be felt to echo *Met.* 5.568: *verto(r)* recurs in the same form and in the same metrical *sedes* as in the earlier passage, and an *os* is again involved in the description.

51 See Bömer (1969–   ) on *Met.* 2.425.

52 So also *Met.* 1.160, 4.219. The change in *Met.* 4.125–6 *arborei fetus aspergine caedis in atram | vertuntur faciem* becomes a supernatural and permanent transformation a little later at *Met.* 4.158–65.

53 It is relevant to note here Galinsky's (1975), 62–3, persuasive contention that metamorphosis is the key organisational principle of the poem itself, variously seen in the changes of mood, tone, subject and style within and between stories, in the poem's fluctuating structure, and in its transformation of inherited mythic materials.

54 Note that if one opts not to attach *vultu* to *tristis* ἀπὸ κοινοῦ in *Met.* 5.506, that line, like *Met.* 5.500–1 just above, offers the distinction between inner mood and outward expression: the reactions of mother and daughter may thus be seen as closely identified with each other back in Arethusa's speech, even before the lines under discussion further encourage the association.

55 See Nisbet and Hubbard (1970) on Horace, *Carm.* 1.10, introduction, and F. Williams (1978) on Callimachus, *Ap.* 31 for these features of hymnic form. *Met.* 5.341–5 is noted to be hymnic by Bömer (1969–   ) ad loc.

5 Elegy and epic: a traditional approach

1 See Heinze (1919), 1 = (1960), 308 'Ovid hat den Raub der Proserpina zweimal erzählt, im vierten Buch der Fasten (417–620) und im fünften der Metamorphosen (341–661), beide Male in grosser Ausführlichkeit – die Fastenerzählung ist die längste elegische Erzählung, die wir aus

dem Altertum besitzen –, beide Male ohne dass der Plan der Werke es unbedingt forderte ... Ovid hatte seine beiden grossen Werke gleichzeitig in Arbeit; man fragt sich, was ihn dazu bewegen mochte, ein und denselben Stoff in beiden so ausführlich zu behandeln.' Cf. chapter 2, section vii.

2 I take advantage of Otis's (1970), 50, translation of the key paragraph at Heinze (1919), 10 = (1960), 314–15.

3 Magnus (1920), 1039; Otis (1970), 23 (reprinting his 1966 words). The essentially respectful criticism of Heinze's work in the intervening years is surveyed by Little (1970), 65 n. 1.

4 Tränkle's judicious (1963) article constituted the first serious challenge to Heinze's position. See then Bernbeck (1967), esp. 127–31; Anderson (1969), 352–4; Little (1970); Galinsky (1975), esp. vii–viii; Barsby (1978), 27 and 31–2; and Knox (1982), soon to be published in new form as a Supplement to the *Proceedings of the Cambridge Philological Society*.

5 Heinze himself was aware that the *Fasti* was weightier than the average elegy: see Heinze (1919), 17 = (1960), 320 'die Elegie, selbst so ernster Tendenz, wie es die Fasten sind ...' However, this was not an aspect of its generic identity which he pursued very far in his monograph. Cf. Barsby's (1978), 27, criticism '... in pursuing the contrast between elegy and epic he neglected the further comparisons which can be made within elegy itself'.

6 See e.g. Little (1970), 68 'Heinze's discussion is marked by a confusion of thought intolerable in a work of scholarship, and reduces a critic to impatience and frustration.'

7 Little (1970), 77–105.

8 Little (1970), 68–77.

9 Besides Little, see esp. Galinsky (1975), viii: 'The generic terminology has imposed its limitations even on those who have disagreed with Heinze or, more recently, with Otis, as they have characterized the *Metamorphoses* as an anti-epic, para-epic, mock epic, epic *sui generis*, or even as elegiac. In this fashion, label is simply replaced by counter-label and the generic approach to the *Metamorphoses* is accepted in the process ... To push distinctions and categories of this kind too far may satisfy the scholarly urge to tidy up and impose order on the baffling variety of the *Metamorphoses*, but it tells us little about vital characteristics of the poem itself.' However, the anti-generic trend is not universal: von Albrecht (1977), 78, is still happy to argue with Heinze on Heinze's terms (he is criticised for doing so by Gold (1979), 450).

10 All of Ovid's extant works except the *Metamorphoses* are in elegiac couplets, viz. *Amores*, *Heroides*, *Medicamina Faciei Femineae*, *Ars Amatoria*, *Remedia Amoris*, *Fasti*, *Tristia*, *Ibis*, *Epistulae ex Ponto*. He used hexameters, however, in his abbreviated translation of Aratus (probably early in his career: see chapter 1, p. 13); and his lost *Medea* was another non-elegiac venture.

11 I should make clear at the outset that it is exclusively in the traditional sense (i.e. to label literary forms like 'elegy' and 'epic') that I use here the terms 'genre' and 'generic'; my concern is not with the completely different categories, also conventionally labelled 'genres', whose importance has been rediscovered by Prof. Francis Cairns.

12 Heinze (1919), 19–20 = (1960), 322.

13 See Nisbet and Hubbard (1970) on Horace, *Carm.* 1.33.2; also Brink (1971) on Horace, *A.P.* 75–8. On elegy and the θρῆνος, see Harvey (1955), 168–72. The true etymology of ἔλεγος is uncertain: see Chantraine s.v. ἔλεγος. For the etymologies from ἔλεος, εὖ λέγειν and ἒ ἒ λέγειν, see e.g. *Etym. Magn.* 326.48ff.; the one from εὖ λέγειν is attributed to the first-century B.C. Alexandrian scholar Didymus: see Orion, *Etym.* 58.7ff. (Sturz).

14 See the compelling interpretation of Catullus 65.12 by Wiseman (1969), 17–18 'The twelfth line of this poem is the only passage in our collection of Catullus' poems with an apparently explicit programmatic content: addressing his dead brother, the poet promises *semper maesta tua carmina morte canam* ... The promise is not to keep writing about the brother's death, but to keep writing *carmina maesta* – which means ... to keep writing elegiacs. And, of course, the rest of our collection *is* in elegiacs.'

15 See *Tristia* 5.1 with Nagle (1980), 22–3.

16 See Anderson (1973), 69 and n. 11, on this elegiac plaintiveness in the *Heroides*.

17 Little (1970), 75–6.

18 With this part of the discussion cf. Heinze (1919), 3–4 = (1960), 309–10.

19 The stress on lamentation here stands out all the more clearly when this simile is measured against the differently nuanced comparison in the *Homeric Hymn to Demeter* which may have suggested it: see chapter 3, p. 62 earlier. The *Hymn* is more obviously relevant to the present inquiry in other places: see my discussion later in this chapter. See Brunner (1971), 280, for the conformity of the *Fast.* 4.481–2 simile to Heinze's category of 'das ἐλεεινόν'; and, for further discussion, chapter 6, n. 10 below.

20 Heinze (1919), 3–4 = (1960), 310.

21 Heinze characteristically presses the argument to breaking-point, suggesting that its passionate ferocity distinguishes the scene of mourning *itself* (*Met.* 5.471–3) from the 'pure' mourning typical of the *Fasti* version. One might cite in his support passages in the *Fasti* like 4.523 *flent pariter molles animis virgoque senexque*; but it is hard to see how Heinze would account for *Fast.* 4.454 *et feriunt maesta pectora nuda manu*.

22 I.e. 'erzählte Zeit', as opposed to 'Erzählzeit': see Genette (1972), 77–8 = (1980), 33–5.

23 Otis (1970), 52.

24 See D.C. Innes (1979), 165–6.

25 Bucolic poetry itself, of course, comes under the head of the Latin term *epos*. However (*pace* Galinsky (1975), viii) the *forte epos* which sings of kings and wars was perceived as quite different in kind from the *molle atque facetum* of the bucolic Muse: as well as the preface to Virgil, *Eclogue* 6 itself, see Horace, *Serm.* 1.10.43–5 with Fraenkel (1957), 130–1 and n. 5. When I use the word 'epic' in my discussion, I generally mean (in accordance with modern usage) that perceived sub-category of *epos* which one may call 'grand epic'.

26 See e.g. *Il.* 1.5 Διὸς δ' ἐτελείετο βουλή, and Richardson (1974) on *H.Dem.* 9.

27 Cf. Heinze (1919), 7–8 = (1960), 313; Otis (1970), 51; and chapter 3, n. 31 above.

28 For the Callimacheanism common to this tragic *recusatio* and to the epic *recusationes* more usual in Roman poetry, see Thomas (1979), 180–95, esp. 190 and n. 41; also Thomas (1978). Cf. chapter 1, pp. 20 and 22.

29 The humbleness of the *Fasti* dwelling is a talking-point both at *Fast.* 4.515–16 ... *et orat | tecta suae subeat quantulacumque casae*, and at 526 '*surge, nec exiguae despice tecta casae*'.

30 See Heinze (1919), 6–8 = (1960), 312–13 on the power-struggles of *Met.* 5.341ff.; (1919), 19–20 = (1960), 322 for the δεινόν label.

31 Otis (1970), 52–9, esp. 58 'Beneath the solemn epic façade there are – it is quite obvious – very human feelings at work. This is, at one level, a narrative of solemn gods and goddesses, of Hell and Heaven, of violent love and fierce resentment – of all that is serious and intense and can find its fittest expression in epic oratory and narrative. But at another level it is a story of social ambition (Venus), undignified love (Pluto), childish innocence (Proserpina), matronly respectability (Cyane), womanly gossip (Arethusa), maternal outrage (Ceres), and tactful persuasiveness (Jupiter) all reacting upon each other in a quite delightful human comedy.'

32 Otis (1970), 23, quoted in the first section of this chapter.

33 Heinze (1919), 8 = (1960), 313.

6 Elegy and epic: a new approach

1 Cf. McKeown (1984), 183–4, who points out the similar situation in the fourth book of Propertius' elegies (see esp. Propertius 4.1.57–60).

2 It would be perverse, incidentally, not to see here a hinted reference to Ovid's own contemporary work in the *herous pes*. Ovid does indeed make allusion to Augustus' role as the great *Pater* in the *Metamorphoses*, at the very climax of the poem: with *Fast.* 2.131–2 *hoc tu per terras, quod in aethere Iuppiter alto, | nomen habes: hominum tu pater, ille deum* compare *Met.* 15.858–60 *Iuppiter arces | temperat aetherias et mundi regna triformis, | terra sub Augusto est; pater est et rector uterque.*

3 See *Fast.* 3.1–4 *bellice, depositis clipeo paulisper et hasta, | Mars, ades et nitidas casside solve comas. | forsitan ipse roges quid sit cum Marte poetae: |*

a te qui canitur nomina mensis habet, 7–8 *Palladis exemplo ponendae tempora sume | cuspidis: invenies et quod inermis agas. poetae* here is evidently not so much '*a* poet' as '*the* poet', i.e. the elegiac poet of the *Fasti*. On the preface to Book 4, see further section ii of the present chapter.

4 Little (1970), 72–3.

5 For Alexandrian εἰδογραφία, and for interpretation of this part of the *Ars Poetica*, see Brink (1971) on *A.P.* 73–85. Roman interest in the subject dates at least from Accius' *Didascalica*: see Accius fr. 8 Funaioli. It should be noted that Augustan 'mixing' between generic categories is itself an inheritance from the Alexandrians: see Kroll (1924), 202ff. ('Die Kreuzung der Gattungen').

6 Little (1970), 75, writes 'If Ovid emphasises the ἐλεεινόν, he does it not because it is unheroic, and therefore better suited to his idea of what elegy should be, but because it is better suited to a poem ... whose purpose is essentially peaceful[, which] celebrates the *pax deorum* in the spiritual, the *pax Augusta* in the temporal ...' He fails to see that his non-generic reading can actually coexist with the generic one.

7 Ovid's reassertion in this preface of allegiance to his roots in love elegy is full of (often ironical) verbal allusion to his farewell to love elegy in *Amores* 3.15. The opening words of *Amores* 3.15 *quaere novum vatem, tenerorum mater Amorum* are closely echoed in *Fast.* 4.1, and effectively eaten in *Fast.* 4.8 and 14; *Fast.* 4.9 echoes *Am.* 3.15.3–4 *quos ego composui, Paeligni ruris alumnus, | (nec me deliciae dedecuere meae)* and *Fast.* 4.10 echoes *Am.* 3.15.18 *pulsanda est magnis area maior equis;* finally, note the brazenness of *Fast.* 4.7 after *Am.* 3.15.15–16 *culte puer puerique parens Amathusia culti, | aurea de campo vellite signa meo.*

8 On these features of elegiac composition see Heinze (1919), 75–6 = (1960), 363; von Albrecht (1977), 78; and Wilkinson (1963), 133–4. In the present study one can interestingly contrast the analysis of an instance of continuous hexameter composition (*Met.* 5.379–91) in chapter 2, section iii.

9 For this usage, especially favoured by Ovid, see *TLL* 1.1756.12ff., *OLD* s.v. *alternus* lc. An instance at [Ovid], *Ep. Sapph.* 5–6 is quoted in chapter 5, p. 103. Compare also the physical peculiarity of the personified Elegia at *Am.* 3.1.8 *et, puto, pes illi longior alter erat.* Note, finally, the reading of Propertius 1.10.9–10 adumbrated by Ross (1975), 83–4. I am indebted on this point to a discussion with Dr Maria Wyke.

10 The passage may draw still further programmatic attention to its elegiac status in *Fast.* 4.481–2 *quacumque ingreditur, miseris loca cuncta querellis | implet, ut amissum cum gemit ales Ityn.* References to the myth of Itys are not uncommon in Latin poetry; but the present couplet seems especially reminiscent of Catullus 65.12–14 *semper maesta tua carmina morte canam, | qualia sub densis ramorum concinit umbris | Daulias, absumpti fata gemens Ityli.* Compare especially Ovid's *amissum cum gemit ... Ityn* with Catullus' *absumpti fata gemens Ityli.* There are also verbal

similarities with a Propertian couplet which itself echoes these Catullan lines: Propertius 3.10.9–10 *alcyonum positis requiescant ora querellis;* | *increpet absumptum nec sua mater Ityn.* If Propertius draws *absumptum ... Ityn* from Catullus, he gives in turn to Ovid those successive line-ends *querellis* and *Ityn.* Allusion to Catullus' lines on Itys would be extremely apt in *Fast.* 4.481–2: not only does the Catullan passage, like the Ovidian one, take the form of a simile expressive of lament; not only is it too in elegiacs; but this is the very passage, it seems (see Wiseman (1969), 17–18, cited in chapter 5, n. 14 above), which constitutes Catullus' announcement of his new vocation as elegiac poet. The idea of applying a bird simile to the searching Ceres has been argued (chapter 3, p. 62; cf. chapter 5, n. 19) to come from lines 43–4 of the *Homeric Hymn to Demeter*: is Ovid's newly mournful interpretation of that simile to be traced to one of the most important elegiac programmes in Latin?

This is slightly conjectural; but note also the prompt to any generalising tendency available in the word *querellis*, which is not only *expressive* of elegiac lament, but sometimes almost constitutes a *technical description* of elegiac lament: see Anderson (1973), 69 and n. 11, and cf. Horace's *querimonia* cited in chapter 5, p. 103.

11 On a rather different tack, perhaps one may also see the *per ... vices* and *alternis* which characterise the pattern of Ceres' *miseris ... querellis* here as prefiguring the alternating pattern of the existence, half in the upper world and half in the lower, which awaits her daughter at the end of the story (*Fast.* 4.613–14). *alternis ... perit* in 486 is especially suggestive in this regard.

12 See Bömer (1969–) on *Met.* 5.344. Bömer takes *possim* to be equivalent to an 'unreal' *possem*, as sometimes happens in classical Latin poetry (see Bömer (1969–) on *Met.* 1.363). However, there seems to be no reason not to take it as a regular 'ideal' subjunctive.

13 See the *editio princeps* of the Gallus papyrus by Anderson, Parsons and Nisbet (1979). The (partly lost) hexameter and the pentameter quoted here constitute the first couplet of what appears to be a four-line epigram, which continues fragmentarily ....]. *aṭur iḍem tibi, non ego,* *Vịsce| ..].........l. Kato, iudice te vereor.*

14 For the influence of Gallus, *P. Qaṣr Ibrîm* 6–7 on subsequent poetry see Hinds (1983), including discussion (45–7) of Virgil, *Ecl.* 9.35–6, *Ecl.* 10.2–3 and Propertius 4.7.83. Since the writing of that article, my Gallan research has further benefited from the comments of Prof. Francis Cairns and Mr Stephen Heyworth.

15 The 'fairly clear echo' of Gallus, *P. Qaṣr Ibrîm* 6–7 in *Am.* 1.3.20 was first noted by Hollis (1980), 542. For a fuller discussion than that which I offer here, see Hinds (1983), 48–9. For the first three poems of *Amores* 1 as a connected programmatic sequence, see Kenney (1982), 420.

16 See Anderson, Parsons and Nisbet (1979), 149–50.

17 The echo was first noted by Barchiesi (1981), 163. My discussion here essentially reproduces Hinds (1983), 49–52.

18 For the alliteration of *domina deicere digna* in Gallus, *P. Qaṣr Ibrîm* 7 as an archaic feature, see Anderson, Parsons and Nisbet (1979), 149.

19 Ovid's modification of his source is satisfyingly organic: the elegiac *domina*, who is often treated as a *dea* by her poet-lover (see e.g. Lilja (1965), 186–92), becomes in Ovid's hexameters a *real dea*. I owe this point to a discussion with Dr Anna Wilson at the Liverpool Latin Seminar.

20 Compare especially the first half of *Met.* 5.345 *carmina digna dea* with the second half of *Am.* 1.3.20 *carmina digna sua*.

21 The *Homeric Hymns* were, or (in the case of the later ones) posed as, preludes to epic recitation: see Richardson (1974), 3–4 and comm. on *H.Dem.* 1–3 and 495. For the epic nature of the poetry introduced by such hymns, see *H.Hom.* 32.18–20 σέο δ' ἀρχόμενος κλέα φωτῶν | ᾄσομαι ἡμιθέων ὧν κλείουσ' ἔργματ' ἀοιδοὶ | Μουσάων θεράποντες ἀπὸ στομάτων ἐροέντων. For their association with poetry contests, see *H.Hom.* 6.19–20 χαῖρ' ἑλικοβλέφαρε γλυχυμείλιχε, δὸς δ' ἐν ἀγῶνι | νίκην τῷδε φέρεσθαι, ἐμὴν δ' ἔντυνον ἀοιδήν. On the hymnic prefaces of Hesiod, see West (1978) on *Op.* 1–10. The hymn to a god might or might not betray a connexion with the subsequent epic account, and was in any case clearly marked off from it. In the present instance, Calliope's hymnic preface to Ceres combines connexion and lack of connexion: there is a bond with the narrative's main concern, viz. Persephone and Ceres, and specifically with Ceres' infliction of the famine; but there is a strong disjunction from the opening subject, viz. the punishment of Typhoeus.

22 For Calliope as the eldest Muse, cf. e.g. Plato, *Phaedr.* 259D.

23 See Todd (1903), 8–9 and 44–51; Cairns (1984), 149 and n. 83.

24 A brief discussion by Anderson (1968), 102–3, sees Calliope's significance in *Metamorphoses* 5 in terms somewhat akin to these.

25 On relationships between 'frame' and inset narrative in *Metamorphoses* 5 see further nn. 27 and 40 below; and compare the observations on insets in chapter 4, pp. 91ff and n. 47. Segal (1969), 53, commenting on the outermost frame (see parenthesis in text), notes the irony whereby tales of rape 'are told by the easily frightened, virginal Muses (*Met.* 5.273–4 *omnia terrent* | *virgineas mentes*) to the virgin goddess Minerva, who has just come to the "maidens'" mountain, Helicon (254 *virgineum* ... *Helicona*)'. Compare the importance of internal narrator, audience and setting to the stories of Baucis and Philemon and of Erysichthon in *Metamorphoses* 8: Due (1974), 80–1; Crabbe (1981), 2292–3. The classic analysis by Genette (1972), 225–67 = (1980), 212–62, of the traces left in the '*discours narratif*' by the '*instance narrative*' which produces it is especially instructive in the case of inset stories like these.

26 Cf. Leach (1974), 114 'Since the Muses are giving the account, they compress the song of the Pierides into a hasty, distasteful summary while their own lengthy contribution is unfolded in all its detail.'

27 There is certainly something in Leach's (1974), 115, cynical view of the nymph-judges' verdict: 'The nymphs, as might be expected from the honorific treatment given to their kind [i.e. Cyane, Arethusa] in [Calliope's] tale, vote in favour of the Muses'. For the importance of taking account of the audience of an inset narrative, see n. 25 above.

28 For the moral stance which Calliope's song takes against the Pierid's, see Leach (1974), 114; for anticipation of the Pierids' punishment in that of Typhoeus, see Boillat (1976), 118.

29 Anderson (1968), 102–3, sees a concern with more purely literary principles in the Heliconian contest; but he offers no more than a passing observation on the subject. Prof. Dr Heinz Hofmann in a paper entitled 'Ovid's *Metamorphoses*: *carmen perpetuum*, *carmen deductum*' given to an April 1984 Liverpool Latin Seminar on poetic programmes (publication promised in the fifth volume of *Papers of the Liverpool Latin Seminar*) suggests, again without elaboration, that the Pierid song is a representative of the *perpetuum*, and Calliope's of the *deductum* style. As will be seen, his interpretation coincides with mine more fully in the former case than in the latter. Leach (1974), 111–15, on a rather different tack, sees the Pierids' experience on Mount Helicon as part of an essay by Ovid on the limitations of the (human) artist.

30 Typhoeus (*Met.* 5.321ff.) was originally distinct from the Giants (*Met.* 5.319), as he was from the earlier Titans. However, all these Olympian struggles, viz. Titanomachy, Gigantomachy and Typhonomachy, are subject to confusion and conflation from the fifth century B.C. on: for Titans and Giants, see Hunter (1983), 208 n. 1; for Typhoeus' part, see Fontenrose (1959), 80 and n. 10, 160 and n. 32, 239–41.

31 See D.C. Innes (1979), 165–8; Nisbet and Hubbard (1978) on Horace, *Carm.* 2.12, intr. and comm. on line 7.

32 Besides the instance in Propertius 2.1 noted below, see Propertius 3.9.47ff.; Horace, *Carm.* 2.12.6ff.; Ovid, *Am.* 2.1.11ff., *Met.* 10.149ff., *Trist.* 2.331ff.; [Virgil], *Culex* 26ff.

33 So Nisbet and Hubbard (1978) on Horace, *Carm.* 2.12.7.

34 Cf. Callimachus, *Aet.* fr. 1; Callimachus, *h.* 2.105–13 with F. Williams (1978) ad loc.

35 Cf. Horace, *A.P.* 133–5 with Brink (1971) ad loc.; also Russell (1979), esp. 1–2.

36 For the familiarity of this metaphor in both Greek and Latin, see Brink (1971) on Horace, *A.P.* 27; and Bramble (1974), 57–8 and 156–8. *intumescere* itself is attested as an explicitly literary critical term only in the fifth century A.D. (Sidonius, *Epist.* 4.3.4); but *tumidus*, *tumor*, *turgidus* and *turgere* are all so attested before or in Augustan times, with *tumere* making its first appearance in a literary critical sense in the elder Seneca (*Con.* 9.2.26): see the respective articles in *OLD*.

37 For *non inflati* ... *Callimachi*, see Rothstein (1920–4) on Propertius 2.34.31.

38 See *OLD* s.v. *numerus* 13 and 14. The word *stolidus* too sits happily in a

context of literary critical vilification: cf. the description of the theatre audience at Horace, *Ep.* 2.1.184 as *indocti stolidique*.

39 *Met.* 5.337–9 ... *dedimus summam certaminis uni:* | *surgit et immissos hedera collecta capillos* | *Calliope* .... If a Heliconian setting encourages susceptibility to the smallest hints of poetic programme, can one discern a fleeting reference to Calliope's poetic character, and an anticipation of the aspiration to epic grandeur which will open her recital, in that single, unremarkable word with which she rises to sing, viz. *surgit*? The verb is used in an overtly programmatic way in Propertius 2.10 for the ascent from a humble genre to a grand one: Propertius 2.10.7–12 *aetas prima canat Veneres, extrema tumultus:* | *bella canam, quando scripta puella mea est.* | *nunc volo subducto gravior procedere vultu,* | *nunc aliam citharam me mea Musa docet.* | *surge, anime, ex humili; iam, carmina, sumite vires;* | *Pierides, magni nunc erit oris opus.* And, at the very conclusion of Virgil's *Eclogues*, this programmatic sense of *surgere* seems to be hinted at with an obliquity comparable to what is envisaged in the present passage: *Ecl.* 10.75–6 *surgamus: solet esse gravis cantantibus umbra,* | *iuniperi gravis umbra; nocent et frugibus umbrae. surgamus* here, according to the attractive interpretation of Kennedy (1983), drawing on Berg (1974), 189, implies not only rising from the position characteristic of the pastoral singer, recumbent in the shade of a tree (cf. *Ecl.* 1.1–2): it also presages the poet's move from a genre avowedly humble (*Ecl.* 4.2 *humiles ... myricae*) to something more elevated – perhaps specifically the *fruges* (*Ecl.* 10.76; cf. Ovid, *Am.* 1.15.25) of the *Georgics*.

40 The gross imbalance of length between the coverage given by the Muse-narrator to the Pierid song on the one hand and to Calliope's on the other (noted on p. 128) perhaps makes one wonder if the Muses are unfair to the 'facts' of the Pierid case in other ways too. Otis (1970), 153, opines that the moral distinction between the Pierid's impious tale and the *properatus amor* of Pluto told by Calliope is not quite as clear as the Muses appear to think. Similarly, although the essential theme of the Pierid song, viz. Gigantomachy, is indubitably out of favour amongst the best poets, the concern of the last five lines (i.e. the only ones reported 'verbatim') with metamorphosis can for obvious reasons be argued to be more acceptable. Indeed, the particular transformations recounted here, with their learned and exotic allusion to Egyptian theriomorphic deities (see Gwyn Griffiths (1960), 376), are suggestive, not just of Alexandrian scholarship in general, but specifically of the lost treatment of the Typhon myth in Nicander's *Heteroioumena* (as attested in Antoninus Liberalis 28: see chapter 3, p. 55 and n. 12). Has the Pierid found a way, then, of producing a Gigantomachy with some redeeming features? Does the singer, who in the Muse-narrator's terms shows herself morally reprehensible by belittling the gods (*Met.* 5.320 *extenuat*), actually achieve thereby a touch of Alexandrian *tenue*? For the importance of keeping an eye on narrators, see especially n. 25 above. One might argue that an

unease concerning the extent of the Muses' distance from their rivals is written into the story of the contest from its (Nicandrian) beginnings: as 'daughters of Pieros' the rivals possess a name which elsewhere in the mythological tradition (as was remarked in passing at chapter 1, p. 14) is the property of the Muses themselves.

41 For the *Aeneid* as the main obstacle to Ovid's epic ambitions, see e.g. Kenney (1982), 431–2.

42 Heinze (1919), 7 and n. 2 = (1960), 312–13 and n. 4.

43 For *arma* in such contexts, see e.g. *Am.* 1.1.1, Propertius 1.7.2, 2.1.18; for *bella*, *Am.* 1.1.1, Propertius 2.10.8, 4.6.69, Horace, *A.P.* 73.

44 As a postscript to the verbal echoes noted above, it is worth remarking on a curious correspondence which arises out of the second line of the Virgilian speech. *Aen.* 1.664–5 ... *mea magna potentia, solus | nate patris summi qui tela Typhoea temnis*: the *epitheton a spoliis et victoria* (Servius ad loc.), apparently merely decorative in Virgil's sentence, makes the evocation of that sentence all the more apt here in *Met.* 5.365, where we have just finished hearing about the eponymous victim of the *tela Typhoea* (*Met.* 5.346–55). Pure coincidence, perhaps; but with a shaping genius like Ovid's present, one is rather disposed to admire it as a consciously adept piece of positioning.

45 Venus' and Cupid's intervention at Carthage is directly modelled on Apollonius, *Arg.* 3.83ff., where Aphrodite (at the behest of Hera and Athena) gets her son to shoot an arrow at Medea, to make her fall in love with Jason: see Austin (1971) on Virgil, *Aen.* 1.657–94. One could interpret as an acknowledgement of this ultimate source of his borrowing Ovid's 'restoration' to Cupid of the traditional bow and arrow with which he had operated in the Apollonian version, but which Virgil had suppressed in favour of the subtle device (see G. Williams (1968), 375, 377) of the substitute-Ascanius. For this technique of allusion, see chapter 3, n. 16.

46 For this element in the literary make-up of the *Aeneid*, see McKeown (1984), 185; R.D. Williams (1967), 29–30. For the effect of *parvulus Aeneas* in particular, see Austin (1955) on Virgil, *Aen.* 4.328.

47 For the comparison, see Anderson (1973), 49–68; Kenney (1982), 424–5.

Epilogue

1 On this kind of 'Alexandrian footnote', cf. chapter 3, p. 58 and n. 22.

2 Galinsky (1975), 175, notes the Ovidian 'self-irony'; and he also observes how Orpheus' *vos quoque iunxit Amor* addressed in *Met.* 10.29 to Persephone and Dis, by echoing Venus' *iunge deam patruo* addressed in *Met.* 5.379 to Amor, sharpens the recall here of the *Metamorphoses* 5 account.

WORKS CITED

(i) Standard works of reference

Chantraine   P. Chantraine, *Dictionnaire étymologique de la langue grecque, histoire des mots*. Paris, 1968–80.

Ernout–Meillet   A. Ernout and A. Meillet, *Dictionnaire étymologique de la langue latine, histoire des mots*. 4th edn. Paris, 1959.

LSJ   H.J. Liddell and R. Scott, rev. H. Stuart Jones, *A Greek–English Lexicon*. 9th edn. Oxford, 1925–40.

OCD   *The Oxford Classical Dictionary*. 2nd edn. Oxford, 1970.

OLD   *Oxford Latin Dictionary*. Oxford, 1968–82.

RE   *Paulys Real-Encyclopädie der classischen Altertumswissenschaft*. Stuttgart, 1894– .

TGL   *Thesaurus Graecae Linguae*. 3rd edn. Paris, 1831–65.

TLL   *Thesaurus Linguae Latinae*. Leipzig, 1900– .

(ii) Books and articles

Adams, J.N. (1982). *The Latin Sexual Vocabulary*. London.

von Albrecht, M. (1964). *Die Parenthese in Ovids Metamorphosen und ihre dichterische Funktion*. Spudasmata 7. Hildesheim.

(1977). *Römische Poesie: Texte und Interpretationen*. Heidelberg.

von Albrecht, M., and Zinn, E. (1968), edd. *Ovid*. Wege der Forschung 92. Darmstadt.

Allen, T.W., Halliday, W.R., and Sikes, E.E. (1936), edd. *The Homeric Hymns*. 2nd edn. Oxford.

Allen, W.S. (1973). *Accent and Rhythm*. Cambridge Studies in Linguistics 12. Cambridge.

(1978). *Vox Latina*. 2nd edn. Cambridge.

Alton, E.H., Wormell, D.E.W., and Courtney, E. (1978), edd. *Ovidius, Fasti*. Bibliotheca Teubneriana. Leipzig.

Anderson, R.D., Parsons, P.J., and Nisbet, R.G.M. (1979). 'Elegiacs by Gallus from Qaṣr Ibrîm.' *Journal of Roman Studies* 69:125–55.

Anderson, W.S. (1963). 'Multiple change in the *Metamorphoses*.' *Transactions of the American Philological Association* 94:1–27.

(1968). Review of B. Otis, *Ovid as an Epic Poet*. *American Journal of Philology* 89:93–104.

(1969). Review of E.J. Bernbeck, *Beobachtungen zur Darstellungsart in Ovids Metamorphosen*. *American Journal of Philology* 90:352–5.

(1973). 'The *Heroides*.' J.W. Binns, ed., *Ovid*. Greek and Latin Studies: Classical Literature and its Influence. 49–83. London.

(1977), ed. *Ovidius, Metamorphoses*. Bibliotheca Teubneriana. Leipzig.

Auguet, R. (1972). *Cruelty and Civilization: The Roman Games*. London. Trans. of *Cruauté et civilisation: les jeux romains*. Paris, 1970.

Austin, R.G. (1955), ed. *P. Vergili Maronis Aeneidos Liber Quartus*. Oxford.

(1971), ed. *P. Vergili Maronis Aeneidos Liber Primus*. Oxford.

Barchiesi, A. (1981). 'Notizie sul "nuovo Gallo".' *Atene e Roma* n.s. 26: 153–66.

Barrett, W.S. (1964), ed. *Euripides, Hippolytus*. Oxford.

Barsby, J.A. (1978). *Ovid*. Greece and Rome New Surveys in the Classics 12. Oxford.

Barwick, K. (1925). 'Ovids Erzählung vom Raub der Proserpina und Nikanders Ἑτεροιούμενα.' *Philologus* 80: 454–66.

Bauer, D.F. (1962). 'The function of Pygmalion in the *Metamorphoses* of Ovid.' *Transactions of the American Philological Association* 93: 1–21.

Beare, W. (1957). *Latin Verse and European Song: A Study in Accent and Rhythm*. London.

Berg, W. (1974). *Early Virgil*. London.

Berlin, B., and Kay, P. (1969). *Basic Colour Terms: Their Universality and Evolution*. Berkeley and Los Angeles.

Bernbeck, E.J. (1967). *Beobachtungen zur Darstellungsart in Ovids Metamorphosen*. Zetemata 43. Munich.

Bethe, E. (1904). 'Ovid und Nikander.' *Hermes* 39: 1–14.

Boillat, M. (1976). *Les Métamorphoses d'Ovide: thèmes majeurs et problèmes de composition*. Bern and Frankfurt.

Bömer, F. (1957–8), ed. *P. Ovidius Naso, die Fasten*. Wissenschaftliche Kommentare zu lateinischen und griechischen Schriftstellern. 2 vols. Heidelberg.

(1969–   ). *P. Ovidius Naso, Metamorphosen*. Wissenschaftliche Kommentare zu griechischen und lateinischen Schriftstellern. Heidelberg.

Bramble, J.C. (1974). *Persius and the Programmatic Satire: A Study in Form and Imagery*. Cambridge Classical Studies. Cambridge.

Brink, C.O. (1971), ed. *Horace on Poetry: The 'Ars Poetica'*. Cambridge.

Brunner, T.F. (1971). 'Δεινόν vs. ἐλεεινόν: Heinze revisited.' *American Journal of Philology* 92: 275–84.

Bühler, W. (1960), ed. *Die Europa des Moschos*. Hermes Einzelschriften 13. Wiesbaden.

Cairns, F. (1979). 'Self-imitation within a generic framework: Ovid, *Amores* 2.9 and 3.11 and the *renuntiatio amoris*.' D.A. West and A.J. Woodman, edd., *Creative Imitation and Latin Literature*. 121–41. Cambridge.

(1979a). *Tibullus: A Hellenistic Poet at Rome*. Cambridge.

(1984). 'Propertius and the Battle of Actium (4.6).' A.J. Woodman and

D.A. West, edd., *Poetry and Politics in the Age of Augustus*. 129–68. Cambridge.

Coleman, R.G.G. (1977), ed. *Vergil: Eclogues*. Cambridge Greek and Latin Classics. Cambridge.

Courtney, E. (1980). *A Commentary on the Satires of Juvenal*. London.

Crabbe, A. (1981). 'Structure and content in Ovid's *Metamorphoses*.' H. Temporini and W. Haase, edd., *Aufstieg und Niedergang der römischen Welt*. II.31.4. 2274–2327. Berlin.

Crump, M.M. (1931). *The Epyllion from Theocritus to Ovid*. Oxford.

Curtius, E.R. (1953). *European Literature and the Latin Middle Ages*. Bollingen Series 36. New York. Trans. of *Europäische Literatur und lateinisches Mittelalter*. Bern, 1948.

Dale, A.M. (1954), ed. *Euripides, Alcestis*. Oxford.

Davie, D. (1983). *Collected Poems 1971–83*. Manchester and Ashington.

Diggle, J. (1970), ed. *Euripides, Phaethon*. Cambridge Classical Texts and Commentaries. Cambridge.

Due, O.S. (1974). *Changing Forms: Studies in the Metamorphoses of Ovid*. Classica et Mediaevalia: Dissertationes 10. Copenhagen.

Du Quesnay, I.M.Le M. (1973). 'The *Amores*.' J.W. Binns, ed., *Ovid*. Greek and Latin Studies: Classical Literature and its Influence. 1–48. London.

    (1977). 'Vergil's Fourth *Eclogue*.' F. Cairns, ed., *Papers of the Liverpool Latin Seminar 1976*. 25–99. Liverpool.

    (1979). 'From Polyphemus to Corydon: Virgil, *Eclogue* 2 and the *Idylls* of Theocritus.' D.A. West and A.J. Woodman, edd., *Creative Imitation and Latin Literature*. 35–69. Cambridge.

Eisenhut, W. (1961). '*Deducere carmen*. Ein Beitrag zum Problem der literarischen Beziehungen zwischen Horaz und Properz.' *Gedenkschrift für Georg Rohde*. Aparchai 4. 91–104. Tubingen (= Eisenhut (1975), 247–63).

    (1975), ed. *Properz*. Wege der Forschung 237. Darmstadt.

Evans, H.B. (1983). *Publica Carmina: Ovid's Books from Exile*. Lincoln and London.

Farnell, L.R. (1896–1909). *The Cults of the Greek States*. 5 vols. Oxford.

Fontenrose, J.E. (1939). 'Apollo and Sol in the Latin poets of the first century B.C.' *Transactions of the American Philological Association* 70:439–55.

    (1940). 'Apollo and the Sun-God in Ovid.' *American Journal of Philology* 61:429–44.

    (1959). *Python: A Study of Delphic Myth and its Origins*. Berkeley and Los Angeles.

Fordyce, C.J. (1977), ed. *P. Vergili Maronis Aeneidos Libri VII–VIII*. Oxford.

Förster, R. (1874). *Der Raub und die Rückkehr der Persephone*. Stuttgart.

Fraenkel, E. (1912). *De media et nova comoedia quaestiones selectae*. Diss. Göttingen.

(1957). *Horace*. Oxford.

Fränkel, H. (1945). *Ovid: A Poet between Two Worlds*. Sather Classical Lectures 18. Berkeley and Los Angeles.

Frazer, J.G. (1912). *The Golden Bough*. Part 5: *Spirits of the Corn and of the Wild*. 3rd edn. London.

(1921), ed. *Apollodorus, the Library*. The Loeb Classical Library. 2 vols. London.

(1929), ed. *The Fasti of Ovid*. 5 vols. London.

Galinsky, G.K. (1975). *Ovid's Metamorphoses: An Introduction to the Basic Aspects*. Oxford.

Gatz, B. (1967). *Weltalter, goldene Zeit und sinnverwandte Vorstellungen*. Spudasmata 16. Hildesheim.

Genette, G. (1972). *Figures III*. Collection Poétique. Paris.

(1980). J.E. Lewin, tr., *Narrative Discourse*. Oxford (= Genette (1972), 65–282).

Gilbert, C.D. (1976). 'Ovid, *Met*. 1.4.' *Classical Quarterly* n.s. 26:111–12.

Gold, B.K. (1979). Review of M. von Albrecht, *Römische Poesie*. *American Journal of Philology* 100:449–51.

Gow, A.S.F. (1952), ed. *Theocritus*. 2 vols. 2nd edn. Cambridge.

Gow, A.S.F., and Scholfield, A.F. (1953), edd. *Nicander, the Poems and Poetical Fragments*. Cambridge.

Graefe, R. (1979). *Vela erunt: die Zeltdächer der römischen Theater und ähnlicher Anlangen*. 2 vols. Mainz.

Grisart, A. (1959). 'La publication des Métamorphoses: une source du récit d'Ovide.' E. Paratore, ed., *Atti del convegno internazionale ovidiano* II. 125–56. Rome.

Grube, G.M.A. (1965). *The Greek and Roman Critics*. London.

Gwyn Griffiths, J. (1960). 'The flight of the gods before Typhon: an unrecognised myth.' *Hermes* 88:374–6.

Hagen, H. (1902), ed. *Appendix Serviana*. G. Thilo and H. Hagen, edd., *Servii Grammatici qui feruntur in Vergilii carmina commentarii* III.2. Leipzig.

Hall, F.W. (1897), ed. *The Fourth Verrine of Cicero*. Macmillan's Classical Series. London.

Harvey, A.E. (1955). 'The classification of Greek lyric poetry.' *Classical Quarterly* n.s. 5:157–75.

Haupt, M., Ehwald, R., and von Albrecht, M. (1966), edd. *P. Ovidius Naso Metamorphosen*. Vol. I, 10th edn. Vol. II, 5th edn. Zurich and Dublin.

Heinze, R. (1919). *Ovids elegische Erzählung*. Berichte der Sächsischen Akademie zu Leipzig. Philologisch-historische Klasse. 71.7. Leipzig (= Heinze (1960), 308–403).

(1960). E. Burck, ed., *Vom Geist des Römertums*. 3rd edn. Stuttgart.

Herter, H. (1941). 'Ovids Persephone-Erzählungen und ihre hellenistischen Quellen.' *Rheinisches Museum* 90:236–68.

(1948). 'Ovids Kunstprinzip in den Metamorphosen.' *American Journal of*

Philology 69:129–48 (= von Albrecht and Zinn (1968), 340–61).

Hill, G.F. (1903). *Coins of Ancient Sicily*. Westminster.

Hinds, S.E. (1982). 'An allusion in the literary tradition of the Proserpina myth.' *Classical Quarterly* n.s. 32:476–8.

(1983). '*Carmina digna*: Gallus, *P. Qaṣr Ibrîm* 6–7 metamorphosed.' *Papers of the Liverpool Latin Seminar* 4:43–54.

(1984). '*Cave canem*: Ovid, *Fasti* 4.500.' *Liverpool Classical Monthly* 9:79.

(1985). 'Booking the return trip: Ovid and *Tristia* 1.' *Proceedings of the Cambridge Philological Society* n.s. 31:13–32.

Hollis, A.S. (1970), ed. *Ovid, Metamorphoses Book VIII*. Oxford.

(1980). 'The new Gallus, 8–9.' *Classical Quarterly* n.s. 30:541–2.

Housman, A.E. (1897). 'Ovid's *Heroides* [V].' *Classical Review* 11:425–31 (= Housman (1972), 412–21).

(1972). J. Diggle and F.R.D. Goodyear, edd., *The Classical Papers of A.E. Housman*. 3 vols. Cambridge.

Hunt, J.D. (1980). 'Theatres, gardens and garden-theatres.' *Essays and Studies* n.s. 33:95–118.

(1983). 'Ovid in the garden.' *AA Files* 3. 3–11.

Hunter, R.L. (1983), ed. *Eubulus: The Fragments*. Cambridge Classical Texts and Commentaries 24. Cambridge.

Innes, D.C. (1979). 'Gigantomachy and natural philosophy.' *Classical Quarterly* n.s. 29:165–71.

Innes, M.M. (1955), tr. *The Metamorphoses of Ovid*. Penguin Classics. Harmondsworth.

Jacoby, F. (1950–5), ed. *Die Fragmente der griechischen Historiker*. III.b. Leiden.

Jones, H.L. (1917–32), ed. *The Geography of Strabo*. The Loeb Classical Library. 8 vols. London and Cambridge, Mass.

Kennedy, D.F. (1980). *A Commentary on Culex 1–156, with an Introductory Section Indicating the Poem's Likely Dependence on Cornelius Gallus*. Diss. Cambridge.

(1983). 'Shades of meaning: Virgil, *Eclogue* 10.75–7.' *Liverpool Classical Monthly* 8:124.

Kenney, E.J. (1969). 'On the *Somnium* attributed to Ovid.' ΑΓΩΝ 3:1–14.

(1970). Review of C.P. Segal, *Landscape in Ovid's Metamorphoses*. *Gnomon* 42:418–19.

(1972). Review of F. Bömer, *Metamorphosen I–III*. *Classical Review* n.s. 22:38–42.

(1973). 'The style of the *Metamorphoses*.' J.W. Binns, ed., *Ovid*. Greek and Latin Studies: Classical Literature and its Influence. 116–53. London.

(1976). '*Ovidius prooemians*.' *Proceedings of the Cambridge Philological Society* n.s. 22:46–53.

(1979). '*Iudicium transferendi*: Virgil, *Aeneid* 2.469–505 and its antecedents.' D.A. West and A.J. Woodman, edd., *Creative Imitation and Latin Literature*. 103–20. Cambridge.

(1982). 'Ovid.' E.J. Kenney, ed., *The Cambridge History of Classical Literature*. Vol. 2. *Latin Literature*. 420–57. Cambridge.

Klotz, A. (1940–1). *Livius und seine Vorgänger*. Leipzig/Berlin.

Knox, P.E. (1982). *Ovid's Metamorphoses and the Tradition of Elegy*. Diss. Harvard.

Kroll, W. (1924). *Studien zum Verständnis der römischen Literatur*. Stuttgart.

Leach, E.W. (1974). 'Ekphrasis and the theme of artistic failure in Ovid's *Metamorphoses*.' *Ramus* 3 : 102–42.

Le Boeuffle, A. (1975), ed. *Germanicus: Les Phénomènes d'Aratos*. Collection Budé. Paris.

Lilja, S. (1965). *The Roman Elegists' Attitude to Women*. Annales Academiae Scientiarum Fennicae Ser. B, 135.1. Helsinki.

Little, D.A. (1970). 'Richard Heinze: Ovids elegische Erzählung.' E. Zinn, ed., *Ovids Ars amatoria und Remedia amoris: Untersuchungen zum Aufbau*. 64–105. Stuttgart.

Lodge, D. (1977). *The Modes of Modern Writing*. London.

Loers, V. (1843), ed. *P. Ovidi Nasonis Metamorphoseon Libri XV*. Leipzig.

Luck, G. (1967–77), ed. *P. Ovidius Naso, Tristia*. Wissenschaftliche Kommentare zu griechischen und lateinischen Schriftstellern. Heidelberg.

Ludwig, W. (1965). *Struktur und Einheit der Metamorphosen Ovids*. Berlin.

Lueneburg, A. (1888). *De Ovidio sui imitatore*. Diss. Jena.

Lyne, R.O.A.M. (1978), ed. *Ciris: A Poem Attributed to Vergil*. Cambridge Classical Texts and Commentaries 20. Cambridge.

Maass, E. (1898), ed. *Commentariorum in Aratum Reliquiae*. Berlin.

McKeown, J.C. (1984). '*Fabula proposito nulla tegenda meo*: Ovid's *Fasti* and Augustan politics.' A.J. Woodman and D.A. West, edd., *Poetry and Politics in the Age of Augustus*. 169–87. Cambridge.

Magnus, H. (1920). Review of R. Heinze, *Ovids elegische Erzählung*. *Berliner Philologische Wochenschrift* 40 : 1035–41.

Malten, L. (1910). 'Ein alexandrinisches Gedicht vom Raube der Kore.' *Hermes* 45 : 506–53.

Merkel, R. (1841), ed. *P. Ovidi Nasonis Fastorum Libri Sex*. Berlin.

Miller, F.J., and Goold, G.P. (1977–84), edd. *Ovid, Metamorphoses*. The Loeb Classical Library. Vol. I, 3rd edn. Vol. II, 2nd edn. London.

Montanari, F. (1974). 'L'episodio Eleusino delle peregrinazioni di Demetra: a proposito delle fonti di Ovidio, *Fast*. 4.502–62 e *Metam*. 5.446–61.' *Annali della Scuola Normale Superiore di Pisa: Lettere e Filosofia*. Ser. III. 4 : 109–37.

Nagle, B.R. (1980). *The Poetics of Exile: Programme and Polemic in the Tristia and Epistulae ex Ponto of Ovid*. Collection Latomus 170. Brussels.

Nisbet, R.G.M., and Hubbard, M. (1970). *A Commentary on Horace, Odes Book I*. Oxford.

(1978). *A Commentary on Horace, Odes Book II*. Oxford.

Norden, E. (1913). *Agnostos Theos*. Berlin.

(1926), ed. *P. Vergilius Maro, Aeneis Buch VI*. 3rd edn. Leipzig and Berlin.

Ogilvie, R.M. (1970). *A Commentary on Livy Books I–V*. Repr. with addenda. Oxford.

Otis, B. (1970). *Ovid as an Epic Poet*. 2nd edn. Cambridge.

Owen, S.G. (1915), ed. *P. Ovidi Nasonis Tristium Libri Quinque, Ibis, Ex Ponto Libri Quattuor, Halieutica, Fragmenta*. Scriptorum Classicorum Bibliotheca Oxoniensis. Oxford.

Palmer, A. (1898), ed. *P. Ovidi Nasonis Heroides*. Oxford.

Papathomopoulos, M. (1968), ed. *Antoninus Liberalis, Les Métamorphoses*. Collection Budé. Paris.

Parry, H. (1964). 'Ovid's *Metamorphoses*: violence in a pastoral landscape.' *Transactions of the American Philological Association* 95:268–82.

Pease, A.S. (1920–3), ed. *Cicero, De Divinatione*. University of Illinois Studies in Language and Literature. Urbana.

Pfeiffer, R. (1949–53), ed. *Callimachus*. 2 vols. Oxford.

Plaehn, G. (1882). *De Nicandro aliisque poetis Graecis ab Ovidio in Metamorphosibus conscribendis adhibitis*. Diss. Halle.

Pressler, B. (1903). *Quaestionum Ovidianorum capita duo*. Diss. Halle.

Putnam, M.C.J. (1979). *Virgil's Poem of the Earth: Studies in the Georgics*. Princeton.

Richardson, N.J. (1974), ed. *The Homeric Hymn to Demeter*. Oxford.

Riley, H.T. (1869), tr. *The Metamorphoses of Ovid*. Bohn's Classical Library. London.

Rose, H.J. (1928). *A Handbook of Greek Mythology*. London.

Ross, D.O. (1975). *Backgrounds to Augustan Poetry: Gallus, Elegy and Rome*. Cambridge.

Rothstein, M. (1920–4), ed. *Propertius Sextus, Elegien*. 2nd edn. Berlin.

Russell, D.A. (1979). '*De Imitatione*.' D.A. West and A.J. Woodman, edd., *Creative Imitation and Latin Literature*. 1–16. Cambridge.

Schönbeck, G. (1962). *Der locus amoenus von Homer bis Horaz*. Diss. Heidelberg.

Segal, C.P. (1969). *Landscape in Ovid's Metamorphoses: A Study in the Transformations of a Literary Symbol*. Hermes Einzelschriften 23. Wiesbaden.

Snyder, J.M. (1980). *Puns and Poetry in Lucretius' De Rerum Natura*. Amsterdam.

Soubiran, J. (1972), ed. *Cicéron: Aratea, fragments poétiques*. Collection Budé. Paris.

Steuart, E.M. (1925), ed. *The Annals of Quintus Ennius*. Cambridge.

Syme, R. (1978). *History in Ovid*. Oxford.

Thalmann, W.G. (1984). *Conventions of Form and Thought in Early Greek Epic Poetry*. Baltimore and London.

Thomas, R.F. (1978). 'Ovid's attempt at tragedy (*Am.* 3.1.63–4).' *American Journal of Philology* 99:447–50.

(1979). 'New Comedy, Callimachus, and Roman poetry.' *Harvard Studies in Classical Philology* 83 : 179–206.

Todd, F.A. (1903). *De musis in carminibus Romanorum commemoratis.* Diss. Jena.

Tränkle, H. (1963). 'Elegisches in Ovids Metamorphosen.' *Hermes* 91 : 459–76.

Vahlen, I. (1903), ed. *Ennianae Poesis Reliquiae.* 2nd edn. Leipzig.

Ward-Perkins, J.B. (1981). *Roman Imperial Architecture.* The Pelican History of Art. 2nd edn. Harmondsworth.

Watts, A.E. (1954), tr. *The Metamorphoses of Ovid.* Berkeley and Los Angeles.

West, M.L. (1966), ed. *Hesiod, Theogony.* Oxford.

(1978), ed. *Hesiod, Works and Days.* Oxford.

Wilkinson, L.P. (1955). *Ovid Recalled.* Cambridge.

(1963). *Golden Latin Artistry.* Cambridge.

(1982). 'The *Georgics*.' E.J. Kenney, ed., *The Cambridge History of Classical Literature.* Vol. 2. *Latin Literature.* 320–32. Cambridge.

Williams, F. (1978), ed. *Callimachus, Hymn to Apollo.* Oxford.

Williams, G. (1968). *Tradition and Originality in Roman Poetry.* Oxford.

Williams, R.D. (1967). *Virgil.* Greece and Rome New Surveys in the Classics 1. Oxford.

Wimmel, W. (1960). *Kallimachos in Rom: die Nachfolge seines apologetischen Dichtens in der Augusteerzeit.* Hermes Einzelschriften 16. Wiesbaden.

Wiseman, T.P. (1969). *Catullan Questions.* Leicester.

Wormell, D.E.W. (1979). 'Ovid and the *Fasti*.' *Hermathena* 127 : 39–50.

Zuntz, G. (1971). *Persephone.* Oxford.

INDEX OF PASSAGES DISCUSSED

178

INDEX OF SUBJECTS